T0270968

Unity in Embedded System Design and Robotics

Chapman & Hall/CRC Artificial Intelligence and Robotics Series

Series Editor: Roman Yampolskiy

For more information about this series please visit: https://www.routledge.com/
Chapman--HallCRC-Artificial-Intelligence-and-Robotics-Series/book-series/
ARTILRO

Unity in Embedded System Design and Robotics

A Step-by-Step Guide

Ata Jahangir Moshayedi
Amin Kolahdooz
Liefa Liao

CRC Press
Taylor & Francis Group
Boca Raton London New York

CRC Press is an imprint of the
Taylor & Francis Group, an **informa** business

A CHAPMAN & HALL BOOK

First edition published 2023
by CRC Press
6000 Broken Sound Parkway NW, Suite 300, Boca Raton, FL 33487-2742

and by CRC Press
4 Park Square, Milton Park, Abingdon, Oxon, OX14 4RN

CRC Press is an imprint of Taylor & Francis Group, LLC

© 2023 Ata Jahangir Moshayedi, Amin Kolahdooz, Liefa Liao

Library of Congress Cataloging-in-Publication Data

Names: Moshayedi, Ata Jahangir, author. | Kolahdooz, Amin, author. | Liao, Liefa, author.
Title: Unity in embedded system design and robotics : a step-by-step guide / Ata Jahangir Moshayedi, Amin Kolahdooz, Liefa Liao.
Description: First edition. | Boca Raton : CRC Press, 2022. | Includes bibliographical references and index.
Identifiers: LCCN 2022004724 | ISBN 9781032214771 (hardback) | ISBN 9781032205588 (paperback) | ISBN 9781003268581 (ebook)
Subjects: LCSH: Unity (Electronic resource)--Handbooks, manuals, etc. | Virtual reality--Computer programs--Handbooks, manuals, etc. | Three-dimensional modeling--Handbooks, manuals, etc. | Application software--Development--Handbooks, manuals, etc. | Embedded computer systems--Design and construction. | Robotics.
Classification: LCC QA76.9.C65 M68 2022 | DDC 006.2/2--dc23/eng/20220405
LC record available at https://lccn.loc.gov/2022004724

ISBN: 978-1-032-21477-1 (hbk)
ISBN: 978-1-032-20558-8 (pbk)
ISBN: 978-1-003-26858-1 (ebk)

DOI: 10.1201/9781003268581

Typeset in Minion
by KnowledgeWorks Global Ltd.

To Our Families

*Life is nothing but step-by-step learning. Enjoy
your life and enjoy your learning.
Dedicated to my first step guider father and mother.
My research Life step colleague Sima (my
wife) and Diba (my daughter).
I hope that this step will turn on lights
and knowledge for Diba's life.*

Ata Jahangir Moshayedi

*To my parents. You guys have forever been good
sports and the true inspiration for happiness.
To Fahimeh for always loving and supporting me.
There wasn't a book in the world that could
have prepared you for my eccentricity.*

Amin Kolahdooz

感谢学院各位老师的支持, 是他们辛勤的工作和支
持让我们有时间开展研究, 并且出版本专著
*Thanks to all the teachers for their support. Their
hard work and support helped us to carry out
research and publish this book.*

廖列法 *Liefa Liao*

Contents

List of Tables

List of Figures

Preface

The gaming industry is currently considered one of the most prominent and essential industries in the world. Gaming is used in education, sport, psychology, and sociology to help with productivity and make laborious tasks more entertaining. On the other hand, virtual reality (VR) technology has led to the use and further development of games in human life and other activities. Therefore, it is expected that game engine software will be a part of an engineering student syllabus. Among all game engines, Unity has amassed a large userbase. Unity was designed in 2004 as a software platform for building video games. "Unity wants to be the 3D operating system of the world", says Sylvio Drouin, VP of the Unity Labs R&D team. The Unity game engine was released in 2005 to develop the games by providing better accessibility. Like other software, various versions of Unity have been released and introduced for users. The initial Unity game engine was just made for Mac OS, but later they developed the engine for Microsoft Windows and web browsers. Also, many books were published to help the users use this software in different ways.

As authors of this book, there were various scopes to write about within the context of *Unity in Embedded System Design and Robotics: A Step-by-Step Guide*. Demand on the subject of embedded systems is increasing rapidly, but there are no good books that explain this subject with real projects. Unfortunately, the currently available books try to have limited examples and mostly talk about the different parts and windows in this software that can easily be found in the software help section.

As university lecturers who'd like the new syllabus to include Unity as part of the embedded system design and robotic courses, we feel that writing this book could give students or any other users the ability to learn and start the project with Unity the embedded system.

In this book, Unity is taught based on some practices, and therefore users will learn how to make connections among various parts and challenges during real projects. This book is intended to aid students who want to study and learn in the embedded and robotic fields. So, it is helpful for the students of electrical, control, instrumentation, robotics, and computer sciences. Each chapter contains one project, and the user will experience an actual unique project using the different windows and sections of Unity. Also, to better understand various Unity applications in the real world, the authors add some fantastic projects and learn existing ways of connecting this software to the boards of Arduino and Raspberry Pi.

Unity in Embedded System Design and Robotics: A Step-by-Step Guide is an open gate for any person who wants to learn Unity by example. In this book, Unity is described based on each step's model and image, even in the initial chapter, and important aspects are described. Based on our teaching experience, we believe that by using this method, users will learn faster. It is the reason why we tried to write this book and teach this software by example.

Dr Ata Jahangir Moshayedi
Dr Amin Kolahdoz
Prof Liefa Liao
Ganzhou, China
Spring 2021

About the Authors

 Dr Ata Jahangir Moshayedi is an Associate Professor at Jiangxi University of Science and Technology, China. He received his PhD in Electronic Science from Savitribai Phule Pune University, India.

He is a member of IEEE, a life member of the Instrument Society of India (ISI) and Speed Society of India (SSI), and published in various conferences and journals.

His research interest includes robotics and automation, sensor modelling, bio-inspired robots, mobile robots, embedded system, machine vision-based systems, virtual reality, and artificial intelligence.

Dr Moshayedi has published several papers in various journals and conferences and registered two patents so far in robotic and machine vision. Also, he has written two books. The first book, *Enjoy the Arduino Programming* (Omid Toutian Entekhab ElmiKarbodi and Cheshmehara, 2016), introduces the Arduino to the embedded system designers and is recognised as the first book about Arduino in Iran. His second book *Odors Source Localization System* (LAP Lambert Academic Publishing, 2019), is about the design and development of Gas leak detector robots.

 **Dr Amin Kolahdooz** received his PhD in Manufacturing Engineering from Babol University of Technology, Iran, in January 2015. Between 2011 and 2020, he worked at the University of Khomeinishahr, Iran, where he was a Researcher and Lecturer (2011–2015), Assistant Professor (2015–2020), and also Director of Research and Development (2017–2018). He achieved the best researcher award among academic staff at the University of Khomeinishahr, Iran, twice in 2016 and

2018. He moved to the school of Engineering and Sustainable Development, De Montfort University, UK, in 2020.

Dr Kolahdooz's research is in manufacturing engineering focused on Materials Processes, Industrial Robots, Machine Learning, VR, and AR in Manufacturing. He is also interested in using finite element and optimisation methods to facilitate the design and the production issues. He was involved in different research projects such as designing and fabrication of a SCARA robot to apply 3D-Printing and developing a portable solar power generator. His research projects made him publish one national patent, six books, and more than 50 journal papers in various world-renowned journals so far.

Prof Liefa Liao, received B.E. degree in Computer Science and Technology from Central South University, Changsha, China, in 1997; M.E. degree in automatic control engineering from Jiangxi University of Science and Technology, Ganzhou, China, in 2003; and Ph.D. degree in system management science and engineering from Xi'an Jiaotong University, Xi'an, China, in 2011.

He is currently a Dean and graduate tutor, School of Information Engineering, Jiangxi University of Science and Technology, Ganzhou, China, and a visiting scholar at Rochester University of Technology, NY. He is known as a key young and middle-aged teacher in Jiangxi Province and won the second prize for the 14th Outstanding Social Science Achievement in Jiangxi Province in 2011 and third Prize of the 15th Provincial Outstanding Achievement in Social Science of the Jiangxi Province. He published 50 papers and presided over 4 National Natural Science Foundations on the research of the Relationship between Organizational Learning and Knowledge Level Based on Multi-Agent Simulation, at present, conducting research on artificial intelligence and neural network.

Introduction

VR was initially demonstrated through games but slowly became more influential in other fields like Health, Sport, or Engineering through topics like system design and performance or even system maintenance. Nowadays, the new aspects of VR are shown in embedded systems and robotics and have more practical designs and applications. *Unity in Embedded System Design and Robotics: A Step-by-Step Guide* introduces the Unity game engine.

The vital aspects of the Unity environment are installation method on Windows and Mac, adding the object, importing an asset, making an EXE file, and interfacing with hardware are discussed initially in Chapters 1–11 and then in Chapter 19 with the help of various examples in step-by-step manner give the reader the ability to use this game engine in embedded system design and robotics. The model in this book is illustrated in such a way that the readers can see the result and compare their output after each step. The examples focus on the design that can be used for embedded course students as part of the syllabus and any developer who wants to work on VR subjects.

Authors mainly target the embedded system developer lover from elementary to advanced stages, but other users can also use and enjoy various projects in this book. This book also can be used as a part of embedded course lectures in university for the students to learn the Unity interface and controllers. A number of the figures describe the examples step by step and exciting projects. As this book is written in a simple form, the initial knowledge about C# and C++ is sufficient.

The book chapters are arranged as follow:

Chapter 1: General Information and Essential Parts of Unity. This chapter introduces Unity and presents some history, significant parts, and needed activities in Unity software. It provides the users with instructions on how to download and install the Unity software. This chapter describes the Unity environment and shows the essential parts of Unity windows to give readers the proper overview. The initial chapter provides the reader with a fast introduction and familiarise them with the most useable part of Unity like environment: making an EXE file, orbiting camera, and exporting the 3D file. Therefore, the beginners who are just starting to work with Unity can cover the software fast and learn how to use the feasibility inside Unity.

Chapter 2, Example 1: Spinning Earth. In this chapter, the user learns how to start the project using the Assets and Packages, Menu Bar, and Creating Materials. This chapter finishes with the Create Spinning Earth project.

Chapter 3, Example 2: Wooden Doll Body. This will be the readers' first foray into designing features like an arm, elbow, and knee. To end this chapter, the reader will learn how to make an EXE file and work on an example named Wooden Doll Body.

Chapter 4, Example 3: Create the Semi Jungle Environment. It addresses the user to make the environment with the asset and called the Semi Jungle Environment, and every step is described sufficiently.

Chapter 5, Example 4: Create KUKA Robot. With KUKA being a famous automation company, this chapter will show the step to create KUKA (1) (Robotic Arm), and the reader will learn about making the joint and arm.

Chapter 6, Example 5: Create BAYMAX Body and Movement. It discusses creating the Body model with a shape similar to the BAYMAX character called "BAYMAX Body and Movement". In this example, the reader learns how to give the initial movement around Z-axis for the created character.

Chapter 7, Example 6: Create Two-wheeled Robot with Gripper and Movement. This presents the concept of a two-wheeled Robot combined with a gripper and outlines the steps to create a two-wheeled Robot with Gripper and Movement.

Chapter 8, Example 7: Human Body (REMY CHARACTER) and Movement. The reader will work on a Human Body Movement. It shows how to import the design character and how to move the character automatically and also with the help of a computer keyboard. In this example, the reader starts to become familiar with the importing object and controlling.

Chapter 9, Example 8: Y-BOT Character Movement. The reader will learn how to import and also move the Y-BOT character. Y-BOT is a famous character in 3D games. This example shows how to import this character with Walking, Running, Waving, Dancing, Clapping, Bowing movements, and using the Keyboard to command character movement.

Chapter 10, Example 9: Flower Example with Sound and Image and Keyboard Control. In this chapter, the steps of the Flower example are reviewed and the steps the learner will need to follow in order to add audio and images to a Unity project are discussed. Additionally Keyboard control is also described. In other words, this chapter is aimed to complete Example 3 and review the significant points for the reader.

Chapter 11, Example 10: KUKA_II. In this chapter, the learner will import the KUKA asset. The reader will learn how to import the robot model and have the movement for design by the Keyboard. This chapter can also be considered as the final step of Example 4 but with the imported character.

This book aims to interface the Unity to the real world in the embedded design. Now, the reader can touch the real world with the recent controllers like Arduino and Raspberry Pi in the following chapters.

Chapter 12, Example 11: Communication between ARDUINO and Unity. After a brief discussion about the Arduino board, with the help of two examples of Arduino to Unity and Unity to Arduino, the reader learns how to connect to UNITY and control the object with the Arduino board. In this chapter, a simple object after creation is moved and controlled by a user command from Arduino.

Chapter 13, Example 12: SpongeBob, Control Object by Keyboard and Arduino. To review and learn more in this chapter, the steps to work with the SpongeBob character are described. In this example, after importing the character, the three approaches of the character control in automatic, Keyboard, and Unity modes are described. This chapter will address the computer steps to review and complete the previous chapters.

Chapter 14, Example 13: Object Movement with Kinect. This chapter shows how to connect Unity to Kinect as one of the famous sensors in the game and VR systems. In this chapter, Kinect V1 and Kinect V2 are discussed and described by two examples. Both project aims are to detect the user by Kinect and show its movement in Unity.

Chapter 15, Example 14: Log and Display Joint Coordinates with Kinect. Logging the Joint and arm information in Kinect steps are described, and during this example reader will learn how to log and store the joint information in a CSV file for further process.

Chapter 16, Example 15: Unity and Kinematics. Inverse kinematic review in this chapter as one of the main concepts in robotic with the help of two examples and readers become familiar with this concept and how to use it in the Unity.

Chapter 17: Running Unity Project on Raspberry Pi. The reader will go over the use of Raspberry Pi, known as a small microcomputer in the world. This chapter shows the processes and steps for the readers and teaches how to run Unity in the Raspberry Pi processor.

Chapter 18: Unity and ROS Bridge. The procedure of running the robot operating system (ROS) is shown with an example in this chapter for robotic applications. Therefore, the user can run Unity in Linux and use ROS as the powerful operating system merged with Unity.

Chapter 19, Example 16: Unity and Mobile Sensors Bond. The two types of sensors, Accelerometer and Gyroscope with Unity and Mobile sensors interface, are discussed. Finally, the chapter ends with a car example and navigation by the user's mobile.

Finally, this book ends with the References section.

THE BOOK EXAMPLE GUIDELINE

Chapter	Example Name	Picture	QR Code
02	Example 1: Spinning Earth		
03	Example 2: Create Wooden Doll Body		
04	Example 3: Create the Semi Jungle Environment		
05	Example 4: Create KUKA Robot		

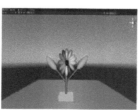

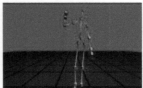 
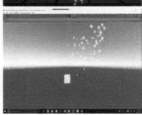

15 Example 14:
Log and Display Joint
Coordinates with
Kinect

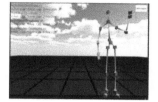

16 Example 15:
Unity and Kinematics
Inverse Kinematics
Fast Inverse
Kinematics

17 Running Unity Project
on Raspberry Pi

No sample code

18 Unity and ROS Bridge

No sample code

19 Example 16:
Unity and Mobile
Sensors Bond

VR COURSE IN EMBEDDED SYSTEM DESIGN AND ROBOTICS

Course Syllabus

English Name:	VR Course in Embedded System Design and Robotics
Course Type:	Elective Course
When Science:	30 + 10 hours
Credits:	3
Adaptation Object:	Robotic engineering, Computer engineering, Information engineering (communication, electrical), Electrical engineering
Prerequisite Courses:	Complex functions, Circuit analysis, Electronic technology, Signals and systems, Digital signal processing, C++ coding, Embedded system, Introduction to robotic

SUGGESTED TEACHING MATERIALS AND REFERENCE BOOKS

- Ata Jahangir Moshayedi, Amin Kolahdooz, & Liefa Liao, *Unity in Embedded System Design and Robotics: A Step-by-Step Guide*, CRC Press, 2023.
- Dan Zhang & Bin Wei, *Adaptive Control for Robotic Manipulators*, CRC Press, 2020.
- Richard Zurawski, *Embedded Systems Handbook Embedded Systems Design and Verification*, CRC Press, 2009.
- Ata Jahangir Moshayedi & Toutian Omid, *Enjoy The Programming With Arduino*, Elemi Karbodi Publication, Chapara, Iran, 2017.

1: COURSE NATURE, PURPOSE, AND TASKS

i. Course Nature

This course is an elective course for undergraduates and postgraduate students majoring in robotic, computer, information, and electrical majoring in engineering. This course meets the design and working with the unity software and teaches students to touch the real world. Students will learn how to integrate the Unity design with various real hardware and work with them during this course. They will real some practical work on kinematics, ROS, etc. to better understand joint and kinematic relations in the robotic world. The main core interest of this course is to integrate the theory and examples to teach students better concepts related to virtual reality (VR), embedded systems, and robotic.

ii. Course Objectives and Tasks

Enable students to learn and study Unity's basic concepts, principles, and processing methods and use the various hardware as the input. They are learning how to start from simple design to the complicated one or use the other techniques to furnish your program environment. Through the study of this course, students will be able to follow the steps, and with the fundamental theories, methods, and practical techniques, and have a specific ability to analyse and solve problems in this field.

2: COURSE CONTENT AND REQUIREMENTS (INCLUDING CRUCIAL POINTS, DIFFICULTIES, SPECIFIC CONTENT, AND THINKING QUESTIONS)

Session 1: General Information and Essential Parts of Unity

Content: In this session, the lecturer introduces Unity and presents some history, significant parts, and needed activity in Unity, like gives the users an address about how to download and install the Unity. Describes the Unity environment and briefly shows the essential part of Unity windows to provide readers with the proper overview. This session offers the students a fast introduction and familiarises them with the most useable part of Unity like environment: making an EXE file, orbiting camera, and exporting the 3D file. Therefore, the beginners who are just starting to work with Unity can cover the software fast and learn how to use the feasibility inside Unity.

Basic Learning Material

1. Understand the main concepts of VR and some introduction to the application.

2. Unity introduction, installation, and its main windows.

3. Understand the basic sections.

4. Learn the composition principle of VR and how to start with simple examples.

Difficulty: Unity installation due to the net speed.

Session 2: How to Start the Program in Unity

Content: The students learn how to start the project using the Assets and Packages, Menu Bar, and Creating Materials, and the session will be finished by learning how to make the EXE file. These activities can be done by Chapter 2, "**Spinning Earth**", and Chapter 3, "**Wooden Doll Body**" of this book.

Basic Learning Material

1. Understand the assets and packages concept.

2. Knowing some windows like Menu bar and Creating Materials.

3. Primary knowledge about C++.

Session 3: How to Develop the Program in Unity

Content: The students learn how to create different environments with various objects and add sound, images, and control the setting by Keyboard. These activities can be done by Chapter 4, **"Create the Semi Jungle Environment"**, and Chapter 10, **"Flower Example with Sound and Image and Keyboard Control"**. Some key points for this session are making objects like flowers, clouds, butterflies, and trees in Unity and designing and adding the sound, image, and giving the movement with the help of a computer keyboard.

Basic Learning Material

1. Understand the assets and packages concept.

2. Knowing some windows like Menu bar and Creating Materials.

3. Extra knowledge about C++.

Session 4: Robotics Part 1

Content: The students will learn the structure of different types of **robots**. They will learn how to create the joints, links in Unity. Some concepts, like the Degree of freedom, etc., will be taught in this session. Using Chapter 5, the **"Create KUKA Robot"** as the famous design in robotic will be considered. Also, in Chapter 6, **"Create BAYMAX Body and Movement"**, the students will learn how to give the initial movement around Z-axis for the created character in Unity.

Basic Learning Material

1. Understand different robot structures.

2. Understand the assets and packages concept in this regard.

3. Create a KUKA Robot Platform.

4. Create BAYMAX Body.

5. Knowing some windows like camera, camera position, and rotation.

6. Coding movement using C#.

Session 5: Robotics Part 2

Content: The students will learn different steps to create a two-wheeled Robot with Gripper and move it in an environment **"Chapter 7"**. Also, the students work on another example to import the design character and move it automatically and with the help of a computer keyboard. Therefore, they become familiar with the importing object and controlling **"Chapter 8"**.

Basic Learning Material

1. Learning some about two-wheeled Robots as the most applicable robot platform.

2. Learning some initial ideas about famous characters in Unity.

3. Understand the assets and packages concept.

4. Knowing some windows like Menu bar and Creating Materials.

5. Improve their knowledge about C++.

Session 6: Robotics Part 3

Content: In this session, students will work on two examples from Chapters 9 and 11. The first example is Y-BOT that is a famous character in a 3D game. Students will learn how to import and move this character in different ways, such as walking, running, waving, dancing, clapping, and bowing using the Keyboard. Also, another view to the KUKA platform but with the imported model can be practised by students. Students will learn how to import the robot model and have the movement for design by the Keyboard as well as moving them automatically.

Basic Learning Material

1. Understanding the assets and packages concept.

2. Learning about some famous characters.

3. Knowing some windows like Menu bar and Creating Materials.

4. Improve their knowledge about C#.

After writing all these chapters, and according to the goal set for this book, in order to connect Unity with the actual world environment in the embedded design, the reader can Touch and use some recent processors such as Arduino and Raspberry Pi in the next chapters with some applicable projects.

The proposed book aims to use Arduino/Pi-based devices, such as input devices, to control entities in Unity and install Unity to run on a Pi. Therefore, Chapters 11–13 explain the connection between Unity and Arduino board, which is a famous platform in embedded system designs. Also, the manner in which to connect Unity to Pi and running sample programs on Pi is described in Chapter 17. As you may know, Pi is known as one of the smallest computers in the world, and the future of VR is running VR environments on small products like Pi and mobile phones. Therefore, this chapter is arranged to motivate the users to use Pi instead of PCs and laptops. Besides, as presented in the proposal form, connecting

Unity to Kinect is introduced to help users act as the developer and enjoy making and inventing various designs in Chapters 13–15.

Furthermore, in Chapter 18, the procedure of setting up and running the ROS into Unity is presented. The use of Unity in robotics is shown in this chapter. Finally, Chapter 19 explains how to connect the sensors in smartphones to Unity.

Session 7: Arduino Board and Connection to Unity Part 1

Content: After a brief discussion about the Arduino board, with the help of two examples of Arduino to Unity and Unity to Arduino, the students will learn how to connect to Unity and control the object with the Arduino board. The lecturer teaches **Chapter 12** with a simple object moved and controlled by a user command from Arduino. The students also learn how to use serial communication and Arduino to attach the Unity design and learn about ARDITY as well as controlling the Unity animation with physical buttons.

Basic Learning Material

1. Learning how to program the Arduino and how to establish serial communication.

2. Learning how to read the Keys as the Digital value in Arduino and show in serial communication.

3. Improving the knowledge of C#.

Session 8: Arduino Board and Connection to Unity Part 2

Content: Review and learn more about the connection between Arduino to Unity. It will be done by practising more exercises with the SpongeBob character (**Chapter 13**). In this example, after importing the character, the three approaches of character control in automatic, Keyboard, and Unity modes are described. This session will address the computer steps to review and complete some previous examples. Students learn how to import and control the designed character, change the colour, and control it with three methods of Keyboard, Automatic, and Arduino.

Basic Learning Material

1. Learning how to program the Arduino.

2. Understand the assets and packages concept.

3. Improving the knowledge of C#.

Session 9: Connect Unity to Kinect

Content: In this session, students learn how to connect Unity to Kinect. Kinect V1 and Kinect V2 will be discussed and described separately with two examples (**Chapters 14 and 15**). Both project aims are to detect the user with Kinect and show its movement in Unity. Also, logging the joint and arm information in Kinect steps must be described, and students learn how to store the joint information in a CSV file. This part can be used in various robotic projects like Puma 560 or any other robot with an arm.

Basic Learning Material

1. Understanding the Assets and packages concept.

2. Increasing knowledge about CSV files and logging data.

3. Improving the knowledge of C++.

Session 10: Inverse Kinematics and Unity

Content: The student will learn the principle of Inverse kinematics. Two examples presented in **Chapter 16** will be done in order for the student to be familiar with the topic.

Basic Learning Material

1. Improving the knowledge about Inverse kinematics.

2. Understand the assets and packages concept.

3. Improving the knowledge of C++.

Session 11: Raspberry Pi and Unity

Content: Raspberry Pi, known as one of the smallest microcomputer in the world. This session shows the processes and steps involved for students and teaches how to run Unity in the Raspberry Pi processor. The students will learn how to install and run his/her Unity design on the Pi. They will learn how to install the Unity on Windows 10 IoT Core Method. Also, the procedure of running the ROS, and therefore the students can run Unity in Linux and use the ROS as the powerful operating system merged with Unity.

Basic Learning Material

1. Improving the knowledge about Raspberry Pi processors.

2. Improving the knowledge about Python command in Pi.

3. Improving the knowledge about ROS.

4. Improving the knowledge about ROS command and installation.

5. Understand the assets and packages concept.

6. Primary knowledge about C++.

3: BASIC REQUIREMENTS FOR COURSE TEACHING

Classroom lectures: Lectures can be done by the instructors using multimedia. Some sessions can be arranged for students to review some useful information, write reports, and discuss the projects in the group.

Homework: Each chapter is arranged 5–8 channel basic theoretical knowledge of the job, but the focus should be on the application and set a considerable amount of work on the machine simulation.

Evaluation method: Examination. Normal scores account for 30%, and written test scores account for 70%. The expected results include:

- **Attendance:** 30%

- **Class practice:** 20%

- **Computer experiment:** 50%

Furthermore, the written test questions include concept questions, short answer questions, and programming questions. The scope of the examination should cover the teaching content and requirements of the syllabus.

4: CLASS HOURS ALLOCATION (CHA)

		CHA				
Sessions	Lectures	Exercise Lesson	Computer Class	Discussion Class	Other	Total
1	2		2			4
2	2		2			8
3	2		2	1		13
4	2		2			17
5	2		2			21
6	2		2	1		26
7	2		2			30
8	2		2			34
9	2		2	1		39
10	2		2			43
11	2		2	1		48
Total	22		22	4		48

General Information and Essential Parts of Unity

DOI: 10.1201/9781003268581-1

1.1 WHAT IS VIRTUAL REALITY

Let's start by looking at the words virtual and reality. The word Virtual means not physically existing as such but made by software to appear to do so, and Reality is known as the human experience. The combination of both terms can be defined as the Near-reality, which can be the environment near the human experience. Virtual Reality (VR) is meant to create a virtual environment using a computer to trigger the senses. In that case, VR is used as a three-dimensional, computer-generated environment that one can discover and interact with. In this environment, the person and system are merged to act together. VR combines different technologies to increase immersive experience like the use of headphones, omnidirectional treadmills, special gloves, etc.

VR allows a person to become anyone, anything, and be anywhere another person can imagine. This digital technology allows a person to step into a digital environment. The environment could be a game or a place where a person just walks around and looks around. The idea is to trick the brain into thinking that that's a new reality. This technology is embedded in various games to put the user in an interactive world, such as in the driver's seat of a car or on the battlefield as a first-person shooter, or even in living in a little town. VR can be a useful tool in many sectors like architecture, sport, medicine, the arts, entertainment, etc.

1.1.1 Key Components in VR

For a user's brain to perceive a virtual environment, some key factors are vital for creating an immersive experience, which are required to give the user a good experience with VR. These components are hardware, trackability, and interactivity. These three components should work together to create a total VR environment for users. Part one, hardware, includes components such as a VR headset (Figure 1.1). This component has two lenses to cover the human eyes combined with a digital screen inside. Currently, there are two kinds of VR headsets. One is used as an accessory that you can plug your smartphone with, which works as a screen, like Google Cardboard or Samsung's Gear VR. The second type has a screen which is connected with a gyroscope and accelerometer that help track the users' head movement and help to tilt their head, like Oculus Rift or HTC Vive. Both types of headsets have lenses that help users focus on the stereoscopic image right up against their faces.

The second part is trackability, which makes mobility possible. This is essential as it is the main difference concerning immersive experience between a VR and a video game or a film. Initially, VR had a delay with trackability, which caused nausea. The ability to track a user's motion, particularly their head and eye movements, allows the image displayed in the

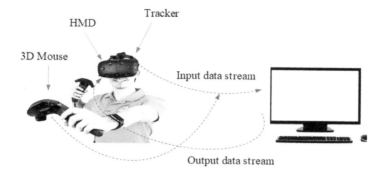

FIGURE 1.1   The basic VR component.

headset to change with the user's perspective. So if the user turns his/her head to the left, the display will render whatever is on the left in that environment. Besides vision, specific VR experiences will include other sensory stimulations like sound and even tactile feedback for touch. The third component is interactivity. This part helps to alter the perception of a user's reality into a certain level of virtual interaction. True interaction should allow a certain degree of user-controlled navigation so the users can walk forwards/backwards or turn through space in the virtual environment in a manner that doesn't feel like they are just watching elaborate 3D movies. Then, when users can freely move within that environment and even interact with things in it, their brains can truly perceive that world accurately. Interactivity is achieved with the use of controllers or even your hands and some other systems. The users actually can perform some activities in VR experience and immerse into the VR. The input device is interfaced with the output devices that are used to provide an immersive experience and the software controls the environment synchronisation.[1]

1.1.2 VR Application

VR is not just a tool for entertainment. There are many other opportunities in this domain where VR makes perfect sense. For example, defence organisations worldwide have started using VR for training and simulations, including combat medics or the air force training system. The flight simulation systems now are much easier and cheaper to train new pilots who practise fighting manoeuvres, shooting objectives, and ejecting, which is in stark contrast to reality where the same activities would cost millions of dollars. Driving schools have started using VR to help prepare students

---

[1] J. Novak-Marcinčin and M. Marcela Kuzmiakova, "Basic Components of Virtual Reality," *Ann. Univ. Petroşani, Mech. Eng.*, vol. 11, pp. 175–182, 2009.

for driving lessons. Surgeons are using VR to practice highly technical surgeries before operating. Businesses are using this technology to give consumers virtual tours of products and locations. Medical students can use VR to study anatomy and practice procedures on an utterly imaginary patient. Some doctors are even using VR to address fears that people have, such as flying in an aeroplane or fear of heights. These individuals can confront their fears in a safe and controlled space, often resulting in dramatic positive progress in real life. Another excellent use case for this technology is around travel meditation, and also in the healthcare space, this technology can be used to help diagnose concussions.

1.1.3 VR History

The date on which VR was invented is a bit of a mystery with some researchers saying that it was discovered in 1935, and some believed it was invented in 1957. The history of VR development can be summarised here.

As you can see in Figure 1.2, in 1935, Stanley Weinbaum, an American Science Fiction Writer, introduced a fictional model of VR in his short story Pygmalion's Spectacles. In his story, the main character meets a professor who created a pair of goggles. The professor can see, smell, hear, and taste with these goggles. In 1960, people started to see gadgets like the sense of Rama, which also included sounds and smells. Then people started to see things like the view master created, which were goggles that would show a picture and build the foundation for VR headsets that we can see now. Morton Heilig, a cinematographer, created the first VR machine, Sensorama, and patented it in 1962. The machine could be used by four people simultaneously and had different facilities such as a stereoscopic 3D screen, stereo speakers, a vibrating chair, and could provide some atmospheric effects. He believed that his machine would be the next generation of cinema. The Sensorama was intended to fully immerse the individual in the film. Six short films were created for his machine. These films are *Belly Dancer, Motorcycle, Helicopter, Dune Buggy, A Date with Sabina*, and *I'm a Coca Cola Bottle*. He also presented the first VR head-mounted display (HMD) in 1960, which was called a Telesphere Mask. The mask could provide wide-vision 3D images and stereo sound without motion tracking. In 1961, two Philco Corp. engineers, Comeau and Bryan, created the first-ever HMD called the **headsight**. The display had two video screens, one for each eye, and a magnetic tracking device. This device was used by military to allow soldiers to remotely look at hazardous situations. The ultimate display was presented in 1965 by Ivan Sutherland, a computer scientist. In his

VR History The 30s &60s

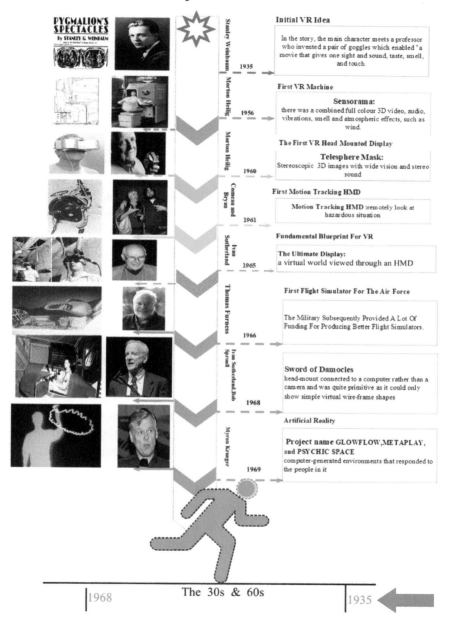

Initial VR Idea

In the story, the main character meets a professor who invented a pair of goggles which enabled "a movie that gives one sight and sound, taste, smell, and touch.

1935

First VR Machine

Sensorama:
there was a combined full colour 3D video, audio, vibrations, smell and atmospheric effects, such as wind.

1956

The First VR Head Mounted Display

Telesphere Mask:
Stereoscopic 3D images with wide vision and stereo sound

1960

First Motion Tracking HMD

Motion Tracking HMD :remotely look at hazardous situation

1961

Fundamental Blueprint For VR

The Ultimate Display:
a virtual world viewed through an HMD

1965

First Flight Simulator For The Air Force

The Military Subsequently Provided A Lot Of Funding For Producing Better Flight Simulators.

1966

Sword of Damocles
head-mount connected to a computer rather than a camera and was quite primitive as it could only show simple virtual wire-frame shapes

1968

Artificial Reality

Project name GLOWFLOW,METAPLAY, and PSYCHIC SPACE
computer-generated environments that responded to the people in it

1969

1968   The 30s & 60s   1935

FIGURE 1.2   VR history from the 1930s to the 1960s.

device, the user was able to interact with objects. In 1966, the first flight VR simulator was created by Thomas Furness. In 1968, a breakthrough in creating a virtual environment came when Ivan postulated in his manuscript that since the human retina can capture and view images in two dimensions (2D), by placing 2D images in front of a viewer, you're able to create an illusory likeness that seems like the viewer can see a 3D image. The idea was to create an HMD that showed the user a three-dimensional image that could change according to the viewer's head motion. This then went on to become the blueprint for recent VR. In this year, he, along with the help of his student, Bob Sproull, could create the first VR-HMD, named The Sword of Damocles. This HMD could connect to a computer rather than a camera. In 1969, Myron Krueger could develop a succession of **Artificial Reality** experiences. He used a combination of computers and video systems based on Video place technology. The projects, such as Glowflow, Metaplay, and Psychic Space, were based on this technology.

General Electric Corporation built a computerised flight simulator in 1972 that featured a 180-degree field of vision by using three screens surrounding the cockpit. The screens surrounded the simulated training cockpit to give trainee pilots a feeling of true immersive experience. In 1975, the first interactive VR platform using Krueger's Video place technology was presented at the Milwaukee Art Center. This platform had video displays, computer graphics, video cameras, projectors, and sensors, but did not use gloves or goggles. In modern terms, it's more like an AR projection and didn't feature any sort of headset. Aspen Movie Map was fabricated by MIT in 1977. From the map, users can virtually wander through Aspen city. They used a video filmed from a moving car to create the impression of moving through the city. Once again, no HMD was part of this setup. The VITAL helmet that could be used by the military was introduced in 1979 by McDonnell-Douglas Corporation. Using a head tracker, pilots could look at primitive computer-generated imagery. Sayre gloves were made by Sandin and Defanti in 1982. These gloves could monitor hand movements using light emitters and photocells. This may have been the start of gesture recognition. In 1985, VPL Research, Inc., was founded by Jaron Lanier and Thomas Zimmerman. The project was for developing VR goggles, EyePhone HMD, and gloves. The term **data glove** came from their DataGlove product. A flight simulator, Super Cockpit, was developed by Furness during 1986–1989. The helmet's tracking system and sensors used in this simulator allowed the pilot to control the aircraft using speech, gestures, and eye movements. NASA signed a contract with Scott Foster in 1989 to investigate and develop the audio element of the

Virtual Environment Workstation Project (VIEW). In this project, real-time binaural 3D audio processing was developed. Interestingly, the technology in these gloves leads directly to the creation of the Nintendo Power Glove (Figure 1.3).

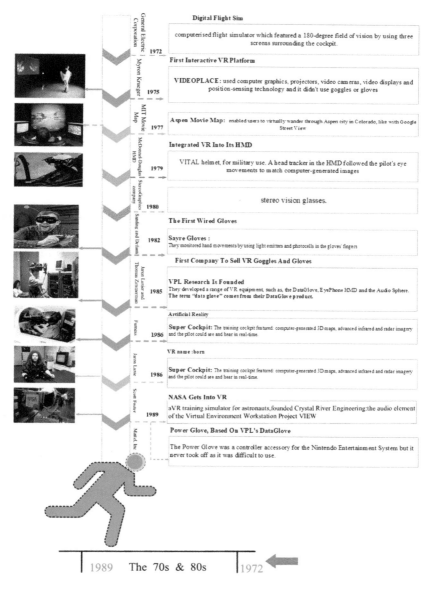

FIGURE 1.3   VR history in the 1970s and the 1980s.

The late 1980s and early 1990s saw organisations such as NASA getting involved in VR by using simulations to train astronauts. It included gloves which were used to simulate tactile feedback (sense of touch). This technology (commonly referred to as haptic technology) inadvertently led to video game companies like Nintendo implementing them into virtual group Arcade games; due to technical issues, it was challenging to implement these consoles, which eventually called for the suspension of manufacture. In 1990, Jonathan Waldern created a VR arcade machine; in 1991, a VR system to drive the Mars robot rovers was designed by Antonio Medina. This system was called **Computer Simulated Teleoperation**. This year, the first trials were conducted by Sega to introduce a VR headset. This headset was meant to be used for arcade games and the Mega Drive console. However, it was never released because of safety issues. Two years later, Sega announced the new VR headset for the Sega Genesis console. Sega also released VR-1 in 1994. It was an arcade motion simulator that moves following what is happening on-screen. The Virtual Boy console, the first portable console with the ability to display 3D graphics, was launched by Nintendo in 1995. The player could play 3D monochrome video games with this console. However, it was a commercial failure because of the lack of software support and coloured graphics, and it was not easy to use. Some home VR headsets, such as Virtual IO by the I-Glasses or VFX1 Headgear by Forte, were released this year. The first attempts to use VR in treatments were made in 1997. In collaboration with Georgia Tech and Emory University, some war zone scenarios were created for veterans to receive exposure therapy for post-traumatic stress disorder (PTSD). This was known as Virtual Vietnam. Science fiction and media have always been ways to guide people as to what the future might look like and be excited at the possibilities of technological advancements or be scared of how these technologies are applied. A common theme in both these possibilities is either a dystopian world or a utopia. The 1999 motion picture *The Matrix*, at its core, is a dystopian work that shows humans, unaware that they live in a simulated world, but, in reality, are only programmed and controlled by intelligent machines to provide them with thermoelectric power. *The Matrix* is now a mainstream pop culture reference as to what alternate reality can look like (Figure 1.4).

The first PC-based cubic room, SAS Cube, which led to Virtools VR Pack, was introduced in 2001. In 2007, Google introduced Street View and Immersive Media. Street View was introduced by Google in a stereoscopic 3D mode. Also, the prototype of the Oculus Rift headset was created

VR History The 90s

Virtuality Group Arcade Machines
VR arcade machine, at the Computer Graphics 90 exhibition in London.

1990

Medina's VR Mars Rover
Computer Simulated Teleoperation: VR system to drive the Mars robot rovers from Earth in supposed real-time despite signal delays between the planets

1991

First Mass-Produced VR Entertainment System
Virtuality: These were VR arcade machines where gamers could play in a 3D gaming world.

1991

Didn't Happened due to the limited processing power
announced that they were working on the SEGA VR headset which would be available for the general public to purchase

The Lawnmower Man Movie: introduced the concept of virtual reality to a wider audience.used virtual reality therapy on a mentally disabled patient. Real virtual reality equipment from VPL research labs was used in the film and the director Brett Leonard, admited to drawing inspiration from companies like VPL.

1992

1993
Sega AS-1: VR glasses The wrap-around protoype glasses had head tracking, stereo sound and LCD screens in the visor

1994
Sega VR-1, an arcade motion simulator that moves in accordance to what's happening on-screen

First Portable Console To Display 3D Graphics
1995
Virtual Boy: it was a commercial failure due to the lack of colour graphics, lack of software support and it wasn't comfortable to use

Landmark VR PTSD Treatment
1997
Virtual Vietnam: VR technology gave therapists unrivaled control over what the patients sees and experiences.

brought the topic of simulated reality into the mainstream.
The Matrix: The film features characters that are living in a fully simulated world, with many completely unaware that they do not live in the real world
1999

| 1999 | The 90s | 1990 |

FIGURE 1.4   **VR history in the 1990s.**

by Palmer Luckey, an 18-year-old entrepreneur at Google. It featured a 90-degree field of vision, which had never been seen before, and relied on a computer's processing power to project the images. In 2012, the founder of the Oculus Rift, Palmer Luckey, kickstarted a campaign to develop his headset prototype. This helped facilitate various other headsets that would be produced in the following years to come. The device calculates head movement and allows the user to experience a virtual four-dimensional experience and considers peripheral vision. Since then, a wide range of industries has set their sights on developing and implementing VR into their mode of operations. However, it wasn't until 2015 when Facebook bought a small company called Oculus that this technology got pushed into the public domain. Soon after, Sony revealed PlayStation VR, a headset to be sold alongside their PS4, which would allow for VR gaming right in someone's home. While the Oculus Rift and PlayStation VR seem superficially similar, the Oculus did not likely bring in tremendous gaming opportunities. Instead, it probably focused on more real world applications that the PS4 will not likely prioritise. There are, of course, other companies working on VR efforts, such as the HTC Vive and the Samsung Gear VR. One of the most significant leaps in competitive gaming was the inclusion of VR spectating into the game Dota 2. Players can put themselves on the battlefield not to play but to merely spectate and watch the events unfold. Entertainment venues across the world like Disneyland and Six Flags have even started to use VR, including the Superman ride in which everyone on the ride wears their headset. You feel like you are in a helicopter when an attack from Lex Luthor makes gravity go crazy. Superman must rescue you with every tilt of the roller coaster feeling like you are falling or flying through the sky.

Nevertheless, just in the last two or three years, technology has improved massively. Users do not need a big heavy-duty two-thousand-dollar computer anymore or hang a bunch of crazy sensors around their room. All users need is a headset, a couple of controllers, and plenty of time to lose themselves in the fantastic VR experiences available on these headsets (Figure 1.5).

1.1.4 VR and AR

A common mistake people make is to use the terms VR and Augmented Reality (AR) interchangeably. VR and AR are two slightly different things. VR and AR are two technologies changing the way we use screens like computers, smartphones, and televisions, creating new and exciting

VR History The 00s - Future

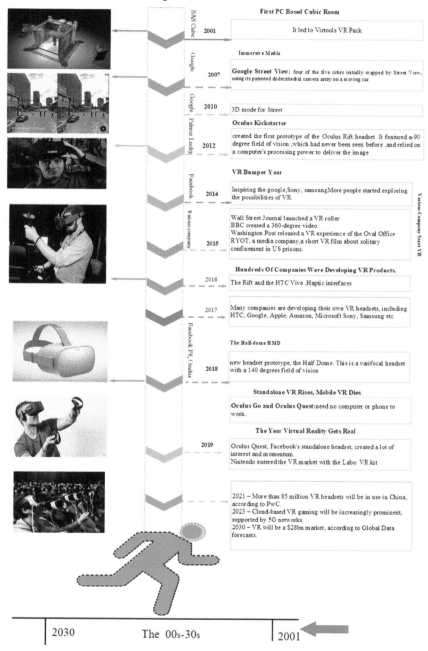

SAS Cube

2001

First PC Based Cubic Room

It led to Virtools VR Pack

Google

2007

Immersive Media

Google Street View: four of the five cities initially mapped by Street View, using its patented dodecahedral camera array on a moving car

Google

2010

3D mode for Street

Palmer Luckey

2012

Oculus Kickstarter

created the first prototype of the Oculus Rift headset .It featured a-90 degree field of vision ,which had never been seen before ,and relied on a computer's processing power to deliver the image

Facebook

2014

VR Bumper Year

Inspiring the google,Sony, samsungMore people started exploring the possibilities of VR

Various company

2015

Wall Street Journal launched a VR roller
BBC created a 360-degree video
Washington Post released a VR experience of the Oval Office
RYOT, a media company,a short VR film about solitary confinement in US prisons.

Various Company Start VR

2016

Hundreds Of Companies Were Developing VR Products.

The Rift and the HTC Vive ,Haptic interfaces

2017

Many companies are developing their own VR headsets, including HTC, Google, Apple, Amazon, Microsoft Sony, Samsung etc

Facebook F8, Oculus

2018

The Half-dome HMD

new headset prototype, the Half Dome. This is a varifocal headset with a 140 degrees field of vision

Standalone VR Rises, Mobile VR Dies

Oculus Go and Oculus Quest:need no computer or phone to work.

The Year Virtual Reality Gets Real

2019

Oculus Quest, Facebook's standalone headset, created a lot of interest and momentum.
Nintendo entered the VR market with the Labo: VR kit

2021 – More than 85 million VR headsets will be in use in China, according to PwC.
2023 – Cloud-based VR gaming will be increasingly prominent, supported by 5G networks.
2030 – VR will be a $28bn market, according to Global Data forecasts.

2030	The 00s-30s	2001

FIGURE 1.5   VR history after 2000s.

interactive experiences. To clarify, VR is replacing your entire reality, so you are immersed in this new world with nothing left from the real world, but AR is just augmenting your reality a little bit. It is adding some things and combining them with the real world, and frequently that will be in the form of an overlay or seeing something on top of a real world object. VR uses a headset with a built-in screen that displays a virtual environment for users to explore. These headsets use head tracking technology, allowing users to look around the environment by simply moving the head. AR is a bit different. Instead of transporting users to a virtual world, it takes digital images and layers them on the real world around them. This is done using either a clear visor or a smartphone. So, with VR, users could explore a world full of specific objects like the flower, dinosaurs, etc., but, with AR, users could see those objects moving through the world around themselves. Both of these technologies are proliferating and being implemented in a variety of different ways.

1.2 WHAT IS UNITY?

Unity is a cross-platform real-time engine developed by Unity Technologies, first announced and released in June 2005 at Apple Inc.'s Worldwide Developers Conference as an OS X-exclusive game engine. As of 2018, the engine has been extended to support 27 platforms. The engine can be used to create both three-dimensional and two-dimensional games and simulations for its many platforms. Industries have adopted the engine outside video gaming, such as film, automotive, architecture, engineering, and construction.

Unity game gives users the ability to create games and experiences in both 2D and 3D. The engine offers a primary scripting API in C# for both the Unity editor in plugin games and drag and drop functionality. Boo was the main programming language for Unity but in August 2017, they decided to use C# as the primary programming language for this engine. Therefore, they used a version of JavaScript called **Unity Script** for Unity 2017.1.

Within 2D games, Unity allows the importation of sprites and an advanced 2D world renderer. With regard to 3D games, Unity allows specification of texture compression, mipmaps, and resolution settings for each platform that the game engine supports and provides support for bump mapping, reflection mapping, parallax mapping, screen-space ambient occlusion (SSAO), dynamic shadows using shadow maps, render-to-texture, and full-screen post-processing effects.

Statistical analysis asserts that in 2018 Unity had created approximately half of the new mobile games in the market and 60 per cent of AR and VR content (Table 1.1).

TABLE 1.1   Specification of the Unity

Developer	Unity Technologies
Initial release	1.0 June 8, 2005; 13 years ago,
Stable release	2019/06/03 /(2019.1.5)
Written in	C++ (Runtime), C# (unity scripting API)
Operating system	MACOS, Windows, Linux
Platform	IA-32, x86-64, ARM
Available in	English
Type	Game Engine
License	Proprietary software
Alexa rank	1,157 (July 2018)
Website	www.unity.com

1.3 UNITY OFFICIAL WEBSITES AND SOCIAL MEDIA

There are various websites and blogs on the Internet for using and learning the Unity environment, such as the links given in Table 1.2.

TABLE 1.2   Some Useful Unity Websites

YouTube page:	https://www.youtube.com/user/Unity3D
Facebook:	https://www.facebook.com/unity3d/
Official page:	https://unity.com/

1.4 SUMMARY OF UNITY'S HISTORY

To view the history of Unity and its development process, you can check the following path: On the Unity Editor toolbar, click the collaborate button. Then open the History window, click history in the Collaborate panel. We introduced Unity application and a route map of that path.

Danish programmer Nicholas Franchise tried to implement his game engine and posted it on the MAC OpenGL board for assistance with a shader system on May 21, 2002. A shader is a programme that gives the look and feel of 3D graphics. It was Joachim Ante (Germany) who responded to Nicholas's post some hours later. They were talking about results that collaborated on the shader while pursuing their game engine. David Helgason knew about the project, and he thought, "*They will do something, so he goes abroad to join them as a developer*". First, they wanted to make it their source of earning, but they saw the need for more good underlining technology. These guys were always thinking, "*We will make good games without the licenses, and we will prove that the game is necessary for the technology*".

At last, they didn't make games but made some tools to provide games. Joachim and Nicholas rent a house in Copenhagen to start their project, and their game development had progressed. For an extra source of income, David worked in a cafe and lived in a down street. At that time, they started developing the most valuable pieces of software for the gaming industry. The main reason of Unity's success was that they supported independent developers who could not buy expensive licenses for developing their games. They knew that they wanted to create some game technology, but they didn't know which form to build. Two years later, the three developers found their mission. They made the definitive tools for 3D applications. After that, they took out a loan to rent an office for their work and then hired some engineers. At first, they weren't looking for a CEO. They then thought that they were going to make up this position. They understood that if they want to succeed, this plan wouldn't work. They posted an advertisement and requested a CEO for a great technology company. After advertising, they received a few applications, but they realised that they were far behind the programme. Helgason said, "*behind the curve, we weren't too far ahead*". In this trio, Helgason was more social than others, so the CEO position was proposed to him.

At this point, the group began to create a business plan called Over The Edge Entertainment (OTEE). PlayStation 2 became very successful in the middleware market when the British game development company modelled Criterion. This model not only has well-built technology but also has leading technology in this industry.

On the other hand, they thought the customer would not feel comfortable enough to buy an expensive license without using it first and realised that casual and online gaming would only grow by focusing on the market. After two years of programming and many nights trying, finally, Unity was near to release. They decided to create a full commercial game for their new engine. They didn't test the power and range of their engines, and also, they could not estimate the number of earnings they will finally have.

David Helgason said that "*No one can remember how we survived that time. We probably didn't eat so much*". OTEE spent five months creating a game called Gooball using the new engine, which was still in the beta version. Gooball was published in March 2005 by Ambrosia Software. Before releasing the official version of the game, the Unity team used the opportunity to split their engine and find the problems and fix the interface. Using the profits they earned from Gooballs, OTEE hired more developers to modify Unity before its first release in June 2005. They wanted to give Unity the best possible chance to move upwards, bring out all bad edges, and provide documentation and support for users. After releasing, the company quickly started the next step and told the developer that "*we *develop tools for developers freely and developers try to identify and may fix the problems of these tools for us".*

At this time, Unity was the child of the game industry. Many game companies were working to create their particular games, but they couldn't sell them properly, and also, they have to throw their engine technologies. The potential customers were concerned that this might happen with Unity too. Before OTEE proved Unity properly, support and update for it would take two years.

The first published version of Unity was only supported on MAC OS X. But it wasn't the full version. Unity needed to make windows and web browsers versions as well. Therefore, Unity brought 3D graphics to the browser in the game industry. In version 1.1, they added a C and C++ plugin and tried to allow the developers to expand their engine by using some hardware and software that Unity did not support at the time. Around this time, the trio felt that their product was up to the estimated value. The Unity team spent the next three months on debugging, optimising, and creating some new processes for old PCs to fix bugs on the graphic cards and driver problems. These activities were compacted with version 1.5, and their most extensive version, Unity 2.0, was released after development for two years. The main goal of this version was to support more products on the window platforms and increase a balance for web players to have an entire stage. To achieve this, the team added support for Microsoft DirectX, which installed the Windows Vista system and recommended OpenGL and Downloaded Extra. Using DirectX in version 2.0 increased their engine speed by about 30 per cent, thus improving overall performance. Other key features added in this release included a web stream, real-time soft shadow networking, the unity asset server, and a new code-based GUI system. Unity 2.0 was released in 2007 at Unite developer conference. Just as the smartphone revolution began, Unity decided to make a version of Unity that works on the iPhone. They released the smartphone version for iPhone in AppStore as an individual product in 2008 and then developed it for a basic and pro version, similar to the base Unity product. It was an important year for them because Unity was now known as Unity Technologies.

They immediately realised that they need an editor for windows as well. They had to disconnect the current editor and rewrite it from scratch to make the platform. Unity technologies released its first version of Unity with windows support in 2009, and the next main release was version 3.0 in September 2010. The Unity 3.0, released with engine graphic features, expanded the engine features for desktop computers and video game consoles. This version had an Android add-on. Some other developments were the integration of Illuminate Labs' Beast Lightmap Tool, Deferred Rendering, a Built-in Tree

Editor, Native Font Rendering, Automatic UV Mapping, and Audio Filters. At that time, Unity users exceeded the 1.3 million developers mark.

This update brought many desired features such as Unification, Beast Lightmapping, Umbra Occlusion Culling, Low-Level Debugging, and FMOD Audio Filter. In a press release, Helgason said, *"By Unity 3.0, we're exhibit that can go faster than any other middleware company, that we're serious about the long term and high technology made simple is a transformation force"*. At that time, more than 200,000 users and developers registered for version 3.0 of Unity. Unity became the first engine for education and the most used technology for the mobile platform. Unity Technologies release its first Beta version for Unity 3.5 on December 22, 2011. The release added support for the Long-Awaited Flash Deployment option. Nicholas Francis said, *"Our version has always been to let developers take their games to as many places as possible and flash deployment greatly further that"*. On February 14, 2012, the Unity team's latest version of Unity 3.5 was published. The following version, Unity 4.0, could support Direct TX-11 and Adobe Flash and was released in November 2012 with a new tool called Mechanic. This version had access to Linux, which is when even Facebook had started to use Unity.

Unity Technologies announced pre-order for Unity 4.0 on June 18, 2012. Once again, the next release carried many new features: Mechanism Animation Technology, Flash Deployment, Linux Publishing Review, and the Shuriken System. Unity Technologies announced that the pre-ordered customers would receive access to the beta list. Helgason said, *"We have been working on Unity 4.0 for a long time and happy for finally available to unveil its imminent arrival and outline its core feature that will change the industry"*.[2] On November 13, 2012, the final release of Unity 4.0 became available for developers. After a long time of waiting, Unity Technologies release its 2D support feature. Before that, Unity developers had to work with some fake 2D features by putting textures on flat planes or using other unconventional techniques. On November 12, 2013, Unity 4.3, as the next version, was released to the public, and the developers could start authoring 2D games and support for sprites and 2D game development. Unity 5.0 was released in 2015 with the goal of global access to the game development engine. This version improved its Lighting and Audio using WebGL and allowed Unity developers to add their games to compatible web browsers with no plugins. Then the developer furnished with some feasibility like Real-Time

---

[2] John Haas, "A History of the Unity Game Engine: An Interactive Qualifying Project" submitted to the Faculty of Worcester Polytechnic Institute in partial fulfillment of the requirements for graduation. Project Advisor: Brian Moriarty, IMGD.: Haas, John. "A history of the unity game engine." *Diss. Worcester Polytechnic Institute* (2014).

FIGURE 1.6   Page of Cloud Build.

Global Illumination, Light Mapping Previews, Unity Cloud (Figure 1.6), a new Audio System, and the Nvidia PhysX 3.3 physics engine. Unity 5.0 introduced Cinematic Image Effects to make Unity games look less generic, with some new gaming features in Facebook introduced in 2016. With Unity support, The Facebook gaming developers could more rapidly spread and issue games to Facebook. From December 2016 onwards, the way Unity was named changed to the year of publication.

The tools of Unity 2017 contained a real-time graphics rendering engine, colour grading, Worldbuilding, live operations analytics, and performance reporting. The next version, Unity 2017.2, highlighted Unity Technologies' plans beyond video games with the new tools such as Timeline, which allowed developers to drag and drop animations into games, and Cinemachine, an intelligent Camera System within games. Also, software such as Autodesk's 3DS Max and Maya got integrated into Unity. Unity 2018 featured the Scriptable Render Pipeline for designers to create high-end graphics with a High-Definition Rendering Pipeline for console and PC experiences using Lightweight Rendering Pipeline for mobile, VR, AR, and mixed reality. Besides, the machine learning tools like Imitation Learning added to Unity equipped the games with abilities to learn from real player habits. Unity also supported Magic Leap and provided templates C# source codes for new developers starting Unity on this version. Finally, in June 2020, the Mixed and Augmented Reality Studio (MARS) was introduced by Unity.

1.5 UNITE

Among the Unity users, Unite is an annual event hosted for developers, publishers, and connoisseurs alike. These conferences allow people to connect with other community members, share knowledge, and utilise resources. The first Unite took place in San Francisco, CA. At Unite events, creativity and interactive learning take centre stage. Users can connect with their fellow artists, creators, and programmers, learn from experts across all forms of entertainment, and walk away with the knowledge and tools they need to boost their creative success (Figure 1.7).

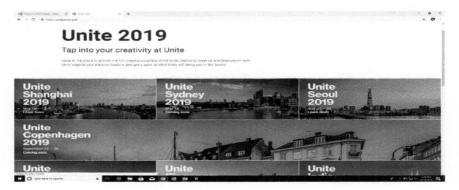

FIGURE 1.7   Unite 2019.

1.6 NOTABLE PUBLICATIONS WITH UNITY

The following top ten games made by using Unity can be listed as follows:[3]

1. Kerbal Space Program
2. Hearthstone: Heroes of Warcraft
3. Wasteland II
4. Battlestar Galactica Online
5. Rust
6. Temple Run Trilogy
7. Escape plan
8. Satellite Reign
9. Assassin's Creed: Identity
10. Deus Ex: The Fall

---

[3] https://unity.com/madewith?_ga=2.203060881.1213607396.1555927100-2040437524.1555313114, https://joyofandroid.com/android-games-made-with-unity/ and https://blog.soomla.com/2015/01/top-10-unity-games-ever-made.html

There are many other ways to learn Unity, and you can use various online tutorials and online books that will help you.

1.7 UNITY DOWNLOAD AND INSTALLATION

This section describes the process to install and download Unity Hub version 2.4.3 and Unity version: 2020.3.5f1c1. The initial work is to download Unity Hub. To install the Unity software, the user can follow the below step.

1.7.1 Step 1: Download Unity

Download Unity from the following link: https://unity3d.com/get-unity/download (Figure 1.8).

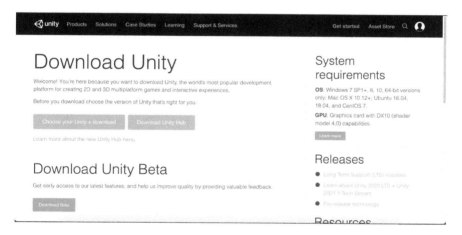

FIGURE 1.8 Download Unity.

For Windows OS: Click on Download Unity Hub and wait for the download to finish, and then open the file (Figure 1.9).

FIGURE 1.9 Download page for Windows.

For Mac OS: The user should wait for the DMG file to finish downloading and then download Unity Hub (Figure 1.10).

FIGURE 1.10   Download page for Mac OS.

1.7.2 Step 2: Install Unity Hub

Open Unity EXE/DMG File [Windows/Mac]

For Windows: Initially, wait for the UAC prompt to come up, then click Yes on UAC prompt and agree to terms and conditions; click Install and wait for it to finish the installation. One can run Unity from this checkpoint or remove the check and click finish. Finally, allow Unity Hub to access the network through the Windows Defender Firewall. Then open Unity Hub from the Desktop Icon or Start Menu (as shown in Figure 1.11).

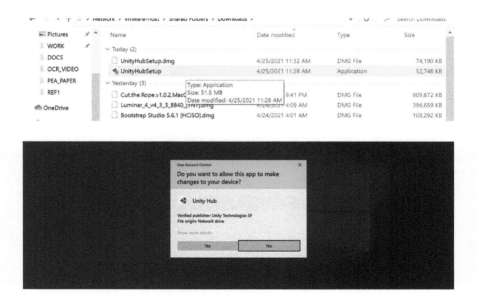

FIGURE 1.11   Installation process for Windows. (*Continued*)

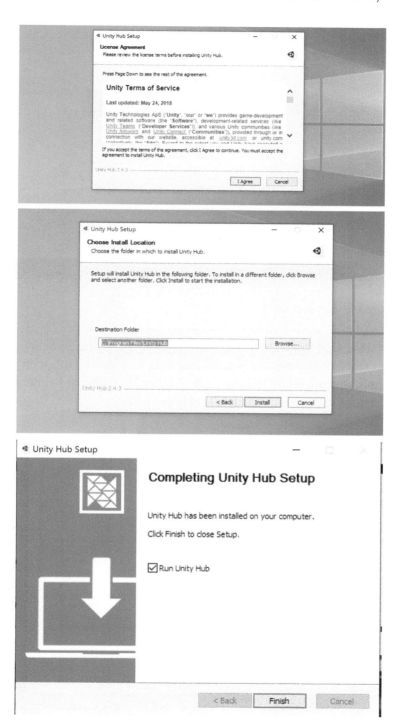

FIGURE 1.11 *(Continued)*

FIGURE 1.11 (*Continued*)

For Mac OS: Open the DMG file, agree to the Terms of Service, and wait to finish verifying. Then drag and drop the Unity Hub Icon inside the Applications Icon. In the end, open Unity Hub from the Launchpad or Applications folder inside the finder (Figure 1.12).

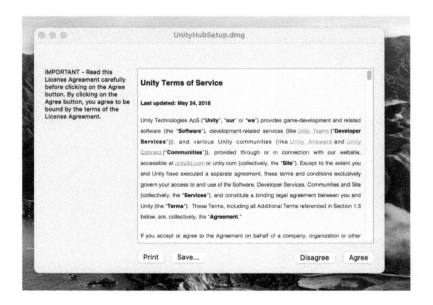

FIGURE 1.12   Installation process for Mac OS. (*Continued*)

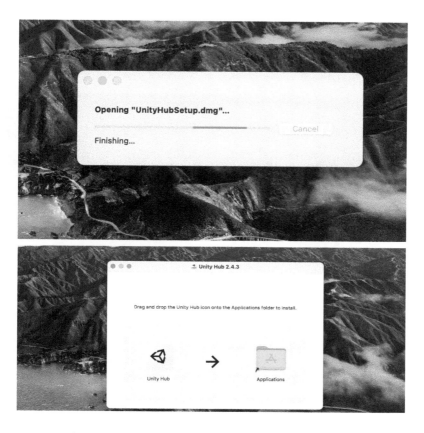

FIGURE 1.12 (*Continued*)

1.7.3 Step 3: Launch Unity Hub

For Windows: Find Unity Hub in the recently added section in Start Menu or Search for it (Figure 1.13).

FIGURE 1.13 How to Unity Hub in Windows.

For Mac OS: Go to Launchpad, find Unity Hub or Press Command + Space, and search for **Unity Hub** (Figure 1.14).

FIGURE 1.14   How to find Unity Hub in Mac OS.

1.7.4 Step 4: Running Unity Hub for the First Time

After opening Unity for the first time, click on the round icon beside the gear-shaped settings icon to log in. If one does not have an account, one must create an account here first. Users can create an account from the following website: https://id.unity.com/ (see Figure 1.15).

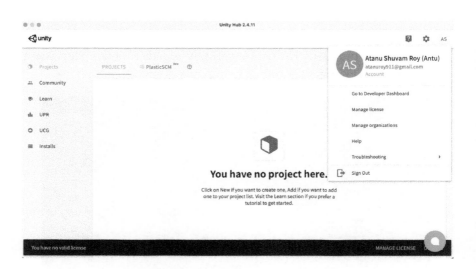

FIGURE 1.15   How to sign into Unity. (*Continued*)

FIGURE 1.15 *(Continued)*

Users can bind their WeChat to Unity for easy login as well (Figure 1.16).

FIGURE 1.16   Bind WeChat to Unity.

After creating the account, the user can sign into the Unity Hub App (Figure 1.17).

FIGURE 1.17   How to log in to Unity.

Input registered email and password or click on WeChat Button to log in (Figure 1.18).

Tips: After registering the account, try to log in with the WeChat option. Because WeChat is not bound to one's account, Unity will tell you to log in with a traditional Email and Password. Upon doing so, it will automatically bind your WeChat account, and you can use it the next time.

FIGURE 1.18   How to log in to Unity by WeChat.

1.7.5 Step 5: Adding New License

After the first login, user sees a prompt like below, "You have no valid license" (Figure 1.19). Click on MANAGE LICENSE or you can also click on Gear Icon (settings) → License Management

FIGURE 1.19   Adding license.

1.7.6 Step 6: Installing the Main Unity 3D Software

Go back to the main dashboard, and from there, click on Installs (Figure 1.20).

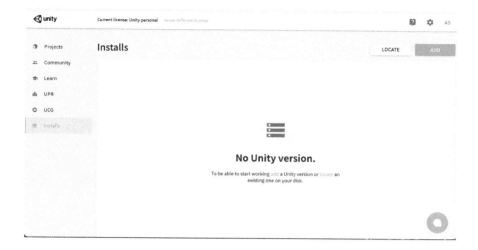

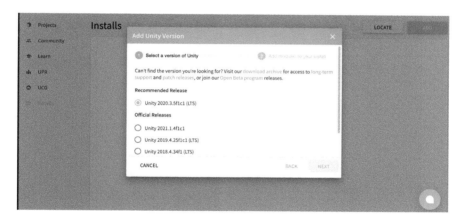

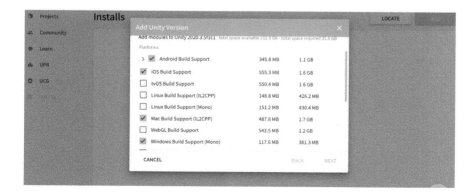

FIGURE 1.20   Main Unity 3D installation. (*Continued*)

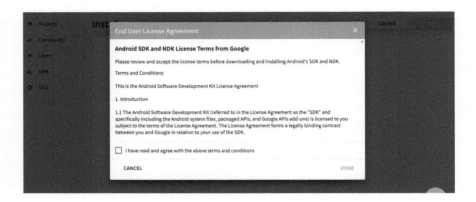

FIGURE 1.20 *(Continued)*

Then click on ADD, select the Recommended Unity Release version, click Next, and select the modules needed for the project to be built and click next. As the next step, accept the EULA and click on Done (Figure 1.21).

FIGURE 1.21 Main menu while installation.

Now the user will see a version of Unity that is downloading and then installed. After this step, the installation is over, and the user will see Figure 1.22.

FIGURE 1.22 Main menu after installation.

1.7.7 Step 7: Creating First Project

To test and create the first project and test the installation, the user can go to the projects tab in the main dashboard and click on NEW (Figure 1.23).

FIGURE 1.23 How to start to create a project.

Set a project name, project location, uncheck PlasticSCM, click on 3D, and then click on Create (Figure 1.24).

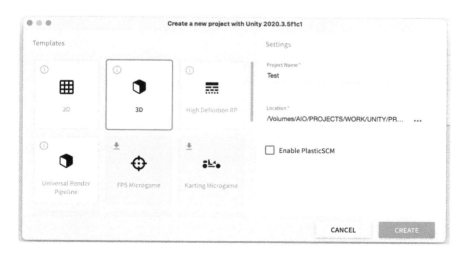

FIGURE 1.24 Create a 3D project.

Now the new workspace as shown in Figure 1.25 opens.

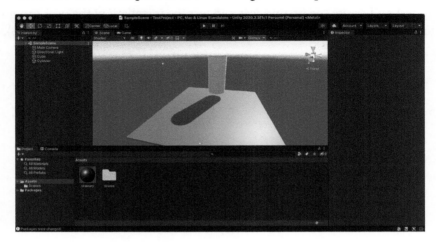

FIGURE 1.25   Main workspace of Unity 3D.

1.8 UNITY INTERFACE AND ENVIRONMENT

Unity is so much more than the world's best real-time development platform – it's also a robust ecosystem designed to enable your success. The Unity editor is comprised of many sub-windows like The Project Window, The Scene View, The Hierarchy Window, The Inspector Window, The Toolbar, and The Game View. Once your new project is created and Unity opens, a window appears as shown in Figure 1.26.

FIGURE 1.26   Main Unity interface.

In brief, the most commonly used are Project Browser(6), Inspector, Game View(3), Scene View(4), and Hierarchy(2) (Figure 1.27, Table 1.3).

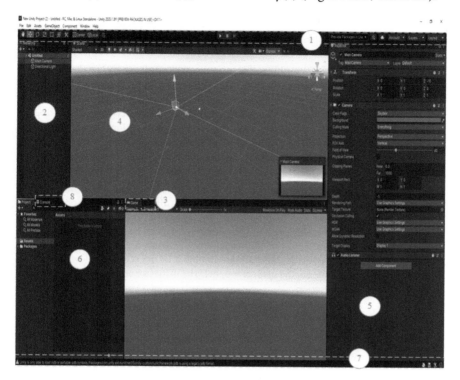

FIGURE 1.27 Environment of Unity.

TABLE 1.3 The Central Unity Windows in Brief

Label	Part	Description
1	The Toolbar	This part offers access to vital working features. On the left, it covers the essential tools for working the Scene view and the GameObjects within it. In the centre are the play, pause, and step controls. The buttons to the right give you access to Unity Collaborate, Unity Cloud Services, and your Unity Account, followed by a layer visibility menu. Finally, the Editor layout menu (which provides some alternate layouts for the Editor windows) allows you to save your custom layouts.
2	The Hierarchy Window	This window has an object for every GameObject in the Scene so the two windows are inherently linked. The hierarchy reveals the structure of how GameObjects are placed or nested. By default, the Hierarchy window lists GameObjects by order of creation, with the most recently created GameObjects at the bottom. We can reorder the GameObjects by dragging them up or down or by making the parent or child GameObjects.

(Continued)

TABLE 1.3   The Central Unity Windows in Brief (*Continued*)

Label	Part	Description
3	The Game Window	This window shows the view that the main camera sees when the game is playing. This means here you can see a preview window of how the game looks like to the player. It is representative of your final game. You will have to use one or more cameras to control what the player sees when playing your game.
4	The Scene Window	This window is where we will create our scenes. This view allows you to navigate and edit your scene visually. The scene view can show a 2D or 3D perspective, depending on the type of project you are working on. We use the scene view to select and position scenery, cameras, characters, lights, and all other kinds of GameObject. Selecting, manipulating, and modifying objects in the scene view are some of the most critical skills you must learn to begin working in Unity.
5	The Inspector Window	The Inspector window allows users to view and edit all the properties of the currently selected object. Since different types of objects have different sets of properties, the layout and contents of the inspector window will vary. In this window, you can customise aspects of each element that is in the scene. You can select an object in the hierarchy window or double click on an object in the scene window to show its attributes in the inspector panel. The inspector window displays detailed information about the currently selected GameObject, including all attached components and their properties, and allows you to modify the functionality of GameObjects in your scene.
6	The Project Window	This window displays the files being used for the game. You can create scripts, folders, etc., by clicking create under the project window. In this view, you can access and manage the assets that belong to your project. All assets in your project are stored and kept here. All external assets, such as textures, fonts, and sound files, are also held here before they are used in a scene. The Favourites section is available above the project structure list where you can maintain frequently used items for easy access. You can drag items from the list of project structures to the Favorites and save search queries.
7	The Status Bar	Provides notifications about various Unity processes and rapid entrees to related tools and settings.
8	Console Window	If you are familiar with programming, you will already know that all the output messages, errors, warnings, and debug messages are shown here. It is similar in Unity, except output messages are done a bit differently than you think. The console window of Unity shows the errors, warnings, and other messages generated by Unity. You can also show your notes in the console using the Debug.Log, Debug.logError, and Debug.LogWarning function.

1.8.1 The Unity Main Windows Part and Section

The components of this software include various parts. We do not need to use all of them. The details of each item mentioned in the examples section are described in detail. In this table, a number is assigned to each item, which you can use to find the location of the item in the software according to Figure 1.28. The components of this software include the various parts listed in Table 1.4.

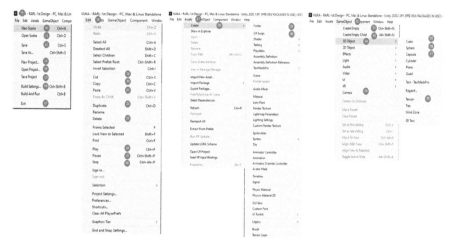

FIGURE 1.28 Main windows of Unity.

TABLE 1.4 The Details of Software Components

No	Section	Location	Description
9	**File**	The top left corner of the main window figure	User will find some essential things like open or save any projects
10	File	New Scene	User can make a new scene from here
11		Open Scene	User can open a saved scene
12		Save	User can Save his/her scene here
13		New Project	User can make a new project from here
14		Open Project	Dropdown menu from File: User can open previously saved project from here
15		Save Project	User can save his/her Project
16		Build Project	User can make an *.Exe file from this menu
17		Exit	User can exit from the application by clicking it
18	**Edit**	The top left corner of the main window figure	User can get the editing menu from here

(Continued)

TABLE 1.4   The Details of Software Components (*Continued*)

No	Section	Location		Description
19		Cut		User can cut anything with the help of this menu
20		Copy		User can copy anything with the help of this menu
21		Paste		User paste cut anything with the help of this menu
22		Duplicate		User duplicate cut anything with the help of this menu
23	Edit	Delete	Dropdown menu from Edit	User delete cut anything with the help of this menu
24		Play		User can play the game by clicking this button in game mode
25		Pause		User can pause/play the game by clicking this button in game mode
26		Step		User can stop/play the game by clicking this button in game mode
27	**Assets**	The top left corner of the main window figure		
28		Create		User can create new folder, script, and many other things
29	Assets	Folder	Dropdown menu from Assets	User can make a new folder
30		Open C# Project		User can open C# source code
31	**Game Object**	The top left corner of the main window figure		
32		Create Empty	Dropdown menu from Assets	User can make a new Empty object
33		Create Empty Child		User can make new Empty objects child
34	Game Objects	3D Object		User can make 3D Object from here
35		Cube		User can make Cube from here
36		Sphere		User can make Sphere from here
37		Capsule		User can make Capsule from here
38		Terrain		User can make Terrain from here
39		Camera		User can change the Camera settings from here

1.9 SOME GENERAL IDEAS FOR PROJECT DEVELOPMENTS

Before starting any project, it is better to review some points. Users need to know how the software works to make progress with their project and achieve the aim of the project. Unity is a user-friendly software if you know what you should do step by step. Therefore, the following steps will give you practical guidelines for any projects you would like to accomplish in Unity.

1.9.1 Step 1: Defining & Writing Your Strategic Aims and the Project's Objectives

A project objective describes the desired results of a project, which often includes a tangible item. A purpose is specific and measurable and must meet the time, budget, and quality constraints. Strategic aims include significant goals you want to reach through your strategies. These can consist of gaining a majority of market share, getting a productivity rate of 90 per cent of capacity, or owning your facilities.

1.9.2 Step 2: Designing and Modelling the Objects

User can build their world in Unity with the help of Unity Editor. ProBuilder is a unique hybrid tool of 3D modelling and level design, optimised for building simple geometry but capable of detailed editing and UV unwrapping. On the other hand, to make better 3D models, users usually use other software such as 3D-Max or Maya. This software offers a rich and flexible toolset to create premium designs with complete artistic control, such as creating massive worlds, visualising high-quality architectural renderings, modelling finely detailed interiors and objects, and bringing characters and features to life-like animation.

1.9.3 Step 3: Programming and Coding

Scripting tells our GameObjects how to behave. A script must be attached to a GameObject in the Scene to be called by Unity. The language that's used in Unity is called C# (pronounced C-sharp). In Unity, the scripts start by laying out the tools you need at the top, usually by declaring variables. Scripts manipulate the variables by using functions. When writing a function, remember that functions start with the returned type of the function initially, followed by the function's name, and then the parameters in the parentheses (if any). Classes are collections of these variables and functions.[3]

1.9.4 Step 4: Extracting the EXE File According to Hardware and Operating System

After finishing the project, developers need to make an EXE file. This file can be run on any system, even without Unity installation. To have the EXE file, you can follow the below steps:

Go to File → Build Settings → Select your platform (win/mac/Linux/Xbox, etc.) → Player settings tab in that dialogue box → Configure your game settings (screen splash, game name, company name, etc.) → Close all windows → Click on Build And Run.

---

[3] https://unity3d.com/learning-c-sharp-in-unity-for-beginners

1.10 UNITY ESSENTIAL ACTIVITY

In this part, we will review some everyday and essential activities which you may need during your Unity project.

1.10.1 How to Use the Asset Store

The Store provides a browser-like interface that allows you to navigate either through a text search or by browsing Asset packages. Asset packages are a handy way of sharing and re-using Unity Projects and collections of Assets (Figure 1.29).

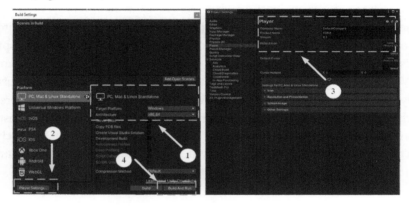

FIGURE 1.29   Extract the EXE file.

To open the asset store, the user can follow the following steps: Open Unity, then click on windows/asset store (ctrl +9) afterwards choose your desired asset (Figure 1.30).

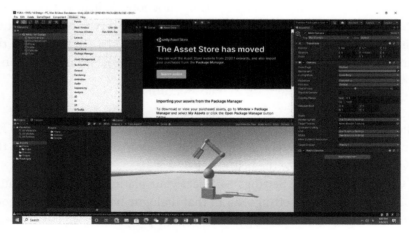

FIGURE 1.30   How to access the asset store.

1.10.2 Orbiting Camera with Script

This Script will move the camera according to the target's movement. The target can be set as the character in the scene. This Script allows movement to the camera with horizontal and vertical keys, and also, the user can move the camera by using a mouse. The target and distance that the camera follows can be set in Unity's UI by following the steps as shown in Figure 1.31. Open the camera game object inspector, then click and drag the Script into the inspector.

FIGURE 1.31   The inspector windows setting.

Then you can change the Distance and Sensitivity of the moving target.

1.10.2.1 Script

```
using UnityEngine;
namespace MenteBacata.ScivoloCharacterControllerDemo
{
    public class OrbitingCamera: MonoBehaviour
    {
        public Transform target;
        public float distance = 5f;
        public float sensitivity = 100f;
        private float yRot = 0f;
        private float xRot = 20f;
        private void Start()
        {
#if UNITY_EDITOR
            // Somehow after updating to 2019.3, mouse axes sensitivity decreased,
but only in the editor.
            sensitivity *= 10f;
#elif UNITY_WEBGL
            // To prevent the mouse axes not being detected when the cursor leaves
the game window.
            Cursor.lockState = CursorLockMode.Locked;
#endif
        }
        private void LateUpdate()
        {
            yRot += Input.GetAxis("Mouse X") * sensitivity * Time.deltaTime;
            xRot -= Input.GetAxis("Mouse Y") * sensitivity * Time.deltaTime;
            xRot = Mathf.Clamp(xRot, 0f, 75f);
            Quaternion worldRotation = transform.parent != null? transform.parent.
rotation : Quaternion.FromToRotation(Vector3.up, target.up);
            Quaternion cameraRotation = worldRotation * Quaternion.Euler(xRot, yRot, 0f);
            Vector3 targetToCamera = cameraRotation * new Vector3(0f, 0f, -distance);
            transform.SetPositionAndRotation(target.position   +   targetToCamera,
cameraRotation);
        }
    }
}
```

1.10.3 Export 3D Files

Unity engine is capable to read the *.fbx, *.dae (Collada), *.3ds, *.dxf, and *.obj files. For more details about exporting 3D files, the user can read the documentation by using the link given in the page footnote.[4] Using the 3D files has some advantages and disadvantages summarised in Table 1.5.

TABLE 1.5   Advantages and Disadvantages of Using 3D File

Advantages	Disadvantages
1. Users can import only the parts of the model that are needed instead of importing the whole model into Unity.	1. Users must re-import models manually if the original file changes.
2. Exported generic files are often smaller than the proprietary equivalent.	2. Users need to keep track of versions between the source file and imported files into Unity.
3. Using exported generic files encourages a modular approach (for example, using different components for collision types or interactivity).	
4. Developers can import these files from software that Unity does not directly support.	
5. After exporting, users can re-import exported 3D files (*.fbx, *.obj) into 3D modelling software after exporting to ensure that all information has been exported correctly.	

Unity can import proprietary files from some 3D modelling software like Autodesk, 3ds Max, Maya, Blender, Modo, and Cheetah3D. But it should be noted that Unity converts proprietary files to *.fbx files as part of the import process, and it's recommended to use fbx instead of directly saving your application files in the project. In some versions like Unity 2019.3, due to unsupported Cinema4D files, it's advised to use Maxon's Cinema4D importer, and then the user can export an fbx file from Cinema4D. In Unity, the Assets saved as *.ma, *.mb, *.max, *.c4d, or *.blend files fail to import unless you have the corresponding 3D modelling software installed on your computer. Everybody who wants to work on the Unity project must install the correct version of the software. For example, suppose you use the **Autodesk® Maya LT™** license to create **ExampleModel.mb** and copy it into your project. In that case, anyone else who wants to open that project needs to have **Autodesk® Maya LT™** that must be installed on their computer too.

---

[4] https://docs.unity3d.com/Manual/3D-formats.html

1.10.3.1 Export OBJ Files

To export any .OBJ file from Unity, the user should follow the steps below:

Step 1: Opening and initialisation

Open Unity and navigate to Asset Folder and create a new folder named Editor in it. It will look like Figure 1.32.

FIGURE 1.32   How to open a new folder on the Asset part.

Step 2: Creating and coding the C# script

Now let's create a new C# script inside this folder and name it as ObjExporterScript. It will look like Figure 1.33.

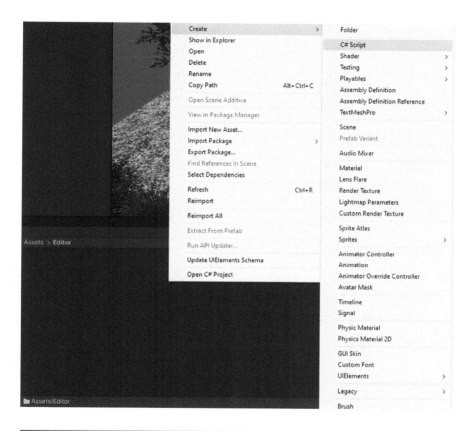

FIGURE 1.33 How to create a C# script.

Now copy and paste the below code inside the Script.

```
using UnityEngine;
using UnityEditor;
using system.Collections;
using System.IO;
using system.Text;
 public class ObjExporterScript
{
    private static int StartIndex = 0;
    public static void Start()
    {
            StartIndex = 0;
    }
    public static void End()
    {
            StartIndex = 0;
    }
    public static string MeshToString(MeshFilter mf, Transform t)
    {
            Vector3 s              = t.localScale;
            Vector3 p                       = t.localPosition;
            Quaternion r           = t.localRotation;
                int numVertices = 0;
            Mesh m = mf.sharedMesh;
            if (!m)
            {
                    return "####Error####";
            }
            Material[] mats = mf.renderer.sharedMaterials;

            StringBuilder sb = new StringBuilder();

            foreach(Vector3 vv in m.vertices)
            {
                    Vector3 v = t.TransformPoint(vv);
                    numVertices++;
                    sb.Append(string.Format("v {0} {1} {2}\n",v.x,v.y,-v.z));
            }
            sb.Append("\n");
            foreach(Vector3 nn in m.normals)
            {
                    Vector3 v = r * nn;
                    sb.Append(string.Format("vn {0} {1} {2}\n",-v.x,-v.y,v.z));
            }
```

```
            sb.Append("\n");
            foreach(Vector3 v in m.uv)
            {
                    sb.Append(string.Format("vt {0} {1}\n",v.x,v.y));
            }
            for (int material=0; material < m.subMeshCount; material ++)
            {
                    sb.Append("\n");
                    sb.Append("usemtl").Append(mats[material].name).Append("\n");
                    sb.Append("usemap ").Append(mats[material].name).Append("\n");
                    int[] triangles = m.GetTriangles(material);
                    for (int i=0;i<triangles.Length;i+=3) {
                    sb.Append(string.Format("f {0}/{0}/{0} {1}/{1}/{1} {2}/{2}/{2}\n",
    triangles[i]+1+StartIndex,triangles[i+1]+1+StartIndex,triangles[i+2]+1+StartIndex));
                    }
            }
            StartIndex += numVertices;
            return sb.ToString();
        }
}
public class ObjExporter : ScriptableObject
{
        [MenuItem ("File/Export/Wavefront OBJ")]
        static void DoExportWSubmeshes()
        {
                    DoExport(true);
        }
        [MenuItem ("File/Export/Wavefront OBJ (No Submeshes)")]
        static void DoExportWOSubmeshes()
        {
                    DoExport(false);
        }
        static void DoExport(bool makeSubmeshes)
        {
                    if (Selection.gameObjects.Length == 0)
                    {
                        Debug.Log("Didn't Export Any Meshes; Nothing was selected!");
                        return;
                    }
                    string meshName = Selection.gameObjects[0].name;
            string fileName = EditorUtility.SaveFilePanel("Export .obj file", "", meshName, "obj");
                    ObjExporterScript.Start();
                    StringBuilder meshString = new StringBuilder();
```

```
                meshString.Append("#" + meshName + ".obj"+ "\n#" +
System.DateTime.Now.ToLongDateString()
+"\n#" + System.DateTime.Now.ToLongTimeString()
                                        + "\n#-------" + "\n\n");
                Transform t = Selection.gameObjects[0].transform;
                Vector3 originalPosition = t.position;
                t.position = Vector3.zero;
                if (!makeSubmeshes)
                {
                        meshString.Append("g ").Append(t.name).Append("\n");
                }
                meshString.Append(processTransform(t, makeSubmeshes));
                WriteToFile(meshString.ToString(),fileName);
                t.position = originalPosition;
                ObjExporterScript.End();
                Debug.Log("Exported Mesh: " + fileName);
        }
        static string processTransform(Transform t, bool makeSubmeshes)
        {
                StringBuilder meshString = new StringBuilder();
                meshString.Append("#" + t.name+ "\n#-------" + "\n");
                if (makeSubmeshes)
                {
                        meshString.Append("g ").Append(t.name).Append("\n");
                }
                MeshFilter mf = t.GetComponent<MeshFilter>();
                if (mf)
                {
                    meshString.Append(ObjExporterScript.MeshToString(mf, t));
                }
                for(int i = 0; i < t.childCount; i++)
                {
                    meshString.Append(processTransform(t.GetChild(i), makeSubmeshes));
                }
            return meshString.ToString();
        }
        static void WriteToFile(string s, string filename)
        {
            using (StreamWriter sw = new StreamWriter(filename))
            {
                    sw.Write(s);
            }
        }
}
```

Step 3: Select and export an OBJ file

The user might need to restart Unity. Now click on File, then Export, and Select the Wavefront OBJ (No Submeshes). The final step is to export it (Figure 1.34).

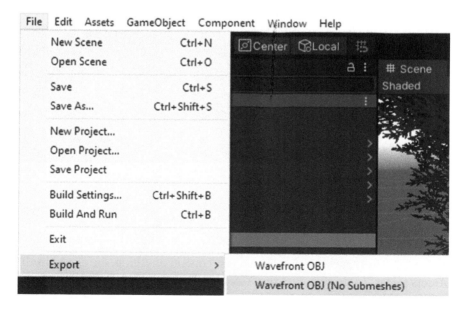

FIGURE 1.34 How to export an OBJ file.

Step 4: Destination folder

Now select the destination folder and save it; it looks like Figure 1.35.

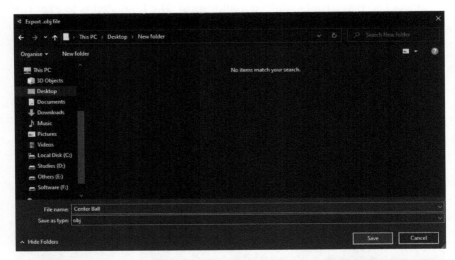

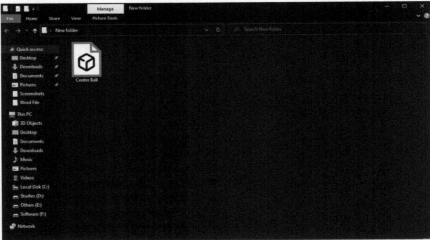

FIGURE 1.35   Find the destination folder.

1.10.4 Downgrading the Project's Unity Version

Unity allows users to export custom folder and even exporting the projects as a package. **Unitypackage** files, which can contain anything, are stored in the **Assets** folder. To do this, find the **Assets → Export Package**. This will bring up a window with a list of all the files in your inspector. To export your entire project, see the button on the export window labelled **All**. Click on this button, and it will automatically select everything within your project hierarchy. To export the package, click the **Export** button (Figure 1.36). This will prompt you to name and save your Unity package file. Be sure to give it a descriptive name.

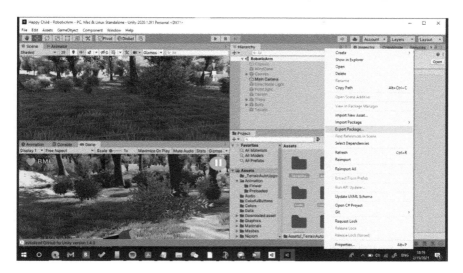

FIGURE 1.36 How to downgrade the project's Unity version.

1.10.5 Opening a Lower Version of Unity

To show the process for this case, the authors use **Unity 2020.1.0f1**, but this can apply to any version of Unity. If you installed **Unity 2020.1.0f1** on your computer, you should be able to find it on the computer's desktop shortcuts. If you have it installed on the desktop, you can skip to **Importing to a New Project**. If you do not have the lower version of Unity installed on your desktop, check to see whether **Unity Hub** is installed on your computer or not.

To use a lower version of Unity successfully, you should be aware of the below points (Figure 1.37).

Point 1: If you do not have this, it can be downloaded from https://unity3d.com/get-unity/download by selecting the **Download Unity Hub** option. Once you have downloaded the installer, open it and follow its instructions.

Point 2: If you do have Unity Hub, you can check to see if you have the correct version installed by going to the **Installs** tab at the top and selecting the Installs option from the menu on the left. If it does not appear, choose the **Official Releases** option on the left, find the correct version (**2020.1.xxx**), and select the **Download** button to its right.

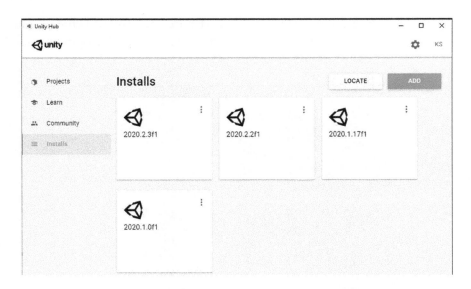

FIGURE 1.37 Different versions of Unity installed on a computer.

After downloading and installing, the version will now be located in the **Installs** tab. The user can go to the Projects tab, find the dropdown, and select the relevant version (Figure 1.38).

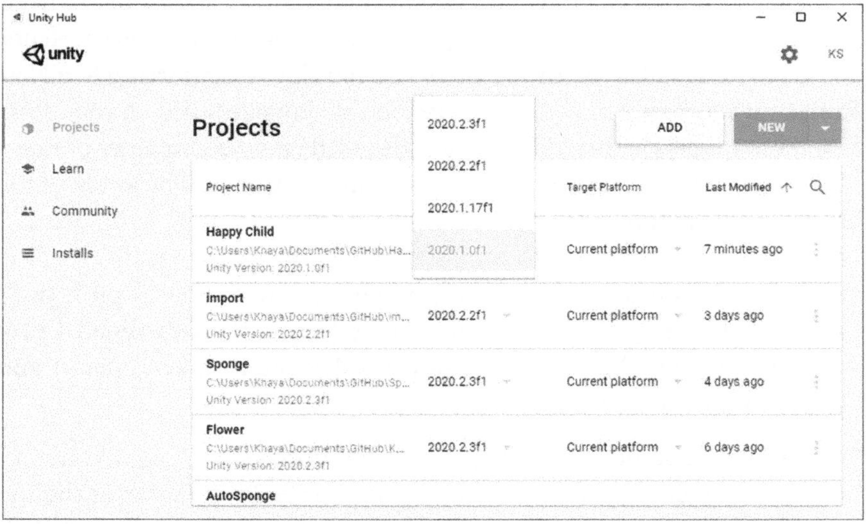

FIGURE 1.38 How to select different versions of Unity.

1.10.6 Importing to a New Project

To import the new project, the user can open the version of Unity he or she wants to use, and in the **Project** tab, select **New**. If the user uses **Unity Hub**, find the **Unity Version** dropdown and make sure that it is the correct version. Set the Project **Template** to match the old Project (it should be **Lightweight VR**). Once all the settings are correct, hit **Create Project**. When the project opens, find **Assets →**
Import-Package → Custom Package. This will prompt the user to find the **.unitypackage** file that was exported earlier. Find your file and import it. A menu will pop up with the hierarchy of assets in the package. This menu should look very similar to the export menu. Make sure you select **All** and hit **Import**. Now all your assets will be in the **Project** tab. Check your scenes to see if everything is still intact. You may have to recreate certain parts, but otherwise, it should build correctly.

1.10.7 Opening Existing Projects

To open an existing project, the user can use Hub or the Unity Launcher.

1.10.7.1 Method 1: Project opening with Unity Hub

To open an existing project with the Hub, the user can follow below steps.

First, open the Unity Hub. Then click on the **Project** on the left-hand side of Hub windows and select the project folder. After that, specify the Unity version for your project. To open it, use the allotted Editor version and the target platform. (If the selected version does not match the project version, Unity will ask for upgrading the version.) To choose the different Editor versions to specify a different target, the user can use the **Advanced Open** dialogue. The **Advanced Open** is accessible by clicking on three dots positioned to the right-hand side of the Project name and selecting the desire version (Figure 1.39).

Besides clicking the Open to the work with the existing Project, Unity Hub has a provision to open your project with any installed unity version of the editor. In this case, if Hub could not find a matching editor version for the project, it displays a cautionary message and guides the user to choose and download the correct version. Also, the users can open the project with their desired version.

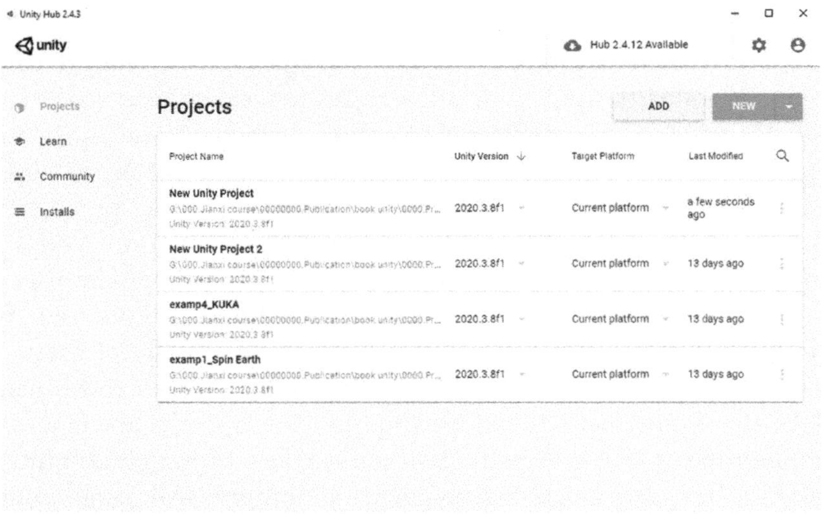

FIGURE 1.39   Open a project from Hub.

1.10.7.2 Method 2: Project opening with from the Launcher

To use this method, users can select the project part from the Home Screen's tab to contain the previously opened project on their computer. Then click on a Project in the list to open it. To view the Home Screen's projects tab from inside the Unity Editor, the users can follow the path: **File → Open Project** (Figure 1.40). In the editor's new installation or opening the project for the first time, the users can click the Open to open the file browser and find the project folder. Remember to open the project folder instead of a specific file.

FIGURE 1.40   Open a project from the Launcher.

UNITY IN EMBEDDED SYSTEM DESIGN AND ROBOTICS
A STEP-BY-STEP GUIDE

CHAPTER 2

Example 1:
Spinning Earth

DOI: 10.1201/9781003268581-2

The first example in Unity is the Spinning Earth, which aims to teach you the general perspectives of Unity by doing a simple example.

2.1 STEP 1: STARTING A NEW PROJECTS

Open Unity (Figure 2.1).

Select New in the top left corner.

Give your project a proper name.

Select an appropriate location.

Depending on the project, you have to select the appropriate template.

Add any relevant Asset Packages that you see fit for your project.

Create the project.

FIGURE 2.1   **Start a new project.**

2.2 STEP 2: LAYOUT SELECTION

We are greeted with the default layout when we start Unity initially (Figure 2.2).

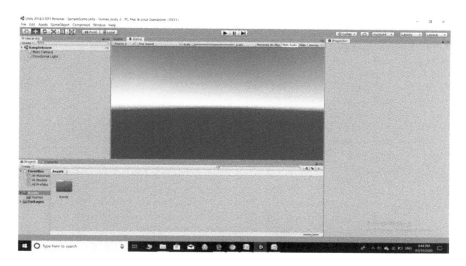

FIGURE 2.2   First view of Unity.

2.3 STEP 3: ASSETS AND PACKAGES INSERTION

After installing Unity, you need to:

Download the post-processing stack form: https://assetstore.unity.com/packages/essentials/post-processing-stack-83912

Download the models: https://assetstore.unity.com/packages/essentials/post-processing-stack-83912

Download the Prefabs: https://www.dropbox.com/s/rruyua26cvzof9x/Prefabs.rar?dl=0

Download the 1.file here: https://www.dropbox.com/s/a0d86y4uc31pcci/1.asset?dl=0

2.4 STEP 4: CREATING MATERIALS

Go to the project window and create a new folder named Materials (Figure 2.3), and follow the path: Right Click → Create → Material.

FIGURE 2.3   Creating materials.

Go to the Inspector window, click on Main maps, and select a colour of your choosing by clicking on Albedo (Figure 2.4). Repeat the same process for different colours and shades. Once configured, click and drag material to the desired object body.

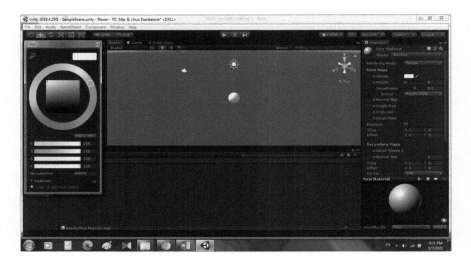

FIGURE 2.4   Select colour.

2.5 STEP 5: CREATE SPINNING EARTH

Start by opening Unity and go to GameObject → 3D Object → Sphere (Figure 2.5).

Then position of the Sphere to be exactly X: 0 Y: 0.5 Z: −7.5 in the Inspector window → Transform → Position.

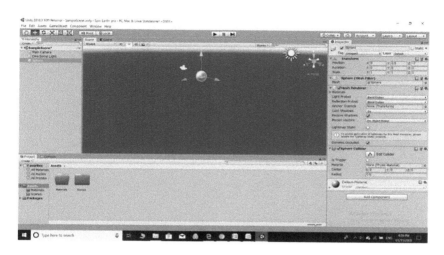

FIGURE 2.5   Select sphere and fix the position.

Now go to the Inspector window through the following path: → Add Component → on the search space type Rigidbody (Figure 2.6) and deselect

FIGURE 2.6   Add Rigidbody.

Use Gravity. The reason for deselecting gravity is to take the physics property of gravity away from the Component. This allows the Component to float freely in the 3D space.

Then again, go to Add Component → on the search space type New Script → Name (Planet_Rotation) → Create and Add (Figure 2.7).

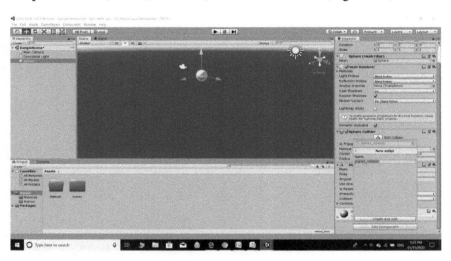

FIGURE 2.7   Add script.

Now, a C# file will be shown into the project window. Right-click on this C# file and open it with any editor (Notepad or Brackets). To apply rotation, users have two different ways to code the item.

2.6 STEP 6: CODE SECTION (FIRST TECHNIQUE)

Copy the following script and save it (Ctrl + S): (Figure 2.8)

```
        using System.Collections;
        using System.Collections.Generic;
        using UnityEngine;
public class planet_rotation: MonoBehaviour
{
        //Start is called before the first frame update
        void Start()
    {

    }
        //Update is called once per frame
        void Update()
    {
        transform.Rotate(0, 0.5f, 0);
    }
}
```

This code has different parts that are as follow:

void update():	This tells Unity to run this code after every frame. This implies that it is perpetually running.
transform.Rotate(0, 0.5f, 0);	**transform.Rotation** will be used to simulate the speed of the earth's rotation. 1st value tells the speed of rotation in X-axis, 2nd value tells the speed of rotation on the Y-axis, 3rd value tells the speed of rotation on the Z-axis. We can use integer or float values for these axes. Add (f) for float value (0.5f).

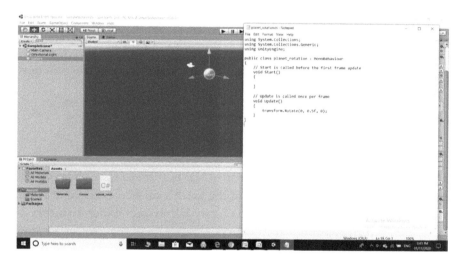

FIGURE 2.8   Save the script.

2.7 STEP 7: CODE SECTION (SECOND TECHNIQUE)

Users can also copy the following script and save it:

```
using System. Collections;
using System.Collections.Generic;
using UnityEngine;
public class planet_rotation: MonoBehaviour
{
  public float speed;

  void Update()
  {
    transform.Rotate(Vector3.up,speed*Time.deltaTime);
  }
}
```

This code also has different parts that are as follow:

public float speed;	This creates a variable called speed that can be accessed in Unity, i.e., it is public. This variable is a data type called float, which is decimal numbers.
Transform.Rotate (Vector3. up, speed* Time.deltaTime);	This is the essential part. **transform.Rotate** tells it to change or transform its rotation in the axis of Vector3.up. **Vector3** refers to a 3D plane, and **up** refers to Y-axis. So, it tells Unity to rotate our Sphere in the Y-axis. Other attributes are also there for Vector3, such as **left** and **right**, which tell Unity to rotate our Sphere in the X-axis. It tells Unity to rotate by the distance of our variable speed multiplied by **Time.deltaTime**. **Time.deltaTime** is the time since the previous frame. The frame rate constantly changes, so if the distance to be covered remains the same, the Sphere would constantly change its speed (Figure 2.9). Remember: $Speed = \frac{Distance}{time}$ or $Distance = Speed \times time$

2.8 STEP 8: FINAL PART

Drag the script from the Assets menu at the bottom to the Sphere on the scene. Now, download any picture of the earth's surface, or a texture of it, from the Internet and save it into the Unity File project folder directory or drag it onto the project folder in Unity → Navigate to the Project window and rename it to Earth.

Then select the Sphere from the Hierarchy window and drag your picture or texture onto the Sphere. Now, navigate to the script in the Inspector and change the speed (Figure 2.10). You can choose your value. Then if you click the play button, you can see spinning Earth.

Now, go to the Project window → Assets → right-click and select create → Material, and rename it to Stars. Then download any star image or texture from the Internet and drag it into the Unity → Project window.

Go to the Inspector window. You will see a dropdown menu called **Shaders**.

Select Skybox → 6 sided (Figure 2.11).

In the Inspector, a series of blank tiles will appear. This is where we insert our texture of stars (downloaded). Insert in each tile (Figure 2.12). Drag the Skybox (Stars folder) near the Sphere.

Then go to the GameObject → UI → Text.

Now, go to the Inspector window → change Anchors to "**top & centre**" (Figure 2.13).

▼ ⬛ ☑**Mesh Renderer**   ▣ ⌐ ⚙,
▶ Materials
  Light Probes | Blend Probes   ↕ |
  Reflection Probes | Blend Probes   ↕ |
  Anchor Override | None (Transform)   ◎ |
  Cast Shadows | On   ↕ |
  Receive Shadows   ☑
  Motion Vectors | Per Object Motion   ↕ |

  Lightmap Static   ☐

  ⓘ To enable generation of lightmaps for this Mesh Renderer, please
     enable the 'Lightmap Static' property.

  Dynamic Occluded   ☑

▼ ⬤ ☑**Sphere Collider**   ▣ ⌐ ⚙,
                        | ⚗ Edit Collider |
  Is Trigger   ☐
  Material | None (Physic Material)   ◎ |
  Center   X | 0 | Y | 0 | Z | 0 |
  Radius | 0.5 |

▼ ⚙ **Rigidbody**   ▣ ⌐ ⚙,
  Mass | 1 |
  Drag | 0 |
  Angular Drag | 0.05 |
  Use Gravity   ☐
  Is Kinematic   ☐
  Interpolate | None   ↕ |
  Collision Detection | Discrete   ↕ |
▶ Constraints

▼ ⬛ ☑**Planet_rotation (Script)**   ▣ ⌐ ⚙,
  Script | ⬛planet_rotation   ◎ |
  Speed | 10 |

  ⬤ Default-Material   ▣ ⚙,
     Shader | Standard   ▼ |

FIGURE 2.9   Speed value in Inspector window.

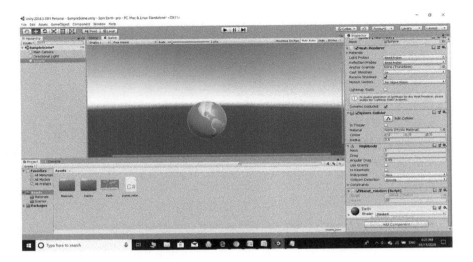

FIGURE 2.10   Change speed value and click the play button.

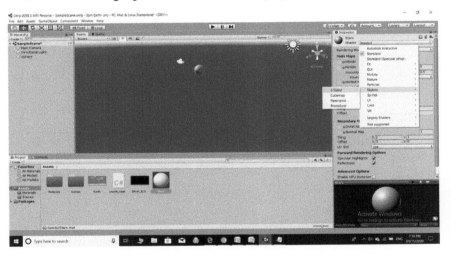

FIGURE 2.11   Select Skybox from Shaders.

Set PosX: 0 PosY: --210 PosZ: 0

Set Width: 1500, Height: 345

Go to the Text (Script) → write the Text (HELLO WORLD!).

Change Font Style → Bold and Italic and Font Size → 70

Set the Alignment → Middle sign, Color → White.

Now, save all these things or click (Ctrl + S).

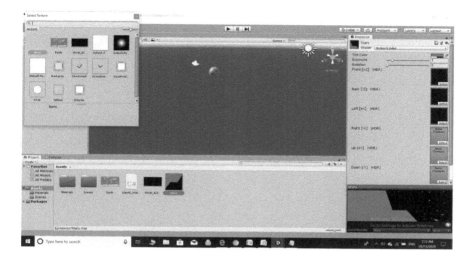

FIGURE 2.12   Add textures for the background.

FIGURE 2.13   Spinning Earth ready.

Click the play button then you can see a Spinning Earth. You can change the speed value or the axis value (X, Y, and Z) to change the speed of sphere rotation.

CHAPTER 3

Example 2: Wooden Doll Body

DOI: 10.1201/9781003268581-3

The second example is about creating the Wooden Doll Body. In this example, the user will learn how to create each part and section of a wooden doll. This example ended with creating the EXE file. To create a character, a user needs some objects. For that, the user should go to the Hierarchy menu, then right-click and select the 3D object.

Then, the user should create body, hands, mouth, nose, feet, and fingers with the Cube, and with a Cylinder, the user can create legs and a neck. Using Sphere, the user can also create head, eyes, shoulder, palm, and elbow.

3.1 STEP 1: CREATING THE PARTS OF A WOODEN DOLL

3.1.1 Creating Body

Select the Cube and insert the values provided in Table 3.1 for the position bar and scale bar (Figure 3.1).

TABLE 3.1 The Position Bar and Scale Bar Data for Body

	X	Y	Z
Position bar	0	−0.98	−3.64
Scale bar	4	9	4

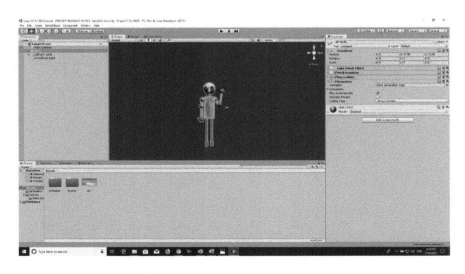

FIGURE 3.1 How to create a body for the wooden doll.

3.1.2 Making Head

Select the Sphere, insert the values provided in Table 3.2 for the position bar and scale bar (Figure 3.2).

TABLE 3.2   The Position Bar and Scale Bar Data for Head

	X	Y	Z
Position bar	0.0025	0.9300001	0
Scale bar	1.25	0.5555556	1.25

FIGURE 3.2   How to create a head for the wooden doll.

3.1.3 Creating Eyes

Select the Sphere, insert the values provided in Table 3.3 for the position bar and scale bar.

TABLE 3.3   The Position Bar and Scale Bar Data for Eyes

	X	Y	Z
Position bar	−0.278	0.04857148	−0.4028572
Scale bar	0.3428571	0.3428571	0.3428571

For the other eye, the user needs to duplicate the first one and change it by clicking on it. In that case, select the second Sphere and put a minus before the magnitude in the Y direction. For the eyeballs, you will follow the same procedure. The only difference is about choosing some new scale bars that should be less than the previous spheres (Figure 3.3).

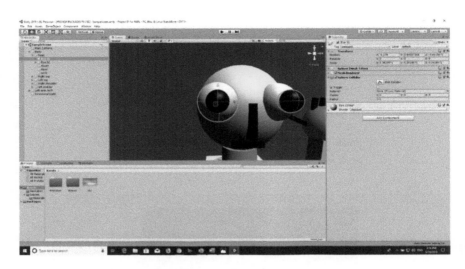

FIGURE 3.3 How to create eyes for the wooden doll.

3.1.4 Creating Mouth

Select the Cube and insert the values provided in Table 3.4 for the position bar and scale bar (Figure 3.4).

TABLE 3.4 The Position Bar and Scale Bar Data for Mouth

	X	Y	Z
Position bar	−0.007	−0.3399999	−0.3714285
Scale bar	0.3	0.5714285	0.02857143

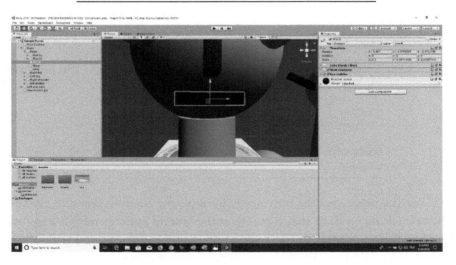

FIGURE 3.4 How to create a mouth for the wooden doll.

3.1.5 Creating Nose

Select the Cube and insert the values provided in Table 3.5 for the position bar and scale bar in the Inspector menu bar (Figure 3.5).

TABLE 3.5   The Position Bar and Scale Bar Data for Nose

	X	Y	Z
Position bar	−0.01	−0.1114287	−0.457
Scale bar	0.05714285	0.2857143	0.1428571

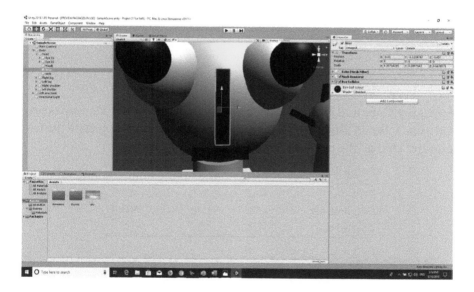

FIGURE 3.5   How to create a nose for the wooden doll.

3.1.6 Creating Neck

Select the Cylinder and enter the Inspector menu bar, and insert the values provided in Table 3.6 (Figure 3.6).

TABLE 3.6   The Position Bar and Scale Bar Data for Neck

	X	Y	Z
Position bar	−0.006	−0.854	0.04599996
Scale bar	0.4	0.4	0.4

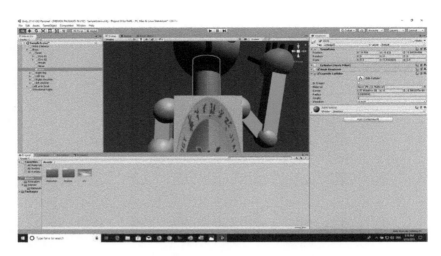

FIGURE 3.6 How to create a head for the wooden doll.

3.1.7 Creating Legs

Select the Cube and go to the Inspector menu bar to insert the values provided in Table 3.7. Then, for the other leg, the user should duplicate the first one and change the position (Figure 3.7).

TABLE 3.7 The Position Bar and Scale Bar Data for Leg

	X	Y	Z
Position bar	−0.27	−1.08	0.01368141
Scale bar	0.175	0.6	0.125

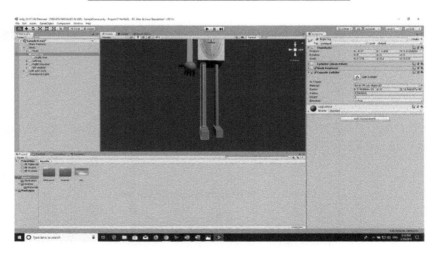

FIGURE 3.7 How to create legs for the wooden doll.

3.1.8 Creating Feet

Select the Cube and enter to the Inspector menu bar and insert the values provided in Table 3.8. For the other foot, duplicate the first one and change its position (Figure 3.8).

TABLE 3.8   The Position Bar and Scale Bar Data for Leg

	X	Y	Z
Position bar	0.08	−1.068	−2.009451
Scale bar	1.428571	0.2	6

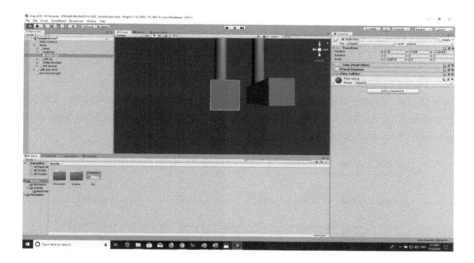

FIGURE 3.8   How to create feet for the wooden doll.

3.1.9 Creating Shoulders

Select the Sphere and enter the Inspector menu bar and insert the values provided in Table 3.9. For the other shoulder, the user should duplicate the first one and change the position (Figure 3.9).

TABLE 3.9   The Position Bar and Scale Bar Data for Shoulder

	X	Y	Z
Position bar	−0.73	0.38	0.01000005
Scale bar	0.175	0.6	0.125

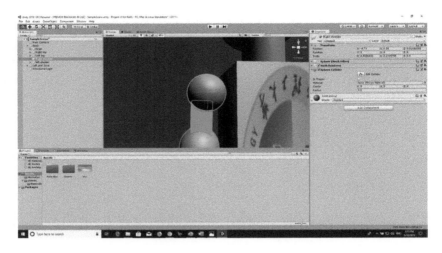

FIGURE 3.9   How to create shoulders for the wooden doll.

3.1.10 Creating Elbow

Select the Sphere and enter the Inspector menu bar and insert the values provided in Table 3.10. For the other elbow, duplicate the first one and change the position (Figure 3.10).

TABLE 3.10   The Position Bar and Scale Bar Data for Elbow

	X	Y	Z
Position bar	−0.187784	−1.422837	−0.003414392
Scale bar	1	1	1

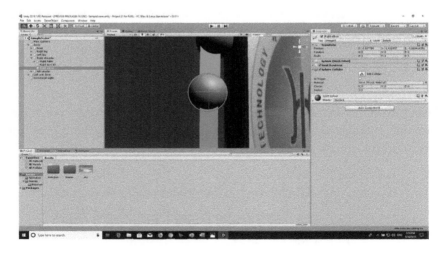

FIGURE 3.10   How to create an elbow for the wooden doll.

3.1.11 Creating Arm Joints

To create the first joint, the user should create an empty Hierarchy menu by right-clicking the mouse button. After that, you have to go to the Inspector menu bar and insert the values provided in Table 3.11 for the position and scale bar, respectively (Figure 3.11).

TABLE 3.11   The Position Bar and Scale Bar Data for Arm Joint

	X	Y	Z
Position bar	4.48	0.31	−3.971714
Scale bar	1	1	1

FIGURE 3.11   How to create arm joints for the wooden doll.

3.2 STEP 2: NESTING ALL THE OBJECTS

Nesting is one of the most important things for creating the moving character. First, the user will nest everything except the main camera, left arm joint, and directional light. After that, the user will nest the eye, mouth, nose, and neck in the head. Then the user will nest left and right feet in the left and right legs. For the left and right shoulders, the user will nest palm, elbow, and arm. For both of the palms, the user will nest fingers in them, and finally, for the left-arm joint, the user will nest the left arm in it.

3.3 STEP 3: MOVING THE OBJECTS

To move the first object, select the left-arm joint in the Hierarchy menu. Then, go to the Inspector menu, add a new component, ANIMATOR, and then create a new animation. After that, when go to the window and select animation, an animation box will appear. At first, in the box, select the timer for 45 seconds and click the record button, and then you will change the joint's rotation for Z to 327.77. Then you will again change the timer to 90 seconds and change the rotation for Z to 450 again. Now, click the record button again to stop the recording. The user can see the movement by clicking the play button in the window of animation.

3.4 STEP 4: FINALISATION AND EXTRACTING EXE FILE

Now, character is ready to move if you play the game; you can see that it's waving. To create the EXE file, you need to do the following steps:

Go to the file → Build setting → Platform → Built and run → Target folder → Select folder (Figure 3.12).

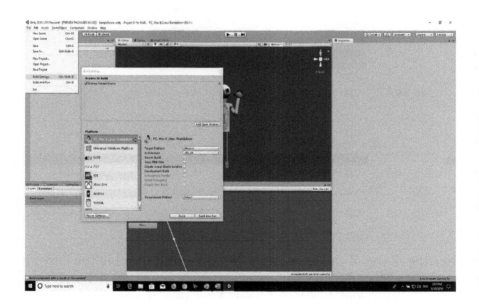

FIGURE 3.12   How to create an EXE file for the wooden doll.

UNITY IN EMBEDDED SYSTEM DESIGN
AND ROBOTICS
A STEP-BY-STEP GUIDE

CHAPTER 4

Example 3: Create the Semi Jungle Environment

DOI: 10.1201/9781003268581-4

The third example describes the steps to make the different characters, like sunflower, butterfly, tree, and cloud, on the same screen. In this example, the developer will learn who to make each character and combine them on the same screen.

4.1 STEP 1: ENVIRONMENT PREPARATION

Start by opening Unity and go to GameObject → 3D Object → Plane.

As Figure 4.1, In Inspector → Transform → Scale, change the scale of the Plane to X: 10, Y: 10, Z: 20.

Also, in Inspector → Transform → Position, change the position of the Plane to X: 0, Y: −4.5, Z: 0.

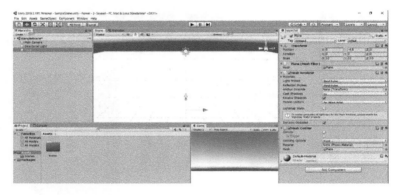

FIGURE 4.1   Create a Plane.

Go to project window → Assets (Figure 4.2).

Right-click into the Assets → Create → Materials.

Rename it to Ground.

FIGURE 4.2   Create Materials.

Click on the Ground. Go to Inspector → Main maps → Albedo (Figure 4.3) and select any colour for the Ground.

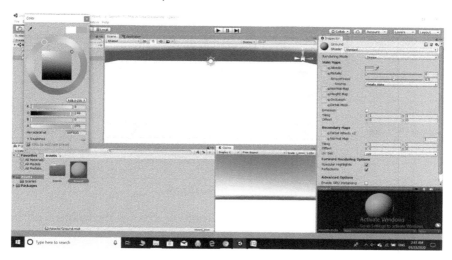

FIGURE 4.3   Select colour for Ground.

Click on Plane from Hierarchy (Figure 4.4), then drag the Ground colour to the Plane.

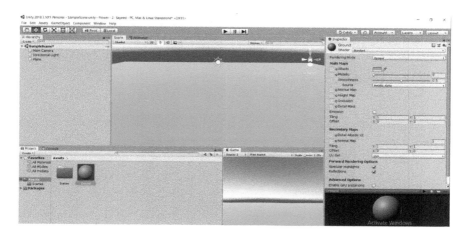

FIGURE 4.4   Add Ground colour.

Click on the Main Camera from Hierarchy (Figure 4.5).

In Inspector → Transform → Position, change the position magnitudes for the Camera to:

X: −0.2, Y: −0.33, Z: 30

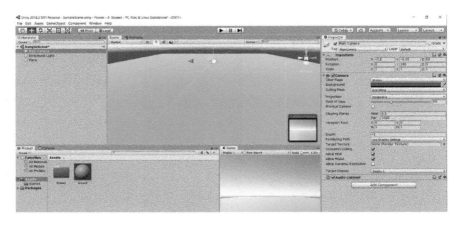

FIGURE 4.5   Fix the Camera rotation and position.

Also, in Inspector → Transform → Rotation, change the rotation of the Camera to:

X: 0, Y: 180, Z: 0

Click on the Directional Light from Hierarchy (Figure 4.6).

In Inspector → Transform → Position, change the position magnitudes for the Light to:

X: 6.2, Y: 3, Z: 3.6

Also, in Inspector → Transform → Rotation, change the rotation of the Light to:

X: 17.2, Y: −105, Z: −48

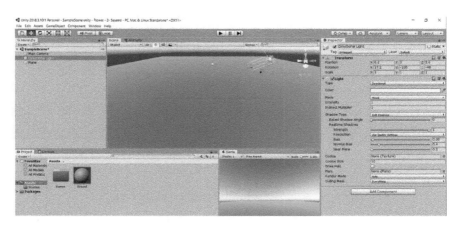

FIGURE 4.6   Fix Directional Light position and rotation.

4.2 STEP 2: MAKING THE FLOWER BASE

Now go to GameObject → 3D Object → Cylinder (Figure 4.7).

Rename it to Base.

Change the position of the Base to, X: −0.67, Y: −4.06, Z: 0, in Inspector → Transform → Position. And also change the scale of Base to X: 4, Y: 0.35, Z: 4, in Inspector → Transform → Scale.

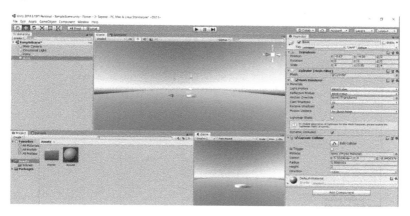

FIGURE 4.7   Create a Base.

Go to Project window → Assets.

Right-click into the Assets → Create → Materials (Figure 4.8).

Rename it to Base.

Click on the Base. Go to Inspector → Main maps → Albedo.

Select any colour for Ground.

Click on Base from Hierarchy and drag the colour to the Base.

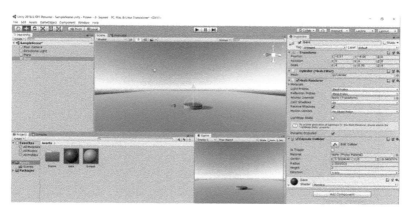

FIGURE 4.8   Select the colour and drag it to Base.

4.3 STEP 3: MAKING THE FLOWER PART DISK FLORETS

Now right on Base from Hierarchy → 3D Object → Sphere (Figure 4.9). Rename it to Head. Then change the position of the Head to X: 0, Y: 14.83, Z: 0, from Inspector → Transform → Position and the scale of the Head, to X: 0.25, Y: 2.86, Z: 0.25, from Inspector → Transform → Scale.

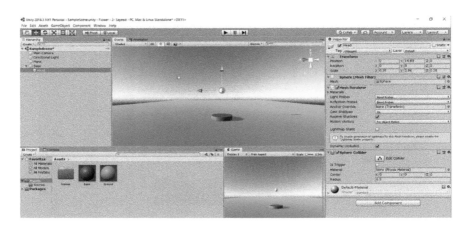

FIGURE 4.9   Create a Sphere (Head).

Now create any colour for Head by going to the Project window → Assets and following the previous steps. Drag the colour to the Head (Figure 4.10).

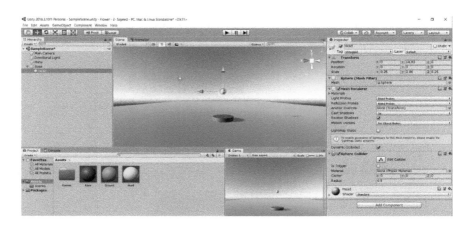

FIGURE 4.10   Select the colour and drag it to Head.

4.4 STEP 4: MAKING THE FLOWER PART INFLORESCENCE

Now right on Head from Hierarchy → 3D Object → Sphere (Figure 4.11). Rename it to P1 and change the position of the P1 to X: 1.353, Y: 0.08, Z: 0 from Inspector → Transform → Position, and the scale of the P1 to X: 1.9, Y: 0.7, Z: 0.5 from Inspector → Transform → Scale.

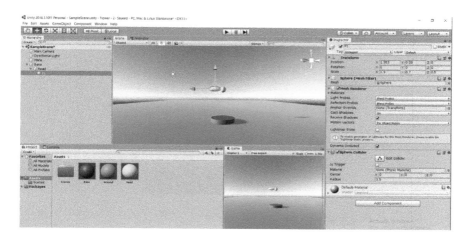

FIGURE 4.11   Create a Sphere (P1).

Now create any colour for P1 into the Project window → Assets by following the previous steps. Drag the colour to P1 (Figure 4.12).

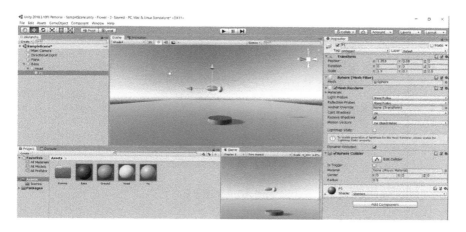

FIGURE 4.12   Select any colour and drag it to P1.

Now right-click on P1 from Hierarchy → Duplicate (Figure 4.13).
Rename it to P2.

Position of the P2 to X: −1.353, Y: 0.08, Z: 0 from Inspector →
Transform → Position.

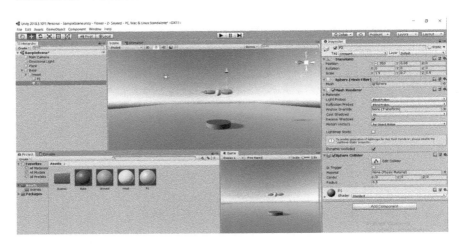

FIGURE 4.13   Duplicate the P1.

Then create any colour for P2 into the Project window → Assets by following the previous steps. Drag the colour to P2 (Figure 4.14).

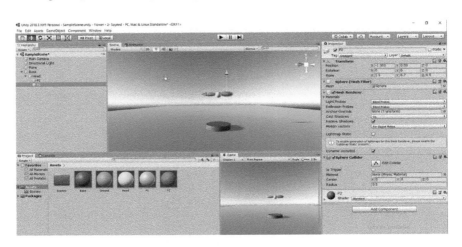

FIGURE 4.14   Select any colour and drag it to P2.

Right-click on P2 from Hierarchy → Duplicate (Figure 4.15). Rename
it to P3.

The position of the P3 must be exactly X: −0.017, Y: −1.34, Z: 0 by going to Inspector → Transform → Position and scale it to X: 0.7, Y: 1.9, Z: 0.5.

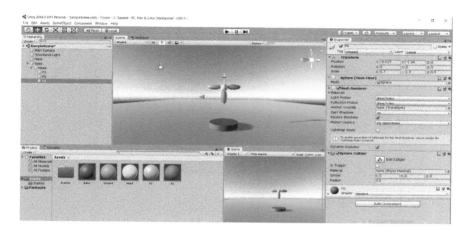

FIGURE 4.15   Create P3.

Create any colour for P3 into the Project window → Assets and drag the colour to P3 as Figure 4.16.

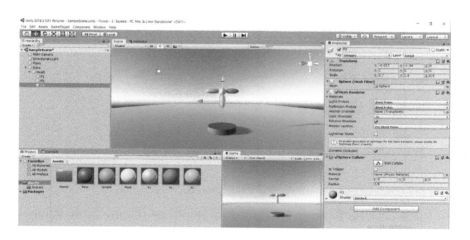

FIGURE 4.16   Select any colour and drag it to P3.

For creating P4, you need to duplicate P3; therefore, right-click on P3 from Hierarchy → Duplicate (Figure 4.17) then rename it to P4.

In Inspector → Transform → Position, change the position of the P4 to X: −0.017, Y: 1.34, Z: 0.

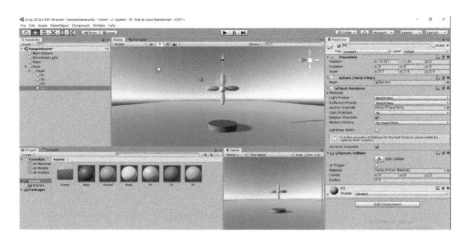

FIGURE 4.17   Create P4.

As Figure 4.18, create any colour for P3 into the Project window →
Assets and drag the colour to P4.

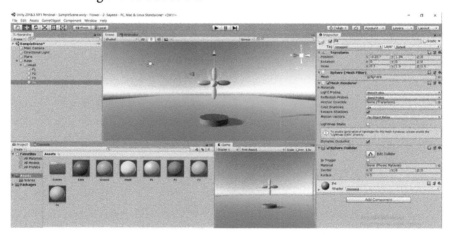

FIGURE 4.18   Select any colour and drag it to P4.

Right-click on P4 from Hierarchy → Duplicate (Figure 4.19). Rename
the new object to P5.

In Inspector → Transform → Position, change the position of the P5 to
X: 1, Y: 0.96, Z: 0.

In Inspector → Transform → Scale, change the scale value of the P5 to
X: 1.9, Y: 0.7, Z: 0.5.

In Inspector → Transform → Rotation, change the rotation value of the
P5 to X: 0, Y: 0, Z: 38.68.

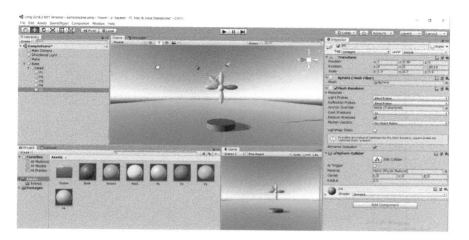

FIGURE 4.19   Create P5.

Again, create any colour for P5 into the Project window →
Assets by following the previous steps and drag the colour to P5
(Figure 4.20).

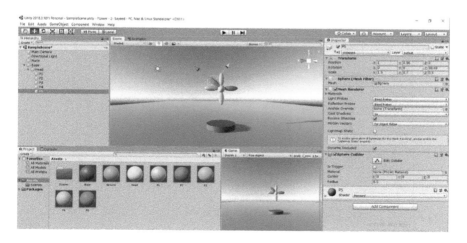

FIGURE 4.20   Select any colour and drag it to P5.

Right-click on P5 from Hierarchy → Duplicate (Figure 4.21). Rename
it to P6. Change the position of the P6 to X: −1, Y: −0.85, Z: 0 from
Inspector → Transform → Position.

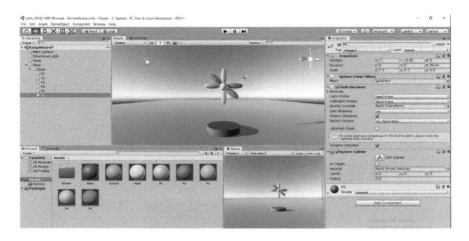

FIGURE 4.21   Create P6.

Now create any colour for P6 from the Project window → Assets by following the previous steps (Figure 4.22). Drag the colour to P6.

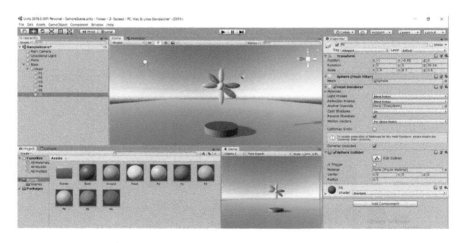

FIGURE 4.22   Select any colour and drag it to P6.

Right-click on P6 from Hierarchy → Duplicate (Figure 4.23). Rename it to P7.

Change the position of the P7 to X: −1, Y: 0.85, Z: 0 from Inspector → Transform → Position and the scale of the P7 to X: 1.9, Y: 0.7, Z: 0.5 from Inspector → Transform → Scale and the rotation of the P7 to X: 0, Y: 0, Z: −34.35 from Inspector → Transform → Rotation.

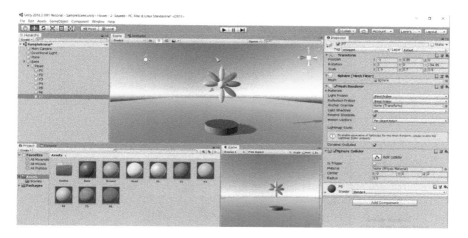

FIGURE 4.23   Create P7.

Again, create any colour for P7 into the Project window → Assets by following the previous steps (Figure 4.24). Drag the colour to P7.

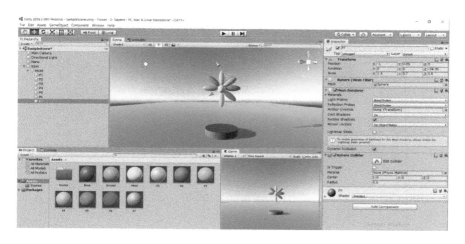

FIGURE 4.24   Select any colour and drag it to P7.

Now right-click on P7 from Hierarchy → Duplicate (Figure 4.25). Rename it to P8.

In the Inspector → Transform → Position, change the position magnitude of the P8 to X: 1, Y: −0.85, Z: 0. Then create a colour for P8 from the Project window → Assets (Figure 4.26). Drag this colour to P8.

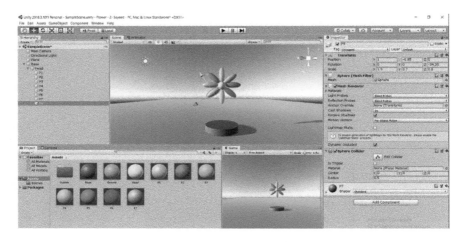

FIGURE 4.25   Create P8.

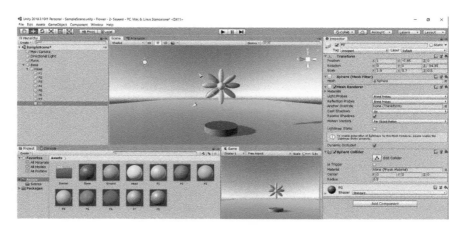

FIGURE 4.26   Select any colour and drag it to P8.

4.5 STEP 5: MAKING A FLOWER – STEM

Now right-click on Base from Hierarchy → 3D Object → Cylinder (Figure 4.27). Rename it to Stem. Change the position of the Stem to X: −0.02, Y: 6.6, Z: −0.125 and the Stem scale to be precise, X: 0.08, Y: 5.72, Z: 0.25, in Inspector → Transform → Position and Scale, respectively. Then create another colour for Stem from the Project window → Assets (Figure 4.28) and drag the colour to Stem.

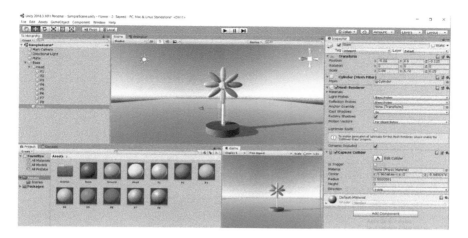

FIGURE 4.27   Create a Cylinder as Stem.

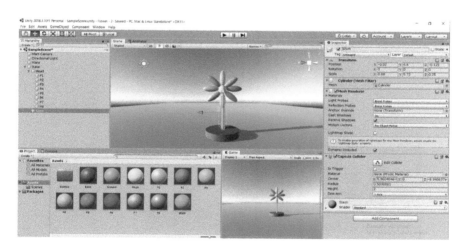

FIGURE 4.28   Select any colour and drag it to Stem.

Right-click on Base from Hierarchy → 3D Object → Capsule (Figure 4.29). Rename it to Leaf base. Change the position of the Leaf base to X: −0.02, Y: 4.12, Z: −0.125 and the scale of the Leaf base to X: 0.375, Y: 0.285, Z: 0.25 from Inspector → Transform → Position and Scale. Then drag the Stem colour to the Leaf base (Figure 4.30).

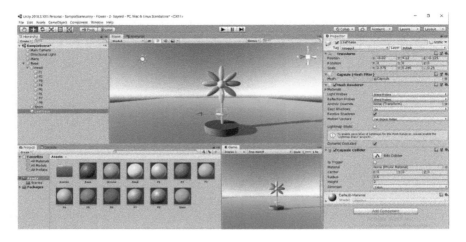

FIGURE 4.29   Create Leaf base.

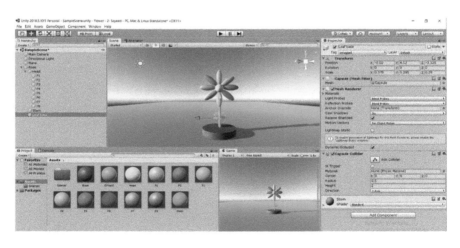

FIGURE 4.30   Drag the Stem colour to the Leaf base.

4.6 STEP 6: MAKING A FLOWER – LEAVES

Then go to GameObject → 3D Object → Cube (Figure 4.31). Rename it to R Leaf Stem.

Position of the R Leaf Stem to be exactly, X: −1.22, Y: −2.27, Z: −0.125 in Inspector → Transform → Position.

The scale of the R Leaf Stem to be exactly X: 0.1, Y: 1, Z: 0.1 in Inspector → Transform → Scale.

Rotation of the R Leaf Stem to be exactly, X: 0, Y: 0, Z: 46.8 in
Inspector → Transform → Rotation.

Then drag the Stem colour to R Leaf Stem (Figure 4.32).

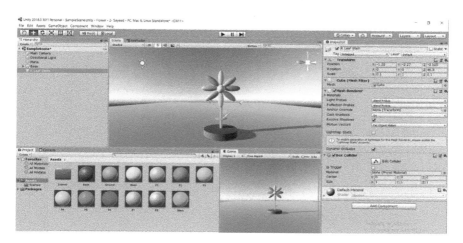

FIGURE 4.31   **Add Right Leaf Stem.**

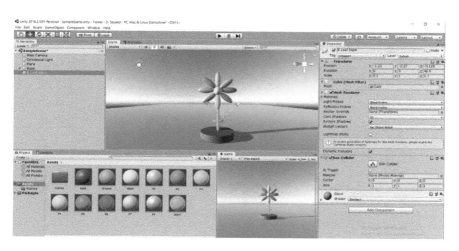

FIGURE 4.32   Add the Stem colour.

Right-click on R Leaf Stem → 3D Object → Sphere (Figure 4.33).
Rename it to Right Leaf. Change the position magnitudes of the Right
Leaf to X: 0, Y: 1.44, Z: −0.125 in Inspector → Transform → Position
and the scale values of the Right Leaf to X: 6, Y: 2, Z: 0.5 in Inspector →
Transform → Scale.

Then drag the Stem colour to Right Leaf (Figure 4.34).

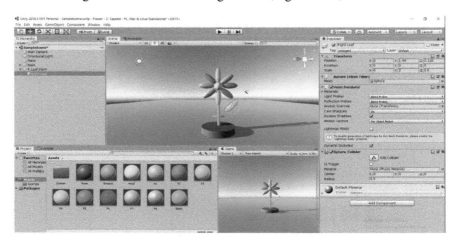

FIGURE 4.33 Create Right Leaf.

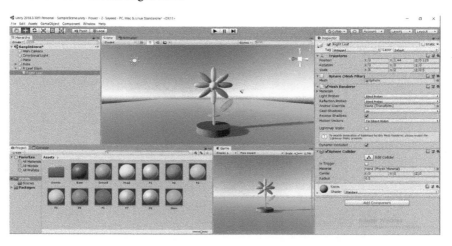

FIGURE 4.34 Add Right Leaf colour.

Right-click on R Leaf Stem → 3D Object → Cube (Figure 4.35).

Rename it to L Leaf Stem.

Position of the L Leaf Stem to be exactly X: 5.85, Y: −0.55, Z: −0.125, in Inspector → Transform → Position.

The scale of the L Leaf Stem to be exactly X: 0.1, Y: 10, Z: 1, in Inspector → Transform → Scale.

Rotation of the L Leaf Stem to be exactly, X: 0, Y: 0, Z: 88.2, in Inspector → Transform → Rotation.

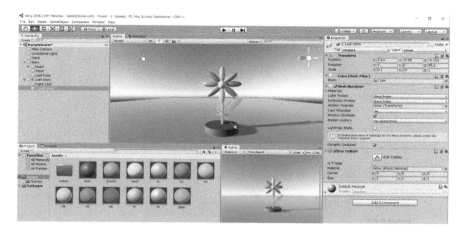

FIGURE 4.35   Add Left Leaf Stem.

Then drag the Stem colour to L Leaf Stem (Figure 4.36).

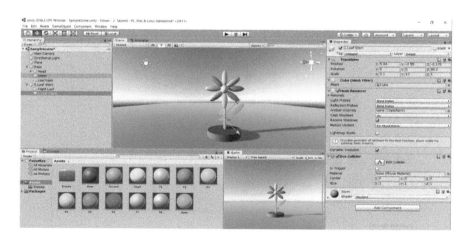

FIGURE 4.36   Add Left Leaf Stem colour.

Right-click on L Leaf Stem → 3D Object → Sphere (Figure 4.37).
Rename it to Left Leaf.
Position of the Left Leaf to be exactly, X: −0.1, Y: −1.24, Z: −0.125, in Inspector → Transform → Position.
The scale of the Left Leaf to be exactly X: 6, Y: 2, Z: 0.5, in Inspector → Transform → Scale.

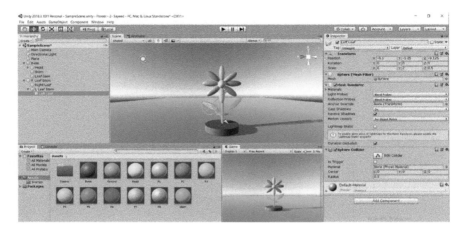

FIGURE 4.37   Add Left Leaf.

Then drag the Stem colour to the Left Leaf (Figure 4.38).

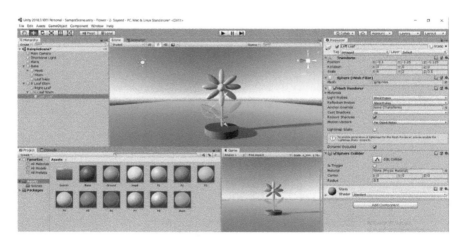

FIGURE 4.38   Add Left Leaf colour.

4.7 STEP 7: MAKING A TREE – STEM

Now go to GameObject → 3D Object → Cylinder (Figure 4.39).

Rename it to Tree Stem(1).

Position of the Tree Stem(1) to be exactly, X: −15.5, Y: −1, Z: −4, in Inspector → Transform → Position.

The scale of the Tree Stem(1) to be exactly X: 0.7, Y: 4, Z: 0.5, in Inspector → Transform → Scale.

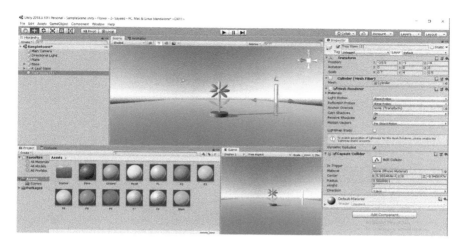

FIGURE 4.39   Add a Tree Stem.

Now create any colour for Tree Stem into the Project window → Assets by following previous steps (Figure 4.40). Drag the colour to Tree Stem.

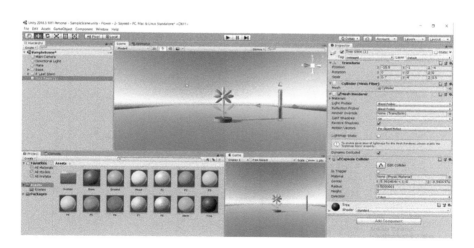

FIGURE 4.40   Add Tree Stem colour.

Right-click on Tree Stem(1) → Duplicate (Figure 4.41). Rename it to Tree Stem(2).

Position of the Tree Stem(2) to be exactly, X: 11.3, Y: −1, Z: −4, in Inspector → Transform → Position.

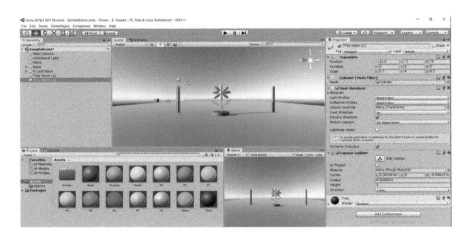

FIGURE 4.41   Add another Tree Stem.

4.8 STEP 8: MAKING A TREES – CROWN

Now go to GameObject → 3D Object → Sphere (Figure 4.42). Rename it to Tree(1).

Position of the Tree(1) to be exactly, X: −15.3, Y: 4.55, Z: −4, in Inspector → Transform → Position.

The Tree(1) scale is exactly X: 7, Y: 7, Z: 6, in Inspector → Transform → Scale.

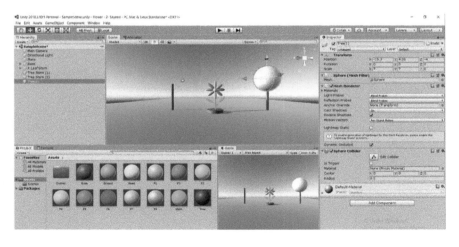

FIGURE 4.42   Add a tree crown.

Create any colour for Tree(1) into the Project window → Assets by following previous steps (Figure 4.43). Drag the colour to Tree(1).

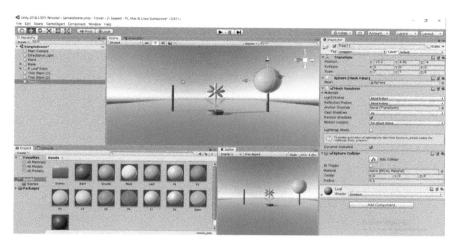

FIGURE 4.43 Add Tree(1) colour.

Right-click on Tree(1) → Duplicate (Figure 4.44). Rename it to Tree(2). Position of the Tree(2) to be exactly, X: 11.3, Y: 4.55, Z: −4, in Inspector → Transform → Position.

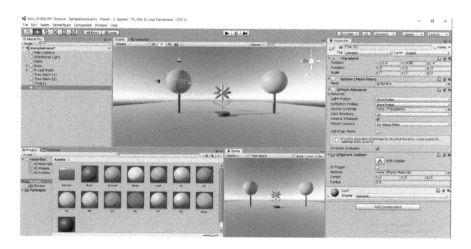

FIGURE 4.44 Add another tree crown.

These four components must be connected to each other. To do this, we need to move the components (Tree Stem(2), Tree(1), and Tree(2)) in the Hierarchy to Tree Stem(1) (Figure 4.45).

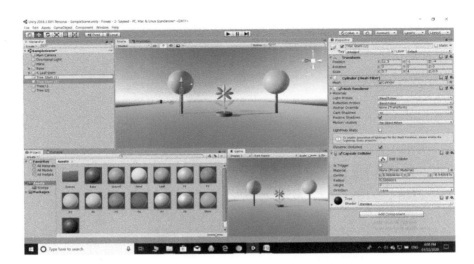

FIGURE 4.45   Connect the components.

4.9 STEP 9: MAKING A BUTTERFLY – HEAD

Go to GameObject → 3D Object → Sphere (Figure 4.46). Rename it to Butterfly – Head.

Position of the Butterfly – Head to be exactly, X: −5.72, Y: 1.62, Z: 0.2, in Inspector → Transform → Position.

Add any colour to Butterfly – Head.

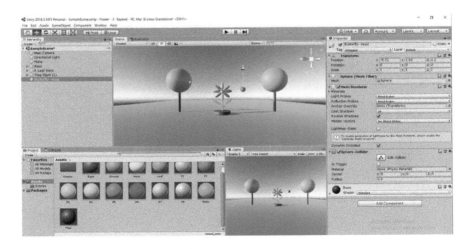

FIGURE 4.46   Add butterfly – head.

4.10 STEP 10: MAKING A BUTTERFLY – BODY

Right-click on Butterfly – Head → 3D Object → Sphere (Figure 4.47). Rename it to Body.

Position of the Body to be exactly, X: −1.33, Y: −1.2, Z: 0, in Inspector → Transform → Position.

The scale of the Body to be exactly X: 3, Y: 0.5, Z: 1, in Inspector → Transform → Scale.

Rotation of the Body to be exactly, X: 0, Y: 180, Z: −46, in Inspector → Transform → Rotation.

Add any colour to the Body.

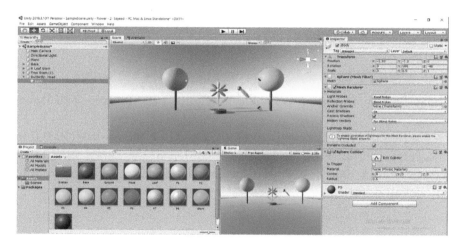

FIGURE 4.47 Add butterfly – body.

4.11 STEP 11: MAKING A BUTTERFLY – TOP WING

Right-click on Butterfly – Head → 3D Object → Sphere (Figure 4.48). Rename it to Top wing.

Position of the Top wing to be exactly, X: −1.64, Y: 0.36, Z: 0, in Inspector → Transform → Position. The Top wing scale is exactly X: 2.5, Y: 1.8, Z: 0.5, in Inspector → Transform → Scale. Rotation of the Top wing to be exactly, X: 0, Y: 180, Z: 65, in Inspector → Transform → Rotation.

Add any colour to Top wing.

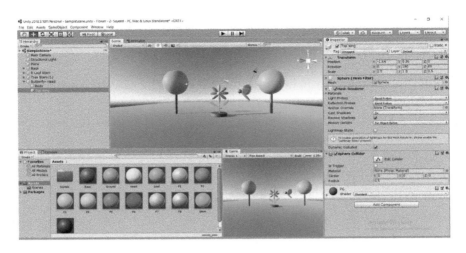

FIGURE 4.48 Add top wing.

4.12 STEP 12: MAKING A BUTTERFLY – DOWN WING

Right-click on Top wing → Duplicate (Figure 4.49). Rename it to Down wing.

Position of the Down wing to be exactly, X: −2.38, Y: −0.68, Z: 0.1, in Inspector → Transform → Position. Rotation of the Down wing to be exactly, X: 0, Y: 360, Z: 7.58, in Inspector → Transform → Rotation. Add any colour to the Down wing.

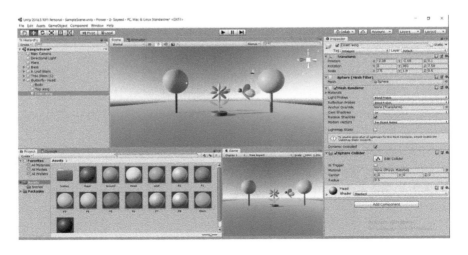

FIGURE 4.49 Add down wing.

4.13 STEP 13: MAKING A CLOUD

Go to GameObject → 3D Object → Sphere (Figure 4.50). Rename it to Cloud.

Fix any position for Cloud and, finally, add colour to Cloud.

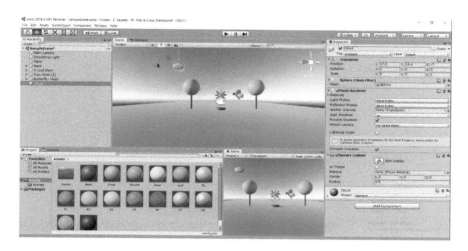

FIGURE 4.50   Add cloud.

Right-click on Cloud → Duplicate (Figure 4.51). Add more Cloud by following the same steps. Only change the position from the Inspection window.

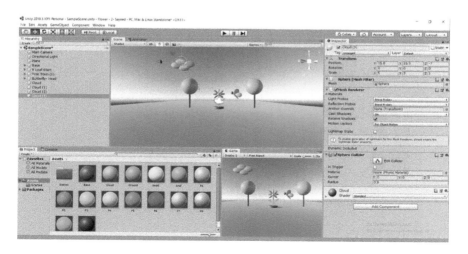

FIGURE 4.51   Add more cloud.

Connect all Cloud components to make more clouds (Figure 4.52). Add as many clouds as you want (Figure 4.53). Save all the things by clicking Ctrl + S.

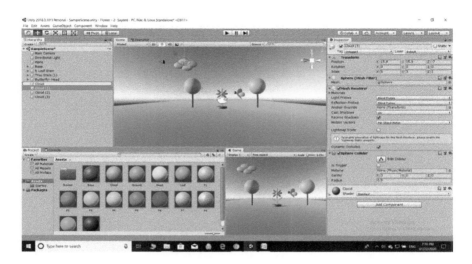

FIGURE 4.52 Connect all cloud components.

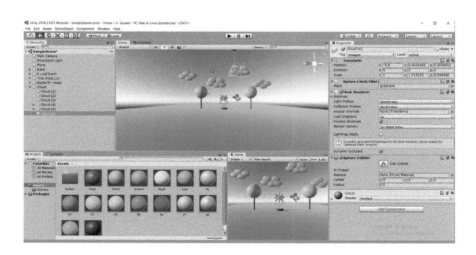

FIGURE 4.53 Add more clouds.

UNITY IN EMBEDDED SYSTEM DESIGN
AND ROBOTICS
A STEP-BY-STEP GUIDE

CHAPTER 5

Example 4: Create KUKA Robot

DOI: 10.1201/9781003268581-5

The fourth example describes the process of making the KUKA robot. This type of robot is used in various applications because of its degree of freedom (DOF). Popular KUKA robots are used for the production of automobiles. These robots are used to assemble vehicle components such as engines, axles, brakes, and steering systems. The accuracy of KUKA's assembly robots ensures all automotive components are assembled correctly for the overall safety of each vehicle. Their long reach enables access to parts at difficult angles and larger workpieces. In contrast, their precise and controlled movements provide the ability to join the most intricate details. In this example, you will learn how to make this robot step by step.

5.1 STEP 1: CREATE A ROBOTIC ARM

Open the Unity and navigate to the path: GameObject → 3D Object → Plane (Figure 5.1).

In Inspector window → Transform → Scale: Scale of the Plane to X: 10, Y: 0.5, Z: 10.

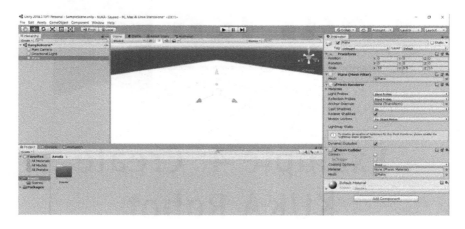

FIGURE 5.1 Select Plane and fix the scale.

Go to Project window → Assets (Figure 5.2).
Right-click into Assets → Create → Folder.
Rename it to Plane.
Double click on the Plane → Create → Materials (Figure 5.3).
Rename it to Ground.

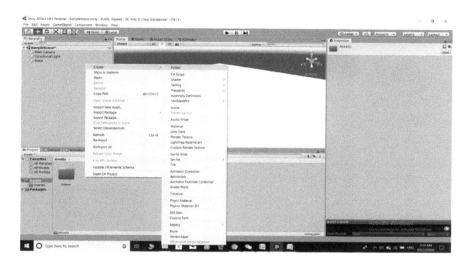

FIGURE 5.2   Create a folder.

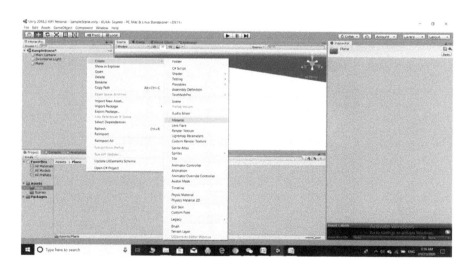

FIGURE 5.3   Create materials.

Now click on the Ground in Plane → Inspector → Main Maps → Albedo (Figure 5.4).

Select a colour for Ground.

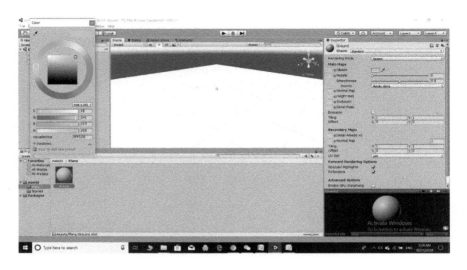

FIGURE 5.4 Select colour for ground.

Then click on Plane from Hierarchy (Figure 5.5). Drag the ground colour to the Plane.

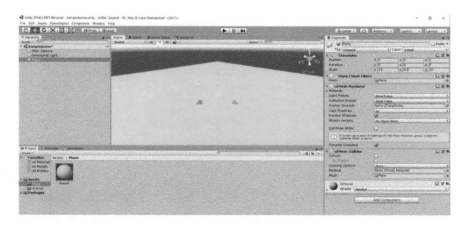

FIGURE 5.5 Drag the colour to the Plane.

5.2 STEP 2: MAKING THE KUKA BASE

Go to GameObject → 3D Object → Cube (Figure 5.6).

In Inspector → Transform, change the following value:

	X	Y	Z
Scale	1.5	2.5	1.5

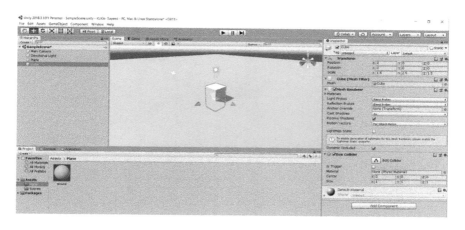

FIGURE 5.6   Create cube as the KUKA base.

Now double click on the Plane window → Create → Materials (Figure 5.7).

Rename it to Cube.

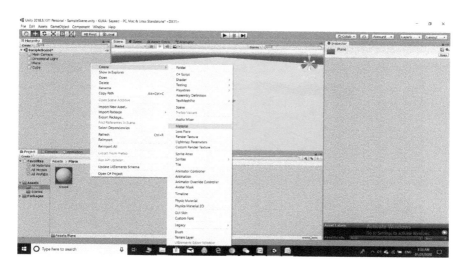

FIGURE 5.7   Create materials for cube.

Click on the Cube in Plane → Inspector → Main Maps → Albedo.

Select a colour for Cube, then click on Cube from Hierarchy and drag the colour to Cube (Figure 5.8).

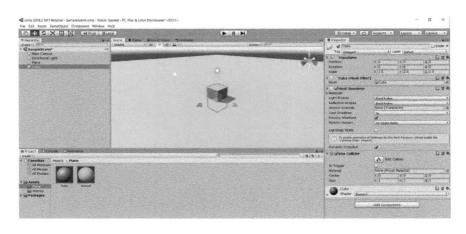

FIGURE 5.8   Drag the colour to cube.

5.3 STEP 3: MAKING THE KUKA ARM

Go to GameObject → 3D Object → Cylinder (Figure 5.9).
In Inspector → Transform → Scale

	X	Y	Z
Scale	1	2.5	1

FIGURE 5.9   Create Cylinder as the robot arm.

5.4 STEP 4: MAKING THE KUKA JOINT

Now go to GameObject → 3D Object → Sphere (Figure 5.10) and rename it to Turn.

Then in Inspector → Transform

Transform	X	Y	Z
Scale	1.5	1.5	1.5
Position	0	3	0

FIGURE 5.10   Add Sphere (Turn) as the robot joint.

Select Turn from Hierarchy (Figure 5.11).
Drag the Cube colour from Project window → Cube to Turn.

FIGURE 5.11   Drag the colour to turn.

5.5 STEP 5: MAKING THE KUKA ARM 2

Now right-click on the Turn → 3D Object → Cube (Figure 5.12). Rename it to Cube(1).

Then in Cube(1) Inspector → Transform.

Transform	X	Y	Z
Scale	0.2	2	0.33
Position	0	0.85	0.55
Rotation	45	0	0

FIGURE 5.12   Create Cube(1) as the second arm.

5.6 STEP 6: MAKING THE KUKA JOINT

Select Cube(1) from Hierarchy (Figure 5.13).

Drag the Cube colour from Project window → Cube to Cube(1).

FIGURE 5.13   Create Sphere(1).

Now right-click on the Turn → 3D Object → Sphere. Rename it to Sphere(1).

In the Sphere(1) from Inspector → Transform

Transform	X	Y	Z
Scale	0.5	0.5	0.5
Position	0	1.61	1.3

5.7 STEP 7: MAKING THE KUKA ARM

Select Sphere(1) from Hierarchy (Figure 5.14).

Drag the Cube colour from Project window → Cube to Sphere(1).

Now right-click on the Sphere(1) → 3D Object → Cylinder. Rename it to Cylinder(1).

Select the Cylinder(1) Inspector → Transform

Transform	X	Y	Z
Scale	0.7	2	0.7
Position	0	1.3	−1.3
Rotation	130	0	0

FIGURE 5.14   Create Cylinder(1) as the third arm.

Select Cylinder(1) from Hierarchy (Figure 5.15).

Drag the Cube colour from Project window → Cube to Cylinder(1).

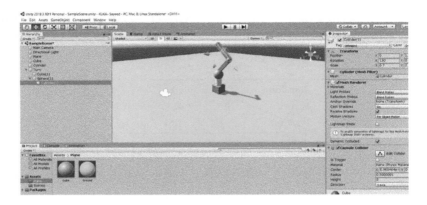

FIGURE 5.15   Drag the colour to Cylinder(1).

5.8 STEP 8: MAKING THE KUKA JOINT

Right-click on the Sphere(1) → 3D Object → Sphere (Figure 5.16). Rename it to Up and Down head.

In Inspector → Transform → Position; change the position of the Sphere (Up and Down head)

	X	Y	Z
Position	0	2.8	−3.1

Select Sphere (Up and Down head) from Hierarchy.
Drag the Cube colour from Project window → Cube to Sphere.

FIGURE 5.16   Create another sphere as the next joint.

5.9 STEP 9: MAKING THE KUKA ARM

Now right-click on the Sphere (named Up and Down head) → 3D Object → Cylinder (Figure 5.17).

Rename it to Cylinder(2).

Select the Cylinder(2) and then in Inspector → Transform

Transform	X	Y	Z
Scale	0.4	0.8	0.4
Position	0	−0.8	−0.6
Rotation	35	0	0

FIGURE 5.17   Create another Cylinder(2).

5.10 STEP 10: CAMERA POSITION AND ROTATION

Click on the Main Camera from Hierarchy (Figure 5.18).

Select the Camera from Inspector → Transform and then make the changes based on the following table:

Transform	X	Y	Z
Position	9	4.2	3.3
Rotation	0	−110	0

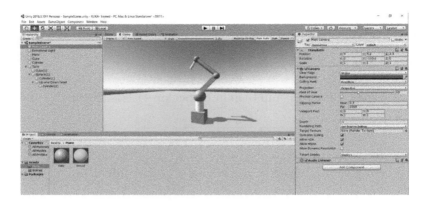

FIGURE 5.18 Fix the camera position and rotation.

5.11 STEP 11: MAKING THE ROBOT GRIPPERS PARTS

Now right-click on the Sphere (Up and Down head) → 3D Object → Cube (Figure 5.19).

Rename it to Gripper.

For the Gripper in Inspector → Transform, make the changes based on the following table:

Transform	X	Y	Z
Scale	2	0.2	0.4
Position	0	−1.5	−1.2
Rotation	37	0	0

Select Gripper from Hierarchy.

Drag the Cube colour from Project window → Cube to Gripper.

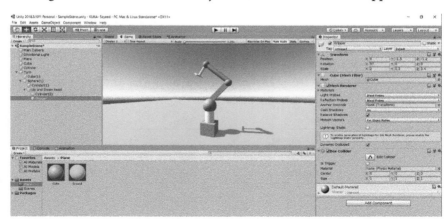

FIGURE 5.19 Create a cube as Gripper.

Now right-click on the Gripper → 3D Object → Cube (Figure 5.20). Rename it to Left.

Select the Left in Inspector → Transform, make the changes based on the following table:

Transform	X	Y	Z
Scale	10	0.8	0.2
Position	0.4	−5.2	−0.14
Rotation	0	90	−87.33

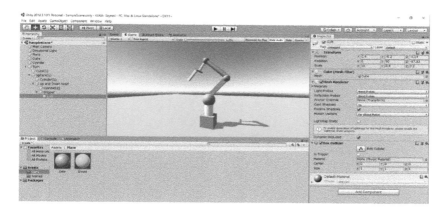

FIGURE 5.20 Create a cube as left.

Select Left from Hierarchy.

Drag the Cube colour from Project window → Cube to Left.

Now again, right-click on the Gripper → 3D Object → Cube (Figure 5.21). Rename it to Right.

Select the Left in Inspector → Transform, make the changes based on the following table:

Transform	X	Y	Z
Scale	10	0.8	0.2
Position	−0.4	−5.2	−0.14
Rotation	0	90	−87.33

Select Right from Hierarchy (Figure 5.22).

Drag the Cube colour from Project window → Cube to Right

FIGURE 5.21   Create another cube as right.

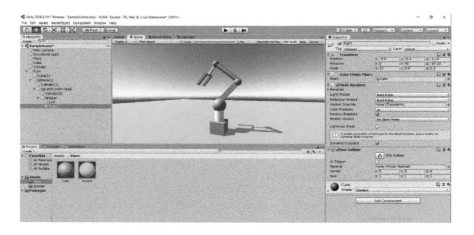

FIGURE 5.22   Drag the colour to the right.

CHAPTER 6

Example 5: Create BAYMAX Body and Movement

DOI: 10.1201/9781003268581-6

In the fifth example, you will learn how to make the body of the BAYMAX robot with all details and then move the object of the designed character.

6.1 STEP 1: CREATE BAYMAX BODY

The steps are started by opening Unity and going to GameObject → 3D Object → Cube (Figure 6.1).

In Inspector window → Transform → Scale, change the value based on the following table:

Transform	X	Y	Z
Scale	1	2	1

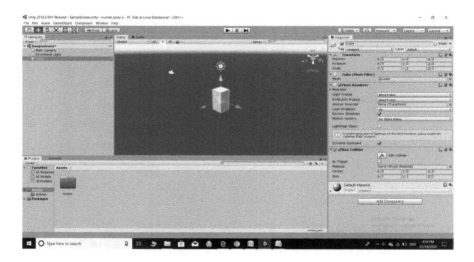

FIGURE 6.1 Select cube and fix the scale.

6.2 STEP 2: CREATE BAYMAX HEAD

Now, follow the path GameObject → 3D → Sphere (Figure 6.2) in the path, Inspector → Transform → Position. Enter the value based on the following table:

Transform	X	Y	Z
Scale	0	1.62	0

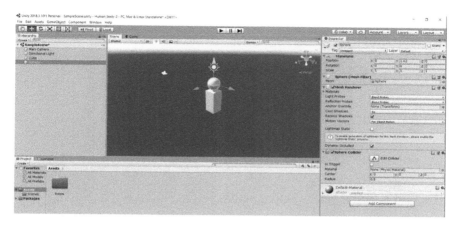

FIGURE 6.2   Select Sphere and fix the position.

6.3 STEP 3: CREATE BAYMAX HAND

Follow the path, GameObject → 3D → Capsule (Figure 6.3).

Select the Inspector → Transform, insert the values for Scale and Position and change the value based on the following table:

Transform	X	Y	Z
Scale	0.4	0.75	0.4
Position	0.78	12	0

FIGURE 6.3   Select Capsule and fix position and scale.

Now, right-click on the **Capsule** in Hierarchy and click Duplicate (Figure 6.4).

FIGURE 6.4   Duplicate the Capsule.

Then, you will see another object named Capsule(1) (Figure 6.5).

Change the position of the **Capsule(1)** in Inspector → Transform → Position, with respect to the following table:

Transform	X	Y	Z
Position	−0.78	12	0

FIGURE 6.5   Fix the Capsule(1) position.

6.4 STEP 4: CREATE BAYMAX LEGS

Right-click on the Capsule in Hierarchy and click Duplicate (Figure 6.6).

You will see the other object, named **Capsule(2)** in Inspector → Transform → Position; change the values based on the following table:

Transform	X	Y	Z
Position	0.3	−1.88	0

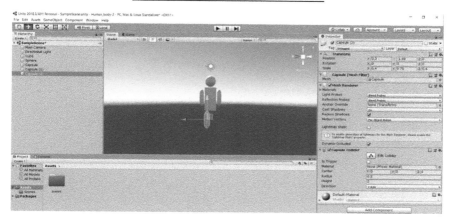

FIGURE 6.6   Again duplicate the Capsule and fix the position.

Once more, right-click on the Capsule in Hierarchy and click Duplicate (Figure 6.7).

For the other object, named **Capsule(3)** in the Inspector → Transform → Position section, make the Capsule value based on the following table:

Transform	X	Y	Z
Position	−0.3	−1.88	0

FIGURE 6.7   Duplicate Capsule and fix the position.

Now, check and ensure the components are aligned in the position using the **Bottom view** from **Pivot** (Figure 6.8).

FIGURE 6.8   Bottom view.

In this stage, all components must be connected. To do this, we need to move the components in the Hierarchy to the body (Cube) (Figure 6.9).

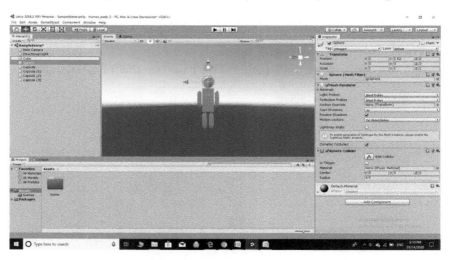

FIGURE 6.9   Connect all components.

6.5 STEP 5: CREATE BAYMAX EYE

Repeat this process to move all the components to the **body** (Cube) (Figure 6.10). After this, right-click on the Sphere → 3D Object → Sphere, and Rename the new created Sphere to **Eye**.

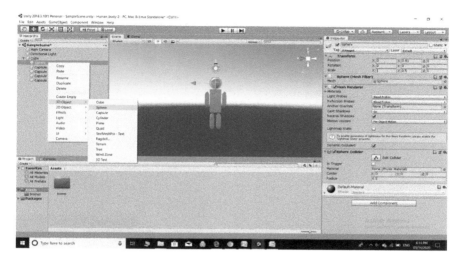

FIGURE 6.10   Select Sphere for eyes.

Then in Inspector → Transform (Figure 6.11), change values of **Eye** based on the following table:

Transform	X	Y	Z
Scale	0.2	0.2	0.2
Position	0.18	0.11	−0.41

FIGURE 6.11   Fix the scale and position of eye(1).

Now, go to the Project window → Assets → right-click into the Assets → Create → Materials (Figure 6.12). Rename it to Eye.

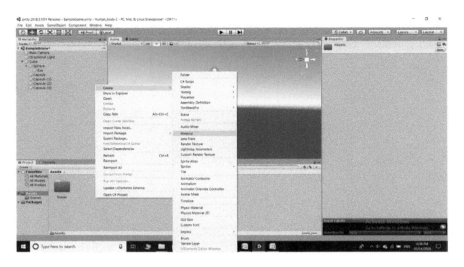

FIGURE 6.12   Create materials for Eye.

Then, to change the Object colour; click on the **Eye** in Assets → Inspector → Main Maps → Albedo (Figure 6.13). Select the black colour for **Eye**.

FIGURE 6.13   Select black colour for Eye.

As the next step, select the **Eye** from Hierarchy and change the position for some time (Figure 6.14). Then drag the colour from Assets to **Eye**.

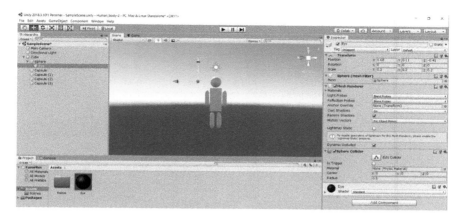

FIGURE 6.14   Drag the colour to Eye.

Then in Inspector → Transform → Position (Figure 6.15), fixed the position of the **Eye** based on the following table:

Transform	X	Y	Z
Position	0.18	0.11	−0.41

FIGURE 6.15   Eye positioning.

Right-click on the **Eye** in Hierarchy (Figure 6.16). Select Duplicate; after that, the user will see another object named **Eye(1)**. The object position should be the change in Inspector → Transform → Position based on the following table:

Transform	X	Y	Z
Position	−0.18	0.11	−0.41

FIGURE 6.16 Duplicate the Eye for creating second one.

6.6 STEP 6: SET THE CAMERA POSITION

Afterwards, click Main Camera in Hierarchy (Figure 6.17) and set the position of Main Camera in Inspector → Transform → Position according to the following table:

Transform	X	Y	Z
Position	0	1	−7

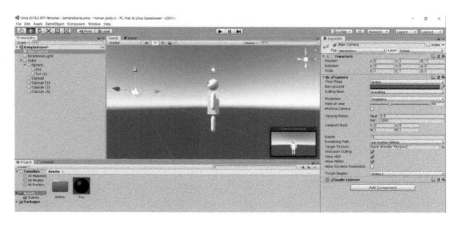

FIGURE 6.17 Fix main camera position.

6.7 STEP 7: ADD THE SCRIPT

Now, click Cube in Hierarchy (Figure 6.18), go to Inspector window and Click Add Component → New Script → name **Rotation_body** → Create and Add.

FIGURE 6.18   Add script.

Then, a C# file will be shown into the project window. The user can open this C# file with any editor like Notepad, Brackets, etc. Copy the following script and save it (Ctrl + S) (Figure 6.19):

```
using System.Collections;
using System.Collections.Generic;
using UnityEngine;
public class Rotation_body : MonoBehaviour
{
    public float mSpeed;
        // Start is called before the first frame update
    void Start()
    {
      mSpeed = 10f;
    }

    // Update is called once per frame
    void Update()
    {
      //transform.Translate(mSpeed * Input.GetAxis("Horizontal") * Time.
deltaTime, 0f,  mSpeed * Input.GetAxis("Vertical") * Time.deltaTime);
        transform.Rotate(5f* Time.deltaTime, 0f,  0f * Time.deltaTime);
    }
}
```

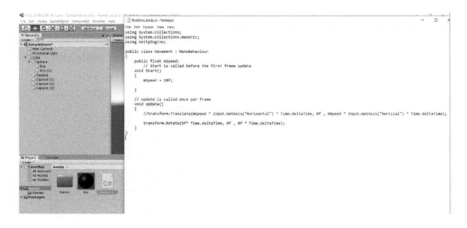

FIGURE 6.19   Save the script.

You can look at the code briefly. The code has different parts that are as follow:

public float mSpeed;	This creates a variable called **mSpeed** which can be accessed in Unity, i.e., public. This variable is a data type called **float**, which is decimal numbers
mSpeed = 10f;	It is reference for rotation speed
transform.Rotate (5f* Time.deltaTime, 0f, 0f * Time.deltaTime);	It is the most important of this script. It tells to fix the speed of rotation (Figure 6.20)

Then click on Cube and drag the script to the Cube in Scene view. To save all the changes, the user can press **Ctrl + S**. Next, go to Game view and click on the Play button to see the rotation of the human body (Figure 6.21).

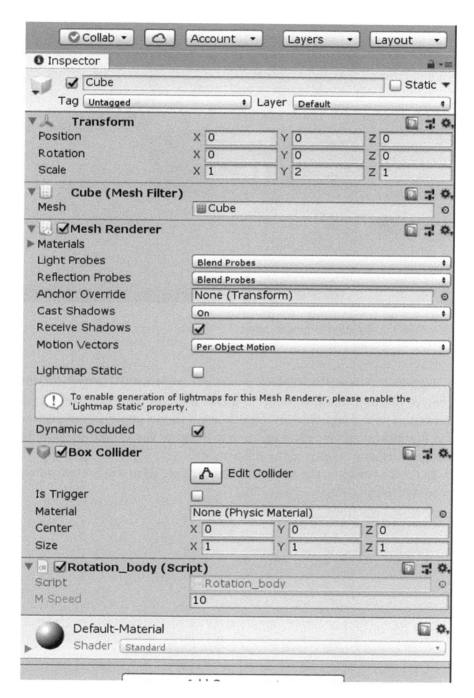

FIGURE 6.20   Change rotation speed.

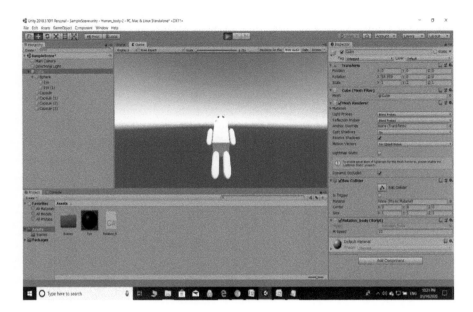

FIGURE 6.21   Rotation of human body.

Figure 6.21 shows the BYMAX model was implemented usefully in this chapter. The user learned how to design the BYMAX model containing the various parts and sections. The importance of this example is to emphasize the significance of how user can learn to integrate the various part and to design from a raw sketch to the entire model.

In the next chapter, the other designs which are related to the two-wheel robot will be analyzed and described.

UNITY IN EMBEDDED SYSTEM DESIGN AND ROBOTICS

A STEP-BY-STEP GUIDE

CHAPTER 7

Example 6: Create Two-wheeled Robot with Gripper and Movement

DOI: 10.1201/9781003268581-7

In this sixth example, creating the two-wheeled robot character with the gripper and the moving object are described.

7.1 STEP 1: INITIAL WORK BEFORE STARTING THE DESIGN

To start this example, first, open the Unity and then following the path GameObject → 3D Object → Cube (Figure 7.1).

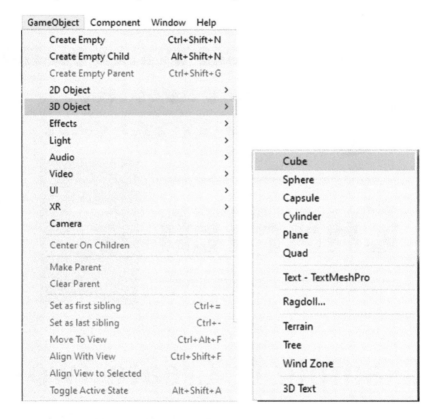

FIGURE 7.1 Selecting a component.

As we need the Assets and Packages, then you need to download the bellow links from the following table:

No	Download	Link
1	Post-processing stack	https://assetstore.unity.com/packages/essentials/post-processing-stack-83912
2	The models	https://assetstore.unity.com/packages/essentials/post-processing-stack-83912
3	The Prefabs	https://www.dropbox.com/s/rruyua26cvzof9x/Prefabs.rar?dl=0
4	The 1.file	https://www.dropbox.com/s/a0d86y4uc31pcci/1.asset?dl=0

7.2 STEP 2: BUILDING THE BODY

As the next step, rename the Cube to Body in the Inspector Window →
Transform → Position (Figure 7.2) based on the following table:

Transform	X	Y	Z
Position	0	1	0

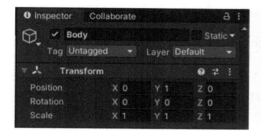 

FIGURE 7.2   Body component.

Then add a new cube, rename it to Head, and change its position
(Figure 7.3) to match the following magnitudes:

Transform	X	Y	Z
Position	1	2	0

FIGURE 7.3   Head component.

Create a Sphere, rename it to WheelL, and change its position (Figure 7.4)
and scale to match the following table co-ordinates:

Transform	X	Y	Z
Position	0	0.5	0.5
Scale	0	0.8	0.8

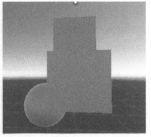

FIGURE 7.4   Setting up the left wheel component.

Create a Sphere, rename it to WheelR, and change its position and scale (Figure 7.5) to change the values based on the following table co-ordinates:

Transform	X	Y	Z
Position	0	0.5	−0.5
Scale	0	0.8	0.8

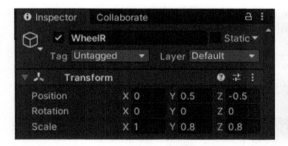

FIGURE 7.5   Setting up the right wheel component.

As a result, once you pass all previous steps, you should have the following model shown in Figure 7.6.

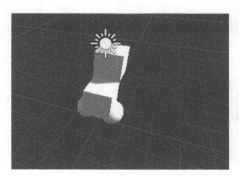
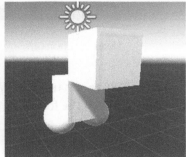

FIGURE 7.6   Robot body.

7.3 STEP 3: MAKING THE NECK, SHOULDER, AND ARMS

Create a Cylinder, rename it to Neck, and change its position and scale magnitude (Figure 7.7) according to the following table:

Transform	X	Y	Z
Position	1.7	2	0
Rotation	0	0.5	90
Scale	0.6	0.3	0.8

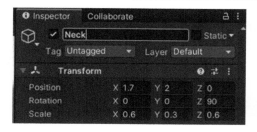 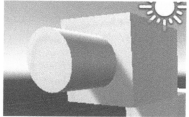

FIGURE 7.7   Neck component.

Then create a Cube, rename it to Shoulder, and change its position and scale (Figure 7.8) to match the following table co-ordinates:

Transform	X	Y	Z
Position	2	2	0
Rotation	0	0	0
Scale	0.2	0.4	2

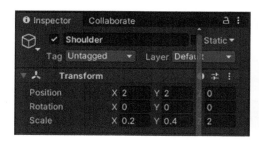 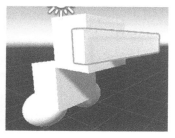

FIGURE 7.8   Shoulder component.

Afterwards, create a Cube, rename it to ArmL, and change its position, rotation, and scale (Figure 7.9) to have the following table co-ordinates:

Transform	X	Y	Z
Position	3	2	0.9
Rotation	0	90	0
Scale	0.2	0	2

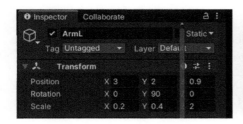

FIGURE 7.9   Left arm component.

Next, create a Cube, rename it to ArmR, and change its position, rotation, and scale (Figure 7.10) based on the following table:

Transform	X	Y	Z
Position	3	2	−0.9
Rotation	0	90	0
Scale	0.2	0.4	2

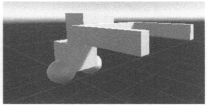

FIGURE 7.10   Right arm component.

After passing all before step, you should have the model as shown in Figure 7.11.

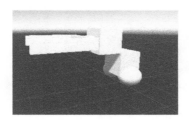

FIGURE 7.11   Final robot arm.

7.4 STEP 4: MAKING THE JOINTS

The joint in Unity used to move objects relative to the connected object. This is important in this project as it creates a perfect hinge effect for the robot arm; for this, we will hide the different components to visualise the different empty child components (Figure 7.12). Then start by setting the real tool to Pivot and Local.

FIGURE 7.12   Show hide component.

And create an Empty Child and rename it to ArmRJoint and change its position, rotation, and scale (Figure 7.13) based on the following values:

Transform	X	Y	Z
Position	2	2	−0.9
Rotation	0	0	0
Scale	1	1	1

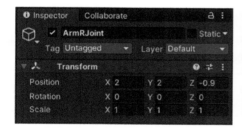
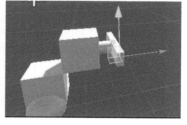

FIGURE 7.13   Right arm joint.

Make an Empty Child and rename it to ArmLJoint and change its values for position, rotation, and scale (Figure 7.14) according to the following table:

Transform	X	Y	Z
Position	2	2	0.9
Rotation	0	0	0
Scale	1	1	1

FIGURE 7.14   Left arm joint.

Create an Empty Child and rename it to "UpAndDownMovement" and change its position, rotation, and scale (Figure 7.15) to match based on the following table:

Transform	X	Y	Z
Position	0.5	1.5	−0.09
Rotation	0	0	0
Scale	1	1	1

FIGURE 7.15   UpAndDownMovement.

Make an Empty Child and rename it to "Rotational Movement" and change its position, rotation, and scale (Figure 7.16) to match the following table:

Transform	X	Y	Z
Position	0.5	1.5	−0.09
Rotation	0	0	0
Scale	1	1	1

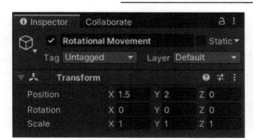
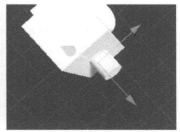

FIGURE 7.16   Rotational movement joint.

Finally, it would help if you moved ArmL into the ArmLJoint followed by the ArmR into the ArmRJoint, then move Shoulder into the neck component.

After that, place the neck component into rotational movement and then move into UpAndDownMovement along with the head component. Finally, move WheelL and WheelR into the body component. The final Hierarchy Tree is shown in Figure 7.17.

 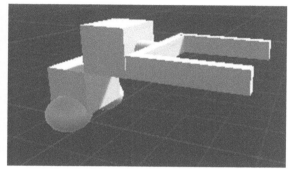

FIGURE 7.17   Hierarchy tree.

7.5 STEP 5: ADDING COLOUR TO THE SCENE

In the next stage, we should use an asset package to decorate our scene. This is available on Unity Assets and is free for use. You can download it from the following link. This will provide the scene as shown in Figure 7.18.

Assets	Link
Nature Starter Kit 2 | 3D Environments | Unity Asset Store	http://assetstore.unity.com/packages/3d/environments/nature-starter-kit-2-52977

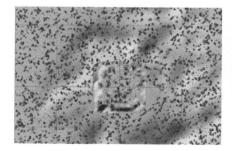 

FIGURE 7.18   Adding colour to scene.

7.6 STEP 6: AUTOMATIC ANIMATION MOVEMENT

To have the Automatic movement, you should go to Window →
Animation → Animation (Figure 7.19). Select UpAndDownMovement,
and then select Create in the Animation window (Figure 7.20).

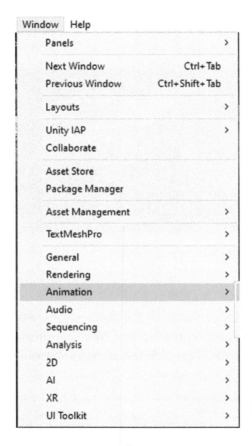

FIGURE 7.19   Add animation.

FIGURE 7.20   Animation window.

Create a new animation clip, named Up and Down Movement. Next, the user should click the red record button in the Animation window and then move the scrubber for 30 seconds (Figure 7.21). The user should go to the inspector and change the UpAndDownMovement components rotation as mentioned in the following table:

Transform	X	Y	Z
Rotation	0	0	−20

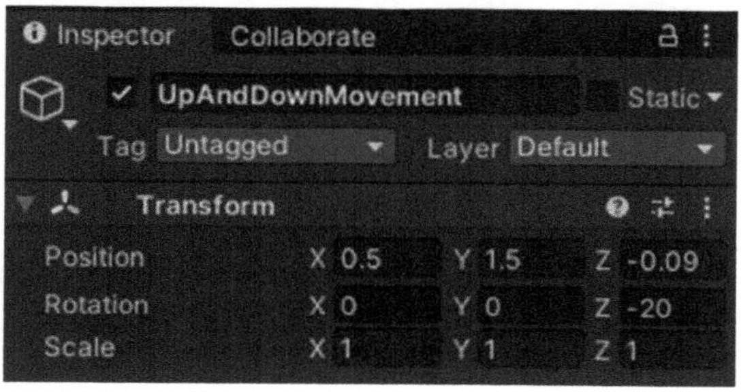

FIGURE 7.21   Rotate component for 30 seconds in the Z direction.

Next, the user should move the scrubber for another 60 seconds (Figure 7.22). Go to the inspector and change the rotation of the UpAndDownMovement component according to the following values:

Transform	X	Y	Z
Rotation	0	0	60

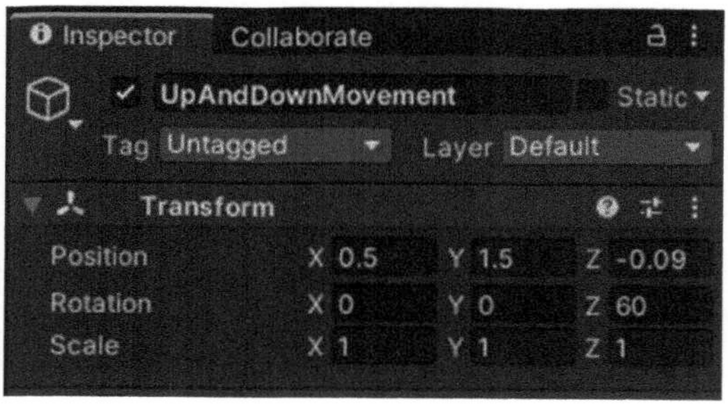

FIGURE 7.22   Rotate component for 60 seconds in the Z direction.

Now select the Rotational Movement component in the Hierarchy window, create a new clip named Rotation.anim then move the scrubber for another 60 seconds (Figure 7.23) and go to the inspector, and change the rotation components like following table:

Transform	X	Y	Z
Rotation	180	0	0

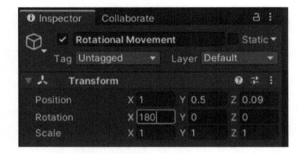

FIGURE 7.23 Rotate component for 30 seconds in the X direction.

Then select UpAndDownMovement and go to Window → Animation → Animator. Reorganise the states and make transitions between them, as shown in Figure 7.24. Afterwards, the plan is ready, and the user can animate it.

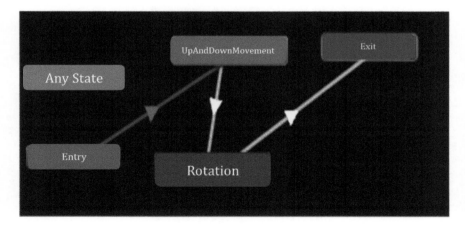

FIGURE 7.24 How to transition among all components.

7.7 STEP 7: MOVING THE ROBOT USING A KEYBOARD

In this step, the user should explore a method for moving the robot using different keys of the keyboard. Our main objective is to move the robot left and right, move the head up and down, and control the gripper by expanding and contracting it. To start, the user needs to make a script for all the different conditions.

7.7.1 Start with the Up and Down Movement

The user must create a new folder within the Assets folder named Scripts, then create two new C# scripts, one with the name of UpandDown and another with the name of Movement (Figure 7.25).

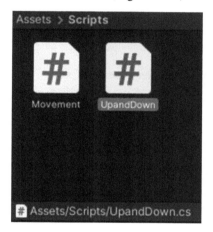

FIGURE 7.25   Create scripts.

Then write the following code on the UpandDown script:

```
using System.Collections;
using System.Collections.Generic;
using UnityEngine;

public class UpandDown: MonoBehaviour
{
  public Animator movementAnim;
  //Start is called before the first frame update
  void Start()
  {

  movementAnim = GetComponent<Animator>();
}
```

```
//Update is called once per frame
void Update()
{
  float moveInput = Input.GetAxis("Vertical");
  if (moveInput > 0f)
  {

    transform.rotation = Quaternion.Euler(0f,0f, moveInput * 20f);
  }
  else if (moveInput < 0f)
  {

    transform.rotation = Quaternion.Euler(0f,moveInput * 0f, moveInput * 20f);
  }
  else
  {

    transform.rotation = Quaternion.Euler(0f, 0f, 0f);
  }

 }
}
```

7.7.2 Left or Right Movement

Next, the user should focus on getting the correct animations for the
Movement script. This script will control the robot's movement whenever
it turns left or right. To do that, the users have to type the following code
into the script. This code will move the robot's body left or right whenever
the users click the left or right arrow button.

```
using System.Collections;
using System.Collections.Generic;
using UnityEngine;

public class Movement: MonoBehaviour
{
  public Animator movementAnim;
  //Start is called before the first frame update
  void Start()
  {
    movementAnim = GetComponent<Animator>();
  }
```

```
//Update is called once per frame
void Update()
{
    float moveInput = Input.GetAxis("Horizontal");
    if(moveInput > 0f)
    {
        transform.rotation = Quaternion.Euler(0f, moveInput * 90f, 0f);
    }
    else if(moveInput < 0f)
    {
        transform.rotation = Quaternion.Euler(0f, moveInput * 90f, 0f);
    }
    else
    {
        transform.rotation = Quaternion.Euler(0f,0f, 0f);
    }
}
}
```

7.7.3 The Gripper Movement

Next, the user should work on the script which will control the gripper. Therefore, create a script for ArmRJoint and ArmLJoint named Grip and GripL, respectively (Figure 7.26).

FIGURE 7.26   Griper movement.

The scripts for Grip and GripL will be as follow:

Grip.cs

```
using System.Collections;
using System.Collections.Generic;
using UnityEngine;

public class Grip : MonoBehaviour
{
    public Animator movementAnim;
    // Start is called before the first frame update
    void Start()
    {
        movementAnim = GetComponent<Animator>();
    }

    // Update is called once per frame
    void Update()
    {
        bool moveInput = Input.GetKey("1");
        if (moveInput == true)
        {
            transform.rotation = Quaternion.Euler(0f, -20f, 0f);
        }
        else
        {
            transform.rotation = Quaternion.Euler(0f, 0f, 0f);
        }
    }
}
```

GripL.cs

```
using System.Collections;
using System.Collections.Generic;
using UnityEngine;

public class GripL : MonoBehaviour
{
    public Animator movementAnim;
    // Start is called before the first frame update
    void Start()
    {
        movementAnim = GetComponent<Animator>();
    }

    // Update is called once per frame
    void Update()
    {
        bool moveInput = Input.GetKey("1");
        if (moveInput == true)
        {
            transform.rotation = Quaternion.Euler(0f, 20f, 0f);
        }
        else
        {
            transform.rotation = Quaternion.Euler(0f, 0f, 0f);
        }
    }
}
```

The users have to add the scripts to their respective components by dragging the scripts to the inspectors of each relevant component (Figure 7.27).

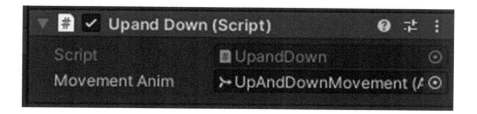

FIGURE 7.27 Dragging the scripts to the inspectors.

7.8 STEP 8: ROBOTIC ARM SCRIPTS

Insert the scripts for each robot sections.

Grip

```
using System.Collections;
using System.Collections.Generic;
using UnityEngine;
public class Grip : MonoBehaviour
{
    public Animator movementAnim;
    // Start is called before the first frame update
    void Start()
    {
        movementAnim = GetComponent<Animator>();
    }
    // Update is called once per frame
    void Update()
    {
        bool moveInput = Input.GetKey("1");
        if (moveInput == true)
        {
            transform.rotation = Quaternion.Euler(0f, -20f, 0f);
        }
        else
        {
            transform.rotation = Quaternion.Euler(0f, 0f, 0f);
        }
    }
}
```

GripL

```
using System.Collections;
using System.Collections.Generic;
using UnityEngine;
public class GripL : MonoBehaviour
{
    public Animator movementAnim;
    // Start is called before the first frame update
    void Start()
    {
        movementAnim = GetComponent<Animator>();
    }
    // Update is called once per frame
    void Update()
    {
        bool moveInput = Input.GetKey("1");
        if (moveInput == true)
        {
            transform.rotation = Quaternion.Euler(0f, 20f, 0f);
        }
        else
        {
            transform.rotation = Quaternion.Euler(0f, 0f, 0f);
        }
    }
}
```

Movement

```
using System.Collections;
using System.Collections.Generic;
using UnityEngine;
public class Movement : MonoBehaviour
{
    public Animator movementAnim;
    // Start is called before the first frame update
    void Start()
    {
        movementAnim = GetComponent<Animator>();
    }
    // Update is called once per frame
    void Update()
    {
        float moveInput = Input.GetAxis("Horizontal");
        if(moveInput > 0f)
        {
            transform.rotation = Quaternion.Euler(0f, moveInput * 90f, 0f);
        }
        else if(moveInput < 0f)
        {
            transform.rotation = Quaternion.Euler(0f, moveInput * 90f, 0f);
        }
        else
        {
            transform.rotation = Quaternion.Euler(0f,0f, 0f);
        }
    }
}
```

UpandDown

```
using System.Collections;
using System.Collections.Generic;
using UnityEngine;
public class UpandDown : MonoBehaviour
{
    public Animator movementAnim;
    // Start is called before the first frame update
    void Start()
    {
        movementAnim = GetComponent<Animator>();
    }
    // Update is called once per frame
    void Update()
    {
        float moveInput = Input.GetAxis("Vertical");
        if (moveInput > 0f)
        {
            transform.rotation = Quaternion.Euler(0f,0f, moveInput * 20f);
        }
        else if (moveInput < 0f)
        {
            transform.rotation = Quaternion.Euler(0f,moveInput * 0f, moveInput * 20f);
        }
        else
        {
            transform.rotation = Quaternion.Euler(0f, 0f, 0f);
        }
    }
}
```

UNITY IN EMBEDDED SYSTEM DESIGN AND ROBOTICS
A STEP-BY-STEP GUIDE

CHAPTER 8

Example 7: Human Body (REMY CHARACTER) and Movement

DOI: 10.1201/9781003268581-8

In this example, the user will learn how to use animation assets and move it. This example can be an initial gate for users to learn how to work with the characters made before.

8.1 STEP 1: DOWNLOAD CHARACTER AND ANIMATION

This example aims to use animation assets. Initially, the user should download the related file and open the Mixamo website from any browser (Google or Firefox) using the following link – https://www.mixamo.com/.

If the user is new to this website, click on **Create an account** and give all the information to create an account. Then verify your account via email (Figure 8.1).

FIGURE 8.1   Create Mixamo account.

In the case of having an account, you can **Log in** to the website, and after that, click on Character, select any of the characters that you like and follow the steps. Here we choose the **REMY** character as the sample (Figure 8.2).

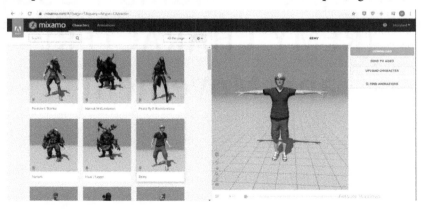

FIGURE 8.2   Select character.

To download the Character, click on DOWNLOAD, follow the path Format → FBX for Unity (.fbx), and click the DOWNLOAD section (Figure 8.3).

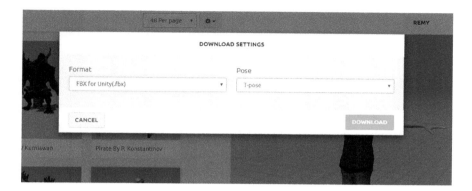

FIGURE 8.3   Download Character.

After completing the download, click on the Animation and write **IDLE** in the search box. Select any idle whichever you want (Figure 8.4).

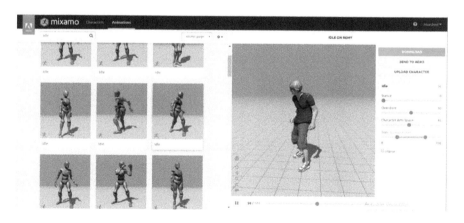

FIGURE 8.4   Select Idle animation.

Also, if you want, you can change any value of **Overdrive** and **Character Arm Space** to have your expected animation. To download the animation, click on the DOWNLOAD and select dropdown, follow the path Skin → Without Skin and click DOWNLOAD (Figure 8.5).

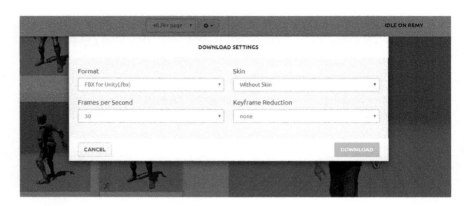

FIGURE 8.5   Download Idle animation.

After that, write **WALK** in the search box and select any walking animation (Figure 8.6). Also, in this part, you can change any value of **Overdrive** and **Character Arm Space** to achieve your expected animation. To make the change in Character, click on the **In Place** of your selected animation and to download the animation, follow the same method as **IDLE** animation.

FIGURE 8.6   Select walking animation.

Later write **JUMP** in the search box. Select any jumping animation and change character by any value of **Overdrive** and **Character Arm Space** to accomplish your expected animation. Then click on the

In Place of your selected animation (Figure 8.7). To download the animation, follow the same method as that of the **IDLE** animation.

FIGURE 8.7   Select jumping animation.

8.2 STEP 2: INSERT THE CHARACTER IN UNITY

As the next step, drag the character and all the animations to Unity by following the path of Unity → Project window → Assets (Figure 8.8).

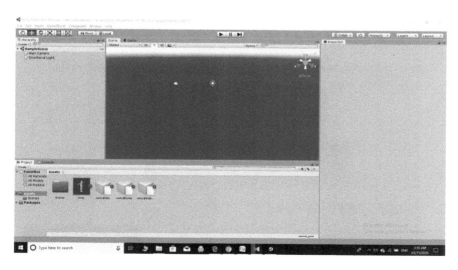

FIGURE 8.8   Drag all downloaded assets.

Now drag the character **REMY** to the Hierarchy (Figure 8.9). Then click on the character **REMY** in the project window. Next, in Inspector → Materials → click on the Textures, right-click on the window → New → Folder. Rename the folder to Textures.

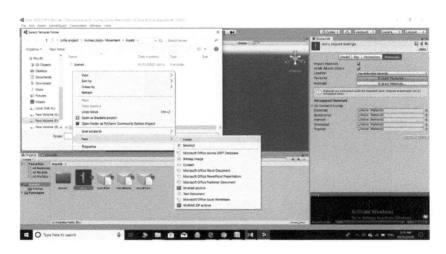

FIGURE 8.9   Create textures folder.

Next, double click on the Textures and click **Select Folder**. Now, wait for processing. After that, click **Fix Now** (Figure 8.10). Then you will see all the textures on the Character's body.

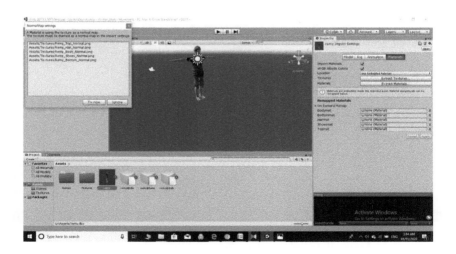

FIGURE 8.10   Fix all textures for the Character.

8.3 STEP 3: CAMERA POSITION SETTING

Click on the Main Camera in Hierarchy (Figure 8.11). In the Inspector window → Transform and set the values based on the following table:

Transform	X	Y	Z
Position	0	2	7
Rotation	0	180	0

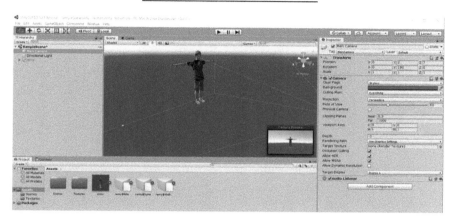

FIGURE 8.11 Fix camera position and rotation.

Now right-click into the Project window → Assets → Create → Animator Controller (Figure 8.12). Rename it to **CH_controller**.

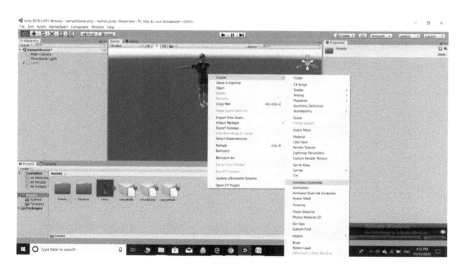

FIGURE 8.12 Create Animator Controller folder.

Then, click on the **REMY** in Hierarchy (Figure 8.13), and drag the **CH_controller** to Inspector → Animator → Controller section.

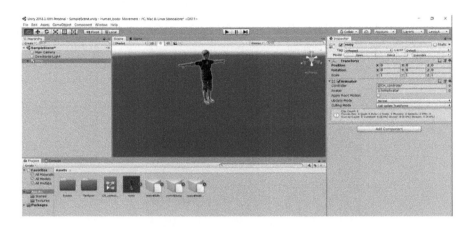

FIGURE 8.13   Set Animator Controller.

Afterwards, go to Window → Animation → Animator (Figure 8.14) and then to Animator → Base Layer (Figure 8.15). Right-click on the Base Layer → Create State → Empty and rename it to **Idle** from Inspector.

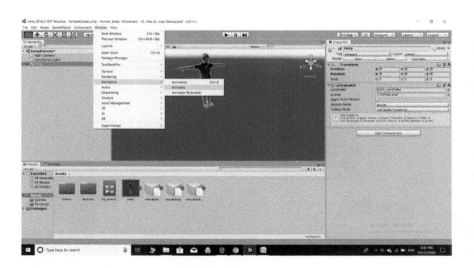

FIGURE 8.14   Open Animator window.

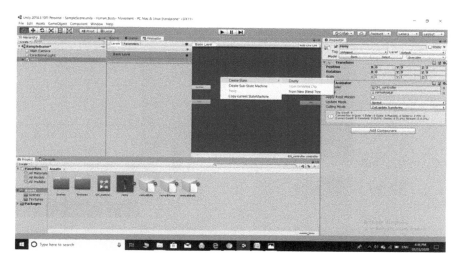

FIGURE 8.15 Create Base Layer folder.

Then, click Motion from Inspector and select **Idle** (Figure 8.16).

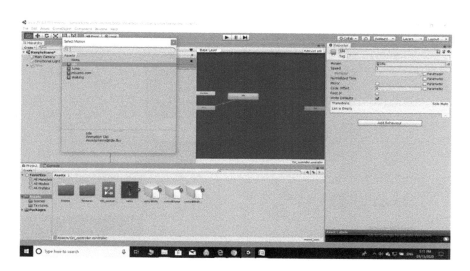

FIGURE 8.16 Select animation-name as Motion.

After that, click on Project → Assets → Idle (Figure 8.17), and then go to Inspector → Animation → click Loop Time.

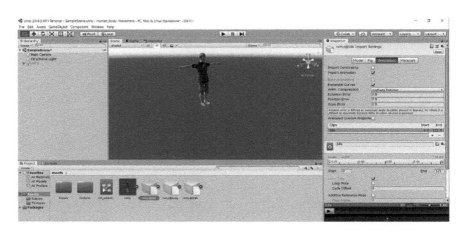

FIGURE 8.17   Select Loop Time (Idle).

8.4 STEP 4: THE CHARACTER WALK MOVEMENT

To have the character movement, then again go to Animator → Base Layer (Figure 8.18). Right-click on the Base Layer → Create State → Empty and then rename it to **Walk** from Inspector.

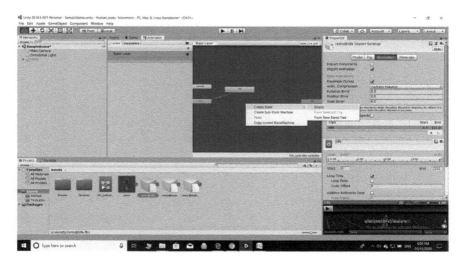

FIGURE 8.18   Create another Base Layer folder.

After that, click Motion from Inspector and select **Walking** (Figure 8.19).

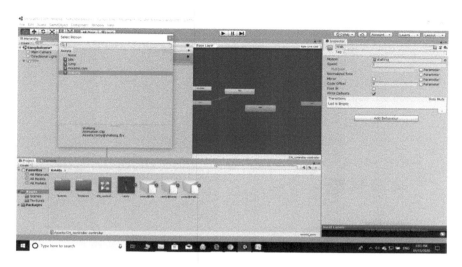

FIGURE 8.19   Select animation-name as Motion.

Then click on Project → Assets → Walk (Figure 8.20), and go to Inspector → Animation → click Loop Time.

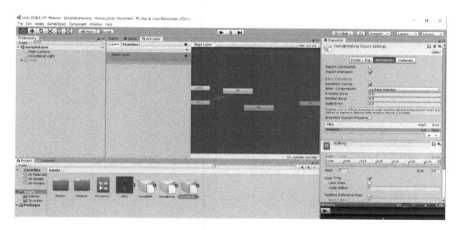

FIGURE 8.20   Select Loop Time (Walk).

Now right-click on the **Walk** from Base Layer (Figure 8.21), select **Make Transition**. Then drag it from **walk** to **Idle**.

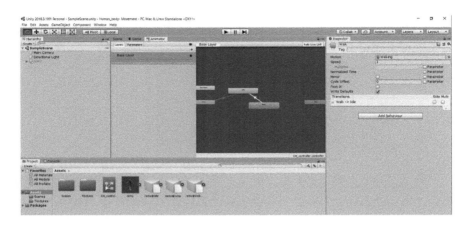

FIGURE 8.21 Make the transition from Walk to Idle.

In the next stage, right-click on the **Idle** from Base Layer (Figure 8.22).

Select **Make Transition**.
Drag it from **Idle** to **Walk**.

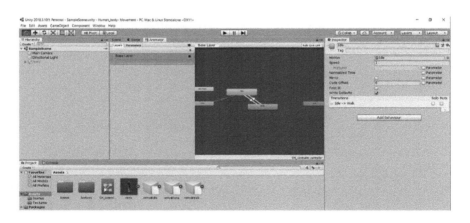

FIGURE 8.22 Make the transition from Idle to Walk.

Then to go Animator → Parameters → click on (+) sign → select Bool (Figure 8.23), and rename it to **isWalking.**

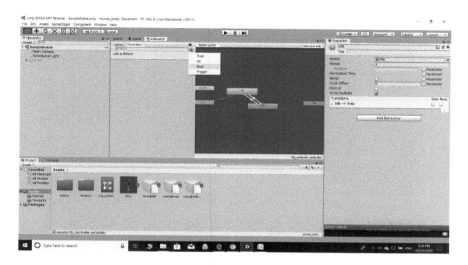

FIGURE 8.23   Select Boolean parameters.

Afterwards, click on the arrow, which has gone **Idle** to **Walk** (Figure 8.24). Deselect the **Has Exit Time** from Inspector. Click (+) sign of the conditions.

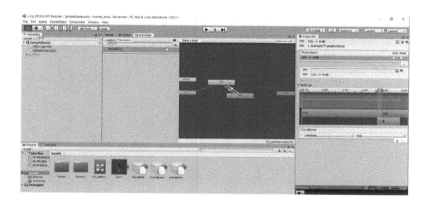

FIGURE 8.24   Deselect exit time and add the condition.

Then click on another arrow that has gone **Walk** to **Idle** (Figure 8.25). Deselect the **Has Exit Time** from Inspector. Click the (+) sign of the conditions and then click on **true**, and select **false**. Drag the **Animator** window beside the **Console**.

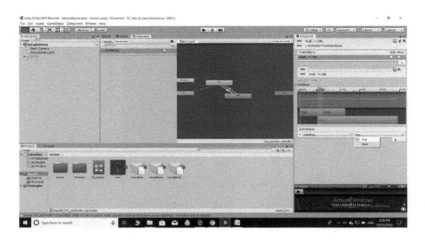

FIGURE 8.25   Deselect exit time and change condition parameters.

Navigate to Animator → Base Layer (Figure 8.26). Right-click on the Base Layer → Create State → Empty.

FIGURE 8.26   Create another Base Layer folder.

Rename it to **Jump** from Inspector, click Motion from Inspector, and select **Jump** (Figure 8.27).

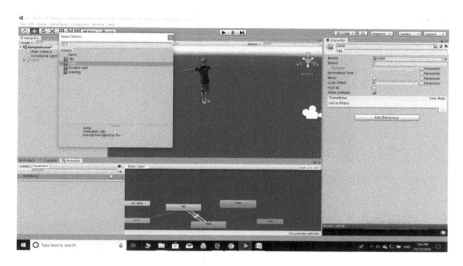

FIGURE 8.27   Select animation-name as Motion.

Now click on Project → Assets → Jump, and go to Inspector → Animation → click Loop Time (Figure 8.28).

FIGURE 8.28   Select Loop Time (Jump).

Then click on Animator → Right-click on the **Jump** from the Base Layer (Figure 8.29). Select **Make Transition**, and drag it from **Jump** to **Idle**; after that, right-click on **Idle** and select **Make Transition**, then drag it from **Idle** to **Jump**.

FIGURE 8.29   Create transition between Jump and Idle.

After that, right-click on the **Jump** from Base Layer. Select **Make Transition**, drag it from **Jump** to **Walk** and right-click on **Walk**. Select **Make Transition**, then drag it from **Walk** to **Jump** (Figure 8.30).

FIGURE 8.30   Create a transition between Jump and Walk.

Then, follow the path Animator → Parameters → click on (+) sign → select Bool (Figure 8.31), and rename it to **isJumping**.

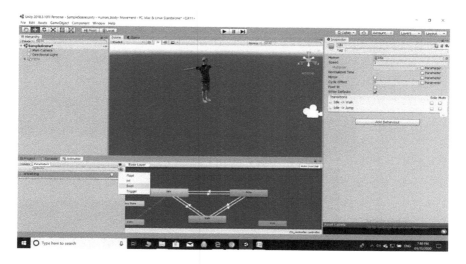

FIGURE 8.31   Create another Boolean parameter.

Now click on the arrow, which has gone **Idle** to **Jump** (Figure 8.32). Deselect the **Has Exit Time** from Inspector. Click (+) sign of the Conditions. Afterwards, click on **isWalking** and select **isJumping**.

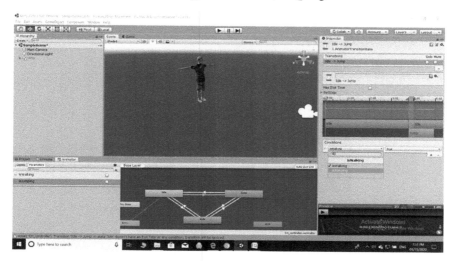

FIGURE 8.32   Add condition (Idle → Jump).

Next, click on the arrow, which has gone **Walk** to **Jump** (Figure 8.33). Deselect the **Has Exit Time** from Inspector, click (+) sign of the Conditions, then click on **isWalking** and select **isJumping**.

FIGURE 8.33   Add condition (Walk → Jump).

Now click on the arrow which has gone **Jump** to **Idle** (Figure 8.34). Deselect the **Has Exit Time** from Inspector, click (+) sign of the conditions two times. Then click on **true** for **isWalking** and select **false**. After that, go to the 2nd condition, click on **isWalking**, select **isJumping** and click on **true** and select **false**.

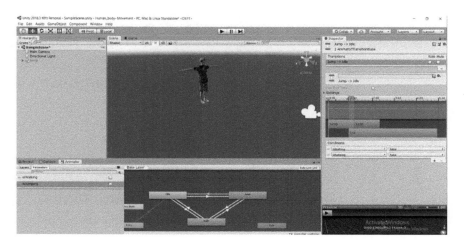

FIGURE 8.34   Add condition (Jump → Idle).

Next, click on the arrow which has gone **Jump** to **Walk** (Figure 8.35). Deselect the **Has Exit Time** from Inspector, click (+) sign of the conditions two times. Go to the 2nd condition and click on **isWalking** and select **isJumping** and click on **true** and select **false**.

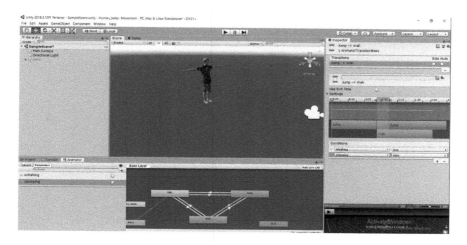

FIGURE 8.35   Add condition (Jump → Walk).

Then, go to GameObject → 3D Object → Plane. Change the values based on the following table (Figure 8.36):

Transform	X	Y	Z
Position	−1	0	0

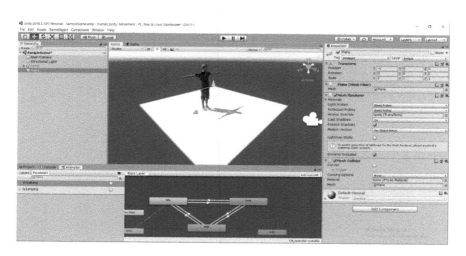

FIGURE 8.36   Create Plane and fix position.

8.5 STEP 5: ADD THE SCRIPT TO CHARACTER

In this step, the Scripts for the movement should add to the project. For this aim, go to Hierarchy → Remy (Figure 8.37) and follow the path of Inspector → Add Component → New Script → write movement.

FIGURE 8.37   Add script.

Then a C# file will be shown into Project → Assets. Double click on the C# file and open it with any editor (Notepad or Brackets). Copy the following script and save it (Ctrl + S) (Figure 8.38):

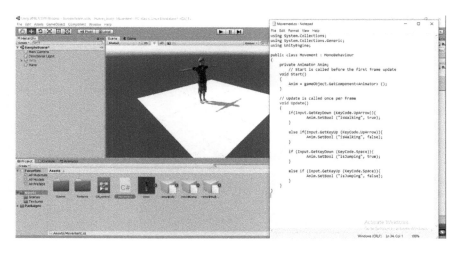

FIGURE 8.38   Save the script.

```
using System.Collections;
using System.Collections.Generic;
using UnityEngine;

public class Movement : MonoBehaviour
{
  private Animator Anim;
// Start is called before the first frame update
  void Start()
  {
    Anim = gameObject.GetComponent<Animator> ();
  }
  // Update is called once per frame
  void Update()
  {
    if(Input.GetKeyDown (KeyCode.UpArrow)){
        Anim.SetBool ("isWalking", true);
  }
  else if(Input.GetKeyUp (KeyCode.UpArrow)){
        Anim.SetBool ("isWalking", false);
  }
  if (Input.GetKeyDown (KeyCode.Space)){
        Anim.SetBool ("isJumping", true);
  }
  else if (Input.GetKeyUp (KeyCode.Space)){
        Anim.SetBool ("isJumping", false);
  }
    }
}
```

The code has different parts that are as follow:

private Animator Anim;	Creates a variable called Anim which can be accessed in Unity, i.e., it is private.
gameObject.GetComponent <Animator> ();	It sets the reference.
	Here, UpArrow button indicates walking and the Space button indicates jumping.
	When we press the UpArrow button, then **isWalking** command will be true, and it starts walking, and when we left this button, then it stops walking.
	When we press the Space button, the **isJumping** command will be true, and it starts jumping. When we left this button, then it stops jumping.

8.6 STEP 6: FINAL STEP AND CHARACTER MOVEMENT

Now save (Ctrl + S) everything and click on the play button, Human Body – Movement Animation is ready. After clicking the play button, you can click and hold the **UpArrow** button or **Space** button to check Character walking and jumping (Figure 8.39).

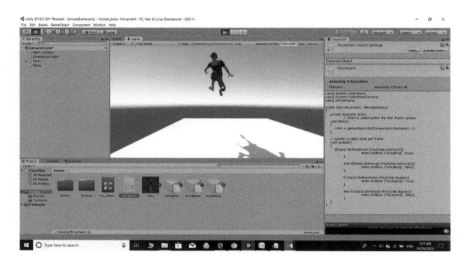

FIGURE 8.39   Play the animation.

UNITY IN EMBEDDED SYSTEM DESIGN
AND ROBOTICS
A STEP-BY-STEP GUIDE

CHAPTER 9

Example 8: Y-BOT Character Movement

DOI: 10.1201/9781003268581-9

In this example, the process to insert the Y Bot Character and add the movement are described. With the help of the Ready character, any user can download and import character and animation from Adobe's Help site Maximo (Link: https://www.mixamo.com). This example shows how to import Y-BOT Character with Walking, Running, Waving, Dancing, Clapping, Bowing movements, and using the keyboard to command the character movement.

9.1 STEP 1: INSERT THE CHARACTER

First, open the Unity Hub and select Projects from the left sidebar (Figure 9.1). Click on the New button. A new window will appear where the user will choose the Templets, Project Name, and saving location. In this case, the user should choose 3D; click on the Create button, then the Unity Editor will be opened (Figure 9.2).

FIGURE 9.1   Unity hub first page.

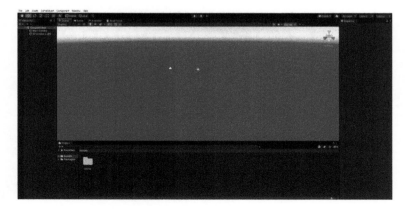

FIGURE 9.2   Unity Editor.

After entering the MAXIMO from the Browser (Link: https://www.mixamo.com), the user can select characters and animations and download them by pressing the DOWNLOAD button (Figure 9.3).

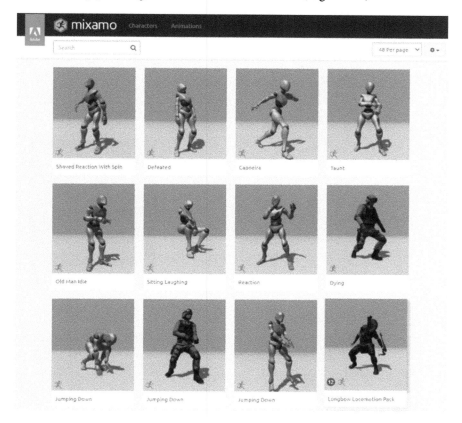

FIGURE 9.3   Main menu of Maximo website.

In this case, the user needs to select Y-BOT as the character. For animation, you should choose Idle, Waiving, Dancing, Clapping, Bowing, Walking, and Running (Figure 9.4), and then import the character and animation in Unity.

To follow the process, you should create two different folders inside the Asset folder by right-clicking inside the Asset folder (Figure 9.5) and name them Maximo and Animation (Figure 9.6).

Now you should drag and drop the previously downloaded animations and characters in the Maximo folder (Figure 9.7). Then click on each character and duplicate the animation by selecting it and pressing **Ctrl + D** and rename them (Figure 9.8). After that, move them into the animation folder by selecting them and drag and drop inside the Animation folder (Figure 9.9).

FIGURE 9.4   **Y-BOT character.**

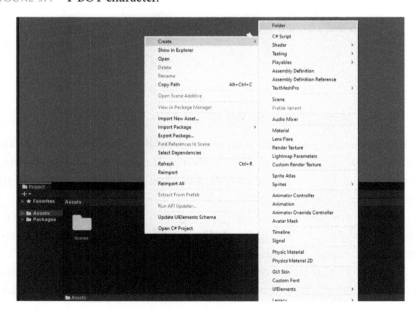

FIGURE 9.5   **How to create the folders.**

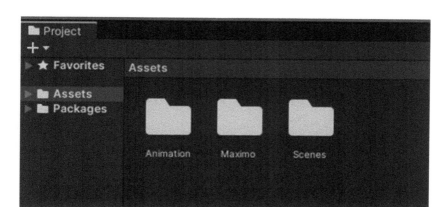

FIGURE 9.6   Naming the folders.

FIGURE 9.7   Add animations and characters to the Maximo folder.

FIGURE 9.8   Duplicate the animations and characters.

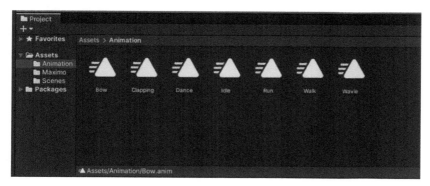

FIGURE 9.9   Add animations and characters to the Animation folder.

Afterwards, go to the Hierarchy menu and create a 3D object called a plane (Figure 9.10). Then let's change the plane scale from the inspector tab to three for X, Y, Z dimension like the following table (Figure 9.11). In the scene window, it will look somewhat like Figure 9.12.

Transform	X	Y	Z
Position	0	0	0
Rotation	0	0	0
Scale	3	3	3

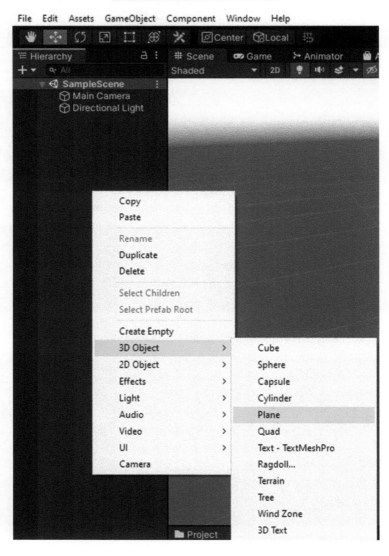

FIGURE 9.10 **Create a plane.**

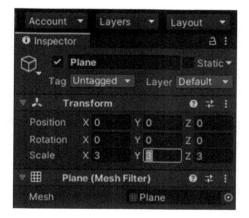

FIGURE 9.11   Change the value.

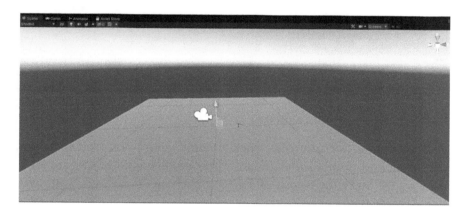

FIGURE 9.12   Result of creating a plane.

Then drag and drop the idle animation character from the Maximo folder to the Hierarchy tab and change the value in inspector windows based on the following table (Figure 9.13).

Transform	X	Y	Z
Position	0	0	0
Rotation	180	0	180
Scale	5	5	5

Next, go to the Animation folder in the Project tab and create an animator called Bot Controller (Figure 9.14).

FIGURE 9.13 Add Idle animation character and change its values.

FIGURE 9.14 Create Bot Controller.

If you click on Bot Controller, a new window will appear called Animator, then drag and drop all the animation inside this window (Figure 9.15). Afterwards, make the transition by right-clicking on each tab from both sides (Figure 9.16).

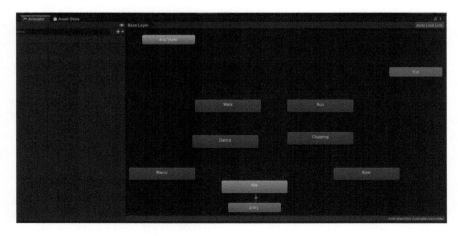

FIGURE 9.15 Animator window.

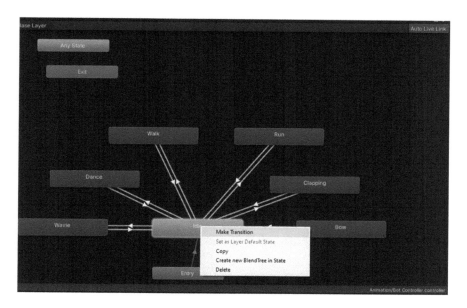

FIGURE 9.16   Making transitions.

And select the animation one by one from the project tab, and in the inspector menu, check the Loop Time box for every animation. Next, from the Hierarchy menu, select the character and add a new component called Animator (Figure 9.17).

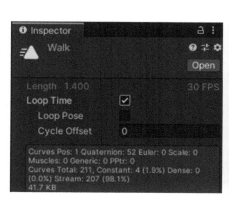

FIGURE 9.17   Select, choose the Loop time.

Next, you should drag and drop the Bot Controller to the controller box in the Animator component from the inspector window (Figure 9.18). Then, click on the Parameters tab in the animator window, click on the dropdown button, and select Bool. After choosing the Bool, a dialogue box will appear where you rename the parameter as **walking** and select the check the box (Figure 9.19).

FIGURE 9.18   Inspector window.

FIGURE 9.19   Choose the Bool. (*Continued*)

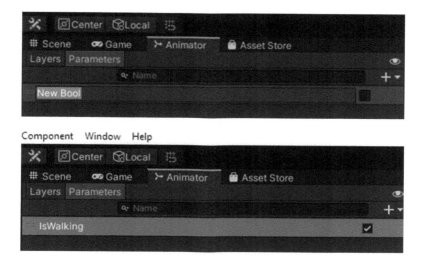

FIGURE 9.19 *(Continued)*

Next, you should add and select the six parameters of isWaving, isDancing, isClapping, isBowing, isWalking, and isRunning as shown in Figure 9.20.

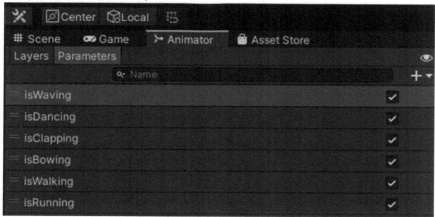

FIGURE 9.20 Add other parameters.

For each transition, choose the parameters and the condition from the inspector tab. Please note that, most importantly, any transition from the initial state is true and returns to the initial state are **false** (Figure 9.21).

FIGURE 9.21 Transition for Waving.

9.2 STEP 2: CHARACTER MOVEMENT BY KEYBOARD

In the next step, the user can use the keyboard to move the specific part of the character body. If you click the play button, our character will move on its own, and you should wait for a long time for each transition, which is very irritating. In the next part, you will make the character move with the help of keyboard buttons.

For example, after a click on the play button:

If we press **1** and hold it, the character will wave Hands.

If we press **2** the character will dance. Again pressing **2** will stop dancing.

If we press **3** and hold it, the character will clap.

If we press **4** and hold it, the character does a formal bow.

If we press **5** and hold it, the character will start walking on the place.

If we press **6** and hold it, the character will start running in the place.

To do these activities, you should follow the discussed steps. Select the character from the Hierarchy menu, and in the inspector, choose Add Component and rename the new script to **AnimationStateController** (Figure 9.22).

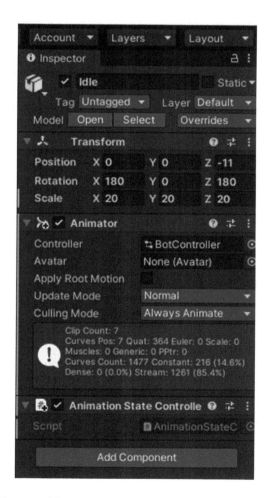

FIGURE 9.22   How to add a new script.

The script will appear in the project tab. Your default C# compiler visual studio will be open (Figure 9.23).

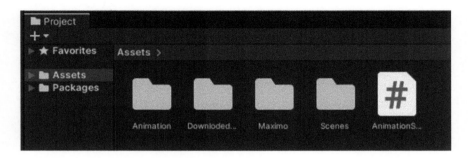

FIGURE 9.23 New script placed on Asset.

In the Visual Studio window, paste the code and save the file. You can change any button or movement, but, for that, you should follow the previous steps accordingly, which are 9, 13, 14, 21 to 23, and 26 to 29. After inserting the code and rerun the program, you should be able to run the character:

```
using System.Collections;
using System.Collections.Generic;
using UnityEngine;

public class AnimationStateController : MonoBehaviour
{
 Animator animator;
 int isWalkingHash;
 int isRunningHash;
 int isWavingHash;
 int isDancingHash;
 int isClappingHash;
 int isBowingHash;

 // Start is called before the first frame update
 void Start()
 {
   animator = GetComponent<Animator>();

   //Increasing Preformance
   isWalkingHash                          =
Animator.StringToHash("isWalking");
   isRunningHash                          =
```

```
Animator.StringToHash("isRunning");
    isWavingHash                        =
Animator.StringToHash("isWaving");
    isDancingHash                       =
Animator.StringToHash("isDancing");
    isClappingHash                      =
Animator.StringToHash("isClapping");
    isBowingHash                        =
Animator.StringToHash("isBowing");

    }

    // Update is called once per frame
    void Update()
    {
    bool            isWalking           =
animator.GetBool(isWalkingHash);
    bool            isRunning           =
animator.GetBool(isRunningHash);
        bool isWaving = animator.GetBool(isWavingHash);
    bool            isDancing           =
animator.GetBool(isDancingHash);
    bool            isClapping          =
animator.GetBool(isClappingHash);
        bool isBowing = animator.GetBool(isBowingHash);
        bool waving = Input.GetKey("1");
        bool dancing = Input.GetKey("2");
        bool clapping = Input.GetKey("3");
        bool bowing = Input.GetKey("4");
        bool walking = Input.GetKey("5");
        bool running = Input.GetKey("6");
        // When Button 1 Is Pressed.
        if (!isWaving && waving)
        {
            // Setting isWaving1 Boolean To True.
            animator.SetBool(isWavingHash, true);

        }
        // When Button 1 Isn't Pressed.
        if (isWaving && !waving)
        {
            // Setting isWaving1 Boolean To False.
            animator.SetBool(isWavingHash, false);

        }
```

```
// When Button 2 Is Pressed.
if (!isDancing && dancing)
{
   // Setting isDancing Boolean To True.
   animator.SetBool(isDancingHash, true);
}
// When Button 2 Isn't Pressed.
if (isDancing && !dancing)
{
   // Setting isDancing Boolean To False.
   animator.SetBool(isDancingHash, false);
}

// When Button 3 Is Pressed.
if (!isClapping && clapping)
{
   // Setting isClapping Boolean To True.
   animator.SetBool(isClappingHash, true);
}
// When Button 3 Isn't Pressed.
if (isClapping && !clapping)
{
   // Setting isClapping Boolean To False.
   animator.SetBool(isClappingHash, false);
}
// When Button 4 Is Pressed.
if (!isBowing && bowing)
{
   // Setting isBowing Boolean To True.
   animator.SetBool(isBowingHash, true);
}
// When Button 4 Isn't Pressed.
if (isBowing && !bowing)
{
   // Setting isBowing Boolean To False.
   animator.SetBool(isBowingHash, false);
}

// When Button 5 Is Pressed.
if (!isWalking && walking)
{
   // Setting isWalking Boolean To True.
   animator.SetBool(isWalkingHash, true);
}
```

```
// When Button 5 Isn't Pressed.
if (isWalking && !walking)
{
   // Setting isWalking Boolean To False.
   animator.SetBool(isWalkingHash, false);
}

// When Button 6 Is Pressed.
if (!isRunning && running)
{
   // Setting isRunning Boolean To True.
   animator.SetBool(isRunningHash, true);
}
// When Button 6 Isn't Pressed.
if (isRunning && !running)
{
   // Setting isRunning Boolean To False.
   animator.SetBool(isRunningHash, false);
}


}
}
```

UNITY IN EMBEDDED SYSTEM DESIGN
AND ROBOTICS
A STEP-BY-STEP GUIDE

CHAPTER 10

Example 9: Flower Example with Sound and Image and Keyboard Control

DOI: 10.1201/9781003268581-10

In this example, you will review the Flower character again. Still, along with the flower character, you will learn how to add sound and image to the environment. Finally, this example will describe the steps to control the created character through the keyboard.

10.1 STEP 1: CREATING FLOWER

To start, open the Unity hub and select Projects from the left sidebar. Then click on the New button. After that, a new window will appear to choose the Templets, Project Name, and save the store location. For example, you should select 3D and click on the Create Button to open the Unity Editor (Figure 10.1).

FIGURE 10.1   Unity editor window.

Now you should create two different folders by right-clicking inside the asset folder. Then name them Animation and Download (Figure 10.2).

Next, go to the Hierarchy menu and create a 3D object called a Plane. Then change the plane scale from inspector tab to 3 for X, Y, Z dimension. Your scene window should like Figure 10.3.

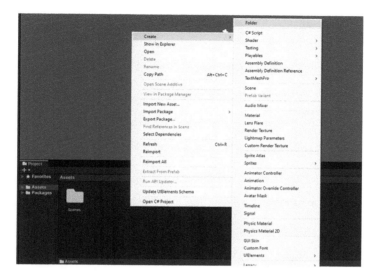

FIGURE 10.2 **Create a new folder.**

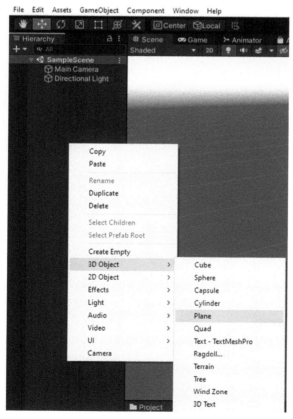

FIGURE 10.3 **Create a plane.** (*Continued*)

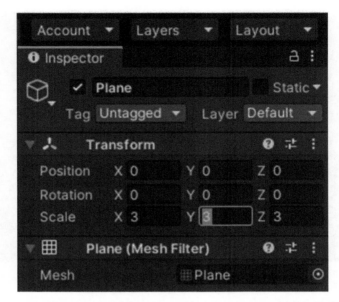

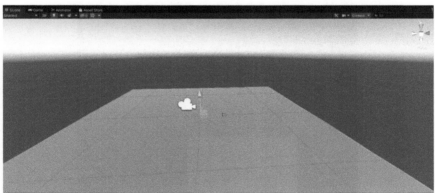

FIGURE 10.3 (*Continued*)

Then, again go to the Hierarchy menu and create a 3D object called a sphere. Change the scale and position (Figure 10.4) with the following table values:

Transform	X	Y	Z
Position	0.54	11.01	−0.33
Rotation	0	0	0
Scale	5	5	5

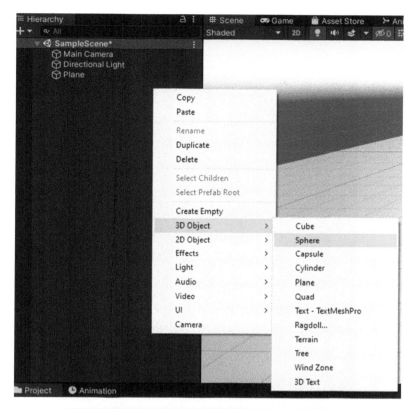

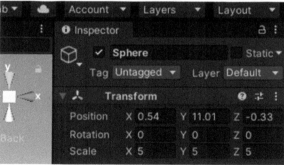

FIGURE 10.4   Create a sphere.

As the next stage, you should create some more sphere as shown in the previous step and change the scale and rotation from the inspector tab based on the last table values to make petals of the Flower (Figure 10.5). In this case, you will have 13 petals. You should see the result for this step in the scene as shown in Figure 10.6.

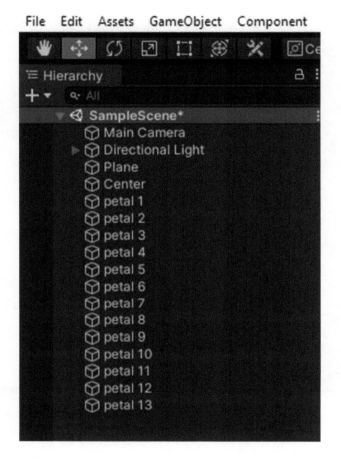

FIGURE 10.5   Create petals.

FIGURE 10.6   The final scene.

You should drag and drop all the petals inside the centre sphere from the Hierarchy tab to nest them inside the centre. When you do that, you should see a figure like Figure 10.7 in the scene view window.

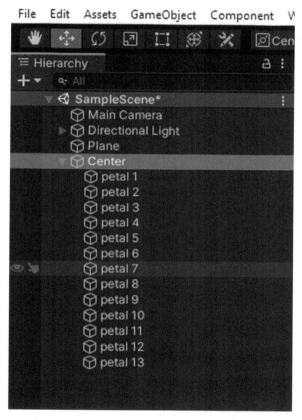

FIGURE 10.7   Add petals to Hierarchy.

Afterwards, one more time, go to the Hierarchy menu and create a 3D object called a cube to use as the pot in your design, as shown in Figure 10.8.

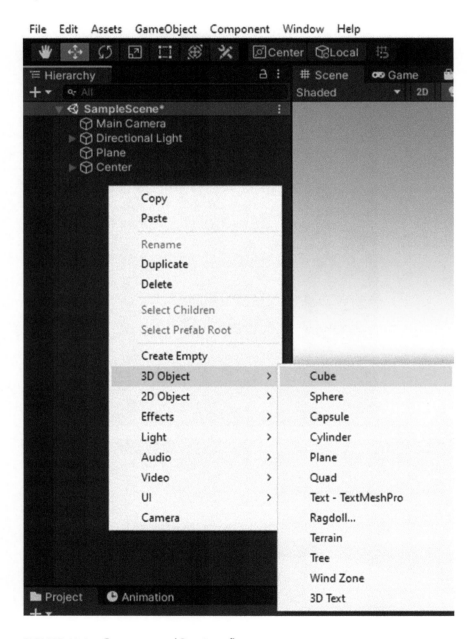

FIGURE 10.8   **Create a pot.** (*Continued*)

FIGURE 10.8   (*Continued*)

It would be best to change the position, scale, and rotation of the cube from the inspector tab as per the following table values (Figure 10.9). This value can be changed, and other values can be selected.

Transform	X	Y	Z
Position	−1.1	6.4	−5.8810
Rotation	0	0	0
Scale	20	5	10

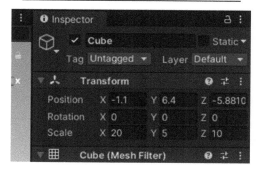

FIGURE 10.9   Change the values.

Again, go to the Hierarchy menu and create a 3D object called Cylinder to use as a Stem. It would help if you changed the position, scale, and rotation of the Cylinder from the inspector (use the value presented in the following table). You should have a figure like Figure 10.10.

Transform	X	Y	Z
Position	−1	24.2	−5.8810
Rotation	0	0	0
Scale	3	16	3

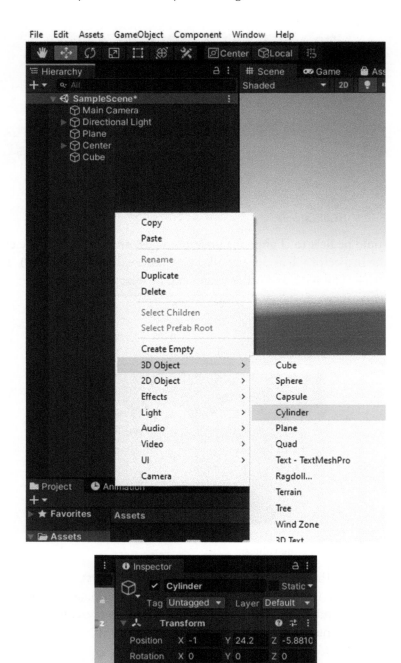

FIGURE 10.10   Create a Stem. (*Continued*)

FIGURE 10.10 (*Continued*)

Again, you should repeat the previous step and change the position, scale, and rotation of the Cylinder from the inspector tab as per the following table. As the next part, you should nest this Cylinder inside the first one in the Hierarchy tab. The scene view window is shown in Figure 10.11.

Transform	X	Y	Z
Position	0	0	−5.729
Rotation	90	0	0
Scale	1	1	0.1875

Once more, make two Cylinders from the Hierarchy tab and rename them as left and right branches. Then change the position, scale, and

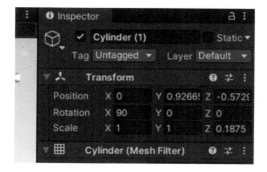

FIGURE 10.11 Create a connection. (*Continued*)

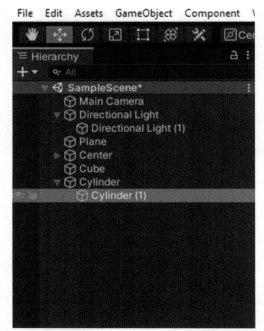

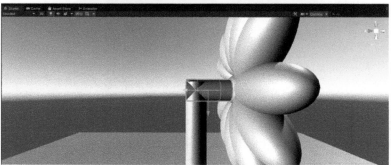

FIGURE 10.11 *(Continued)*

rotation of the Cylinder from the inspector tab like the following table. The overall view is shown in Figure 10.12.

Transform_Left branch	X	Y	Z
Position	8	27.8	−5.9
Rotation	0	0	−50
Scale	2	10	2
Transform_Right branch	**X**	**Y**	**Z**
Position	−9.9	28.1	−6.1
Rotation	0	0	−50
Scale	2	10	2

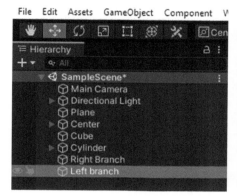

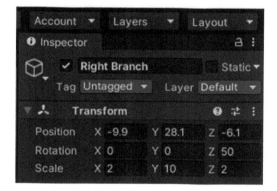

FIGURE 10.12   Create the branches.

Then, go to the Hierarchy menu and create two 3D objects, called sphere and rename them as left and right leaf and nest them inside the left and right branches. Then change the position, scale, and rotation of the sphere from the inspector tab (use the following values). The result is shown in Figure 10.13.

Transform_Left branch	X	Y	Z
Position	21.9	39.7	−5.8810
Rotation	0	0	−50
Scale	8	20	8
Transform_Right branch	**X**	**Y**	**Z**
Position	−22.2	38.8	−5.8810
Rotation	0	0	−50
Scale	8	20	8

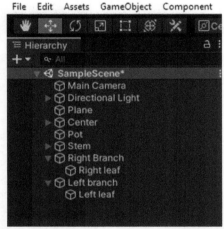

FIGURE 10.13 Create the leafs.

Next, in the project, create 25 material folders and use them for colouring. It will look like Figure 10.14.

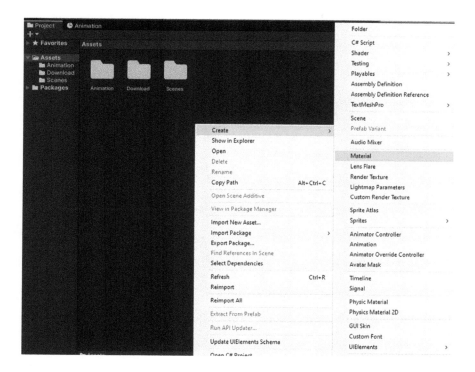

FIGURE 10.14   Create folders for materials.

Now select them by pressing Ctrl and click on each one of them and then move them into the Download folder. When you click on one material in the inspector menu, you can see the colour box (Figure 10.15). If you click on the colour box, a colour selection table will appear. From there, you can choose and change the colour for all materials by any colour.

After that, drag and drop the colours inside the parts. You should have now your final stage on the creating flower (Figure 10.16).

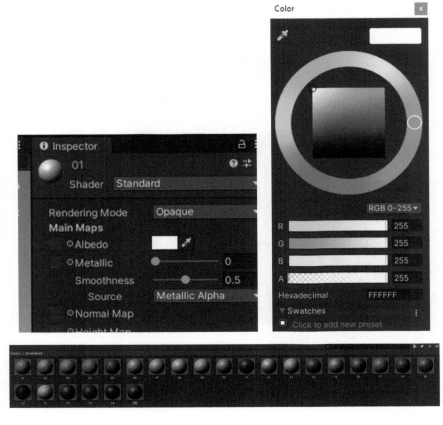

FIGURE 10.15　Assign the colour to parts.

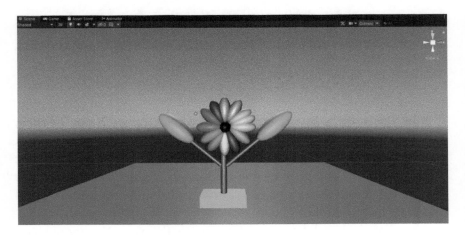

FIGURE 10.16　Final created Flower.

10.2 STEP 2: CHARACTER AUTOMATIC MOVEMENT

Go to the Hierarchy menu, create two empty objects, and rename them as Left branch movement and Right branch movement. Then, nest left and right branches inside them consequently. After that, change the position value like Figure 10.17 and according to the following table.

	Transform	X	Y	Z
Left branch movement	**Transform**	**X**	**Y**	**Z**
	Position	−0.9	21.3	−5.8810
	Rotation	0	0	0
	Scale	1	1	1
Right branch movement	**Transform**	**X**	**Y**	**Z**
	Position	−0.9	21.3	−5.8810
	Rotation	0	0	0
	Scale	1	1	1

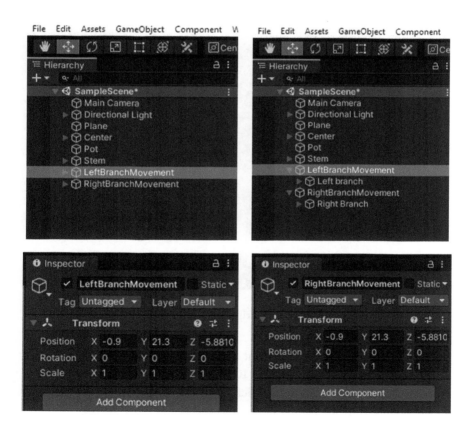

FIGURE 10.17   Create movements for leafs.

Select Left branch movement, and, in the inspector tab, you can see a button called Add Component. From there, you should add Animator and script (Figure 10.18). This part should repeat for both the branches.

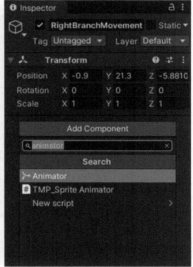

FIGURE 10.18   Add Animator and script.

Now, if the animation tab is not there, click on the window and select animation or press Ctrl+6 (Figure 10.19).

Select LeftBranchMovement, click on the animation tab, and then click on the Create Button. Then rename it to the Left (Figure 10.20).

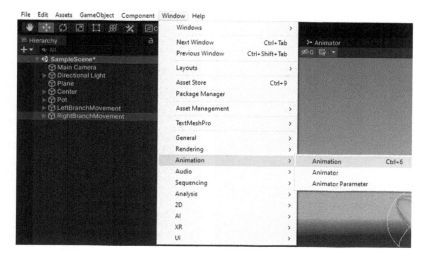

FIGURE 10.19   How to select Animation.

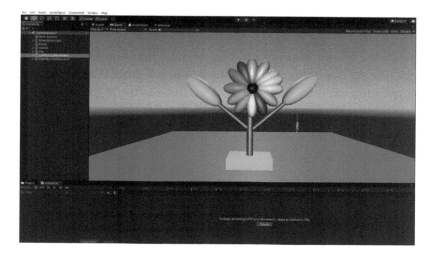

FIGURE 10.20   Rename the leaf branch movement.

Now in the animation tab, click on the record button, and, like Figure 10.21, set the Z-axis rotation to –50 for 1 minute and then set it to 0 for 2 minutes.

Left branch	**Transform**	**X**	**Y**	**Z**
movement	Position	−0.9	21.3	−5.8810
	Rotation	0	0	−50
	Scale	1	1	1

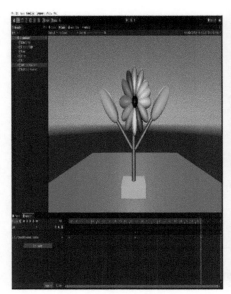

FIGURE 10.21   Record the movement for the left branch.

Select RightBranchmovement, then click on the animation tab and then click on the create button and rename it to Right. After that, in the animation tab, click on the record button and, like Figure 10.22, set the Z-axis

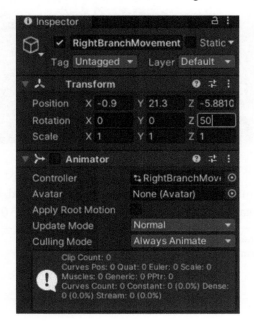

FIGURE 10.22   Record the movement for the right branch.

rotation to –50 for 1 minute and then set it to 0 for 2 minutes. Now, if you click on the play button, the Flower will move automatically.

10.3 STEP 3: ADDING IMAGES AND SOUND

As the next phase, you must Download any 2D asset from the Unity asset store. Because Unity doesn't accept Gif format picture, you should use the images in PNG or JPG format (Figure 10.23).

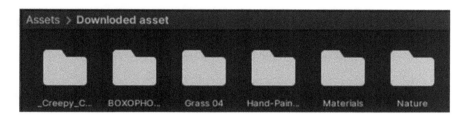

FIGURE 10.23   Downloaded asset.

Then initially, you should navigate to the birds. For that purpose, select the bird and drag and drop it in the Hierarchy tab (Figure 10.24).

FIGURE 10.24   Add birds to Hierarchy.

After that, select the bird, and, from the inspector, change the position and scale values as shown in Figure 10.25.

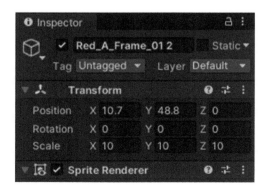

FIGURE 10.25   Change the position and scale of birds.

Next, go to the animation tab and drag and drop the bird's picture in the animation figure (Figure 10.26).

FIGURE 10.26   Drag and drop bird's picture in the Animation.

Then just duplicate the birds from the Hierarchy tab and make a flock (Figure 10.27).

FIGURE 10.27   Duplicate birds.

Afterwards, add background music, create an empty object in the Hierarchy tab, and rename it as music. Then drag and drop any music which is in mp3 format in the Download folder. In this case, name the music as 1 (Figure 10.28).

Then go to the inspector tab and add a component name Audio Source, and, from the Download folder, drag and drop the music file in the Audio clip box (Figure 10.29).

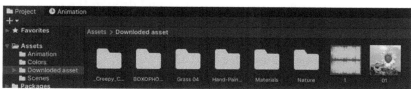

FIGURE 10.28   Add music 1.

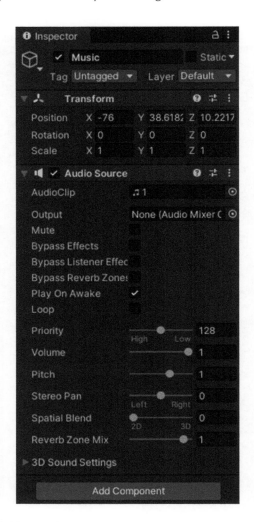

FIGURE 10.29 Add an audio source.

Next, you should create an empty 3D Object called Plane use wall for a picture (Figure 10.30).

You can import any picture just by drag and drop in the Downloaded asset folder (Figure 10.31).

Now you should select the plane and set the scale, position, and rotation and use the following values (Figure 10.32).

The result in the Game view Window should look like Figure 10.33. If you click on the play button, the Flower will move automatically, and background music will be played.

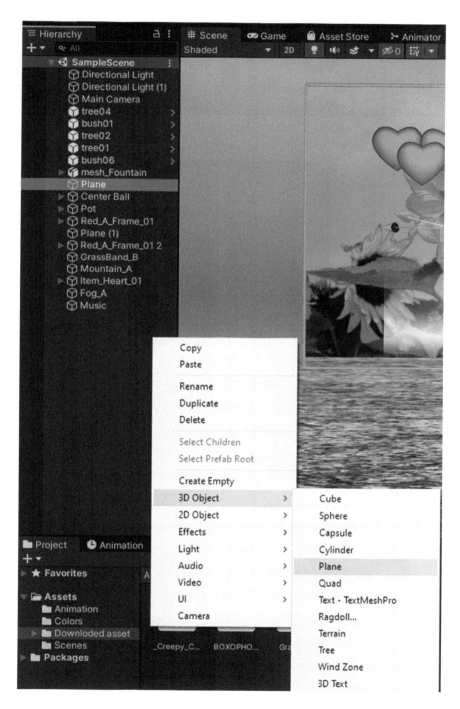

FIGURE 10.30 Create a plane.

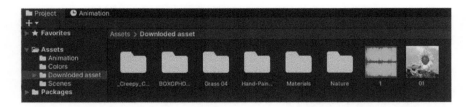

FIGURE 10.31 Import a picture.

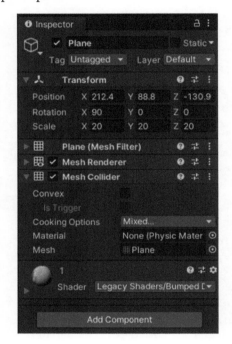

FIGURE 10.32 Change the values.

FIGURE 10.33 The final picture of the project.

10.4 STEP 4: MOVING THE FLOWER WITH KEYBOARD

Moving any character in Unity is a bit tricky. If you click the play button, the character will move on its own so far. In this part, you will learn how to make the Flower to move with the help of keyboard buttons. In this step, you will also learn how to control a different part of the Flower. For example, after a click on the play button:

- If you press **1** and hold it, the Flower's right branch will wave.

- If you press **2** and hold it, the Flower's left branch will wave.

- If you press **3** and hold it, the Flower will spin.

- If you press **6** and hold it, the character will start running in place.

To do these activities, you can follow the following steps:

Select the centre from the Hierarchy tab, click on the Animator tab, and then change the idle Animation to the default one. After that, it makes the transition from both sides. This process should also repeat for Left and Right branch movement (Figure 10.34).

FIGURE 10.34   **Make transition.** (*Continued*)

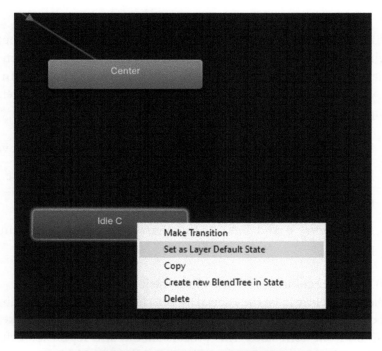

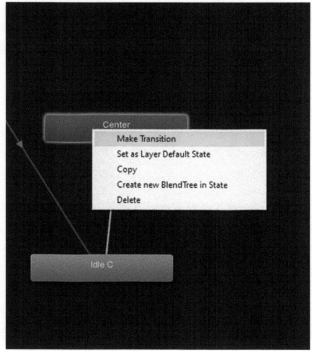

FIGURE 10.34 (*Continued*)

Next, click on the Parameters tab in the Animator window, click on the dropdown button, and select Bool (Figure 10.35).

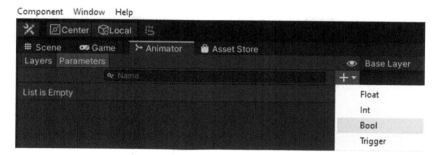

FIGURE 10.35   How to select Bool.

After selecting the bool, a dialogue box will appear, and you have to rename the parameter (Figure 10.36). You can rename it as isSpinning and check the box, and then make for leftBranchMoment and RightBranchmovement.

FIGURE 10.36   Rename the parameters.

Now for each transition, chose the parameters and the conditions from the inspector tab. Most importantly, any transition from the initial state is **true**, and returns to the initial state are **false**. Next, go to the Asset menu and click on the script from Add Component button (Figure 10.37). Paste the following code inside the mentioned place. Now when you click the play button and press 1, the Flower's Right branch will wave. If you press 2, Left branch will wave. If you press 3, the Flower will start spinning.

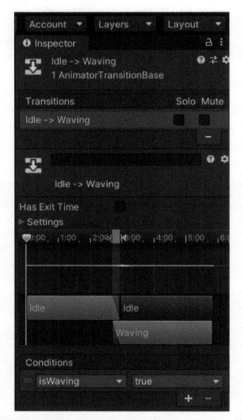

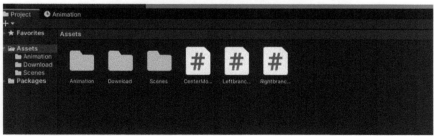

FIGURE 10.37 Create scripts for movements.

MovementController

```
using System.Collections;
using System.Collections.Generic;
using UnityEngine;
public class CenterMovementController :
MonoBehaviour
{
 Animator animator;
 // Start is called before the first frame update
 void Start()
 {
   animator = GetComponent<Animator>();
   //Increasing Preformance
 }
 // Update is called once per frame
 void Update()
 {
   bool spining = Input.GetKey("1");
   // When Button 2 Is Pressed.
   if (spining == true)
   {
   // Setting isWaving1 Boolean To True.
   animator.SetBool("isSpining", true);
   }
 // When Button 1 Isn't Pressed.
 if (waving1 == false)
 {
   // Setting isWaving1 Boolean To False.
   animator.SetBool("isSpining", false);
 }
 }
}
```

LeftBranchMovementController

```
using System.Collections;
using System.Collections.Generic;
using UnityEngine;
public class LeftbranchMovementController :
MonoBehaviour
{
 Animator animator;
 // Start is called before the first frame update
 void Start()
 {
   animator = GetComponent<Animator>();
   //Increasing Preformance
 }
 // Update is called once per frame
 void Update()
 {
   bool waving = Input.GetKey("2");
   // When Button 1 Is Pressed.
   if (waving == true)
   {
   // Setting isWaving1 Boolean To True.
   animator.SetBool("isWaving", true);
   }
 // When Button 1 Isn't Pressed.
 if (waving == false)
 {
   // Setting isWaving1 Boolean To False.
   animator.SetBool("isWaving", false);
 }
 }
}
```

RightBranchMovement Controller

```
using System.Collections;
using System.Collections.Generic;
using UnityEngine;
public class RightbranchMovementController :
MonoBehaviour
{
 Animator animator;
 // Start is called before the first frame update
 void Start()
 {
   animator = GetComponent<Animator>();
   //Increasing Preformance
 }
```

```
// Update is called once per frame
void Update()
{
    bool waving1 = Input.GetKey("1");
    // When Button 2 Is Pressed.
    if (waving1 == true)
    {
        // Setting isWaving1 Boolean To True.
        animator.SetBool("isWaving1", true);
    }
    // When Button 1 Isn't Pressed.
    if (waving1 == false)
    {
        // Setting isWaving1 Boolean To False.
        animator.SetBool("isWaving1", false);
    }
}
}
```

UNITY IN EMBEDDED SYSTEM DESIGN
AND ROBOTICS
A STEP-BY-STEP GUIDE

CHAPTER 11

Example 10: KUKA_II

DOI: 10.1201/9781003268581-11

In this example, you will learn how to add the designed KUKA robot and environment asset inside your project and finally give the movement to the character. Using the asset package, it will decorate your scene and furnish the design to have a more professional environment.

11.1 STEP 1: INSERTING THE ASSET 3D ENVIRONMENTS

The KUKA asset is available on Unity assets and it is free for using. You can download this asset from the following link (Figure 11.1):

> https://assetstore.unity.com/packages/3d/environments/3d-free-modular-kit-85732

FIGURE 11.1   The view of KUKA asset.

To use this, the user should do the following steps (Figure 11.2):

1. Sign in to Unity

2. Click Add to My Assets

3. Then open Unity

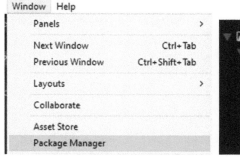 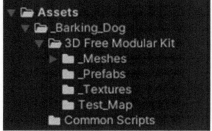

FIGURE 11.2   How to use a downloaded asset. (*Continued*)

FIGURE 11.2   (*Continued*)

4. Go to Window – Package Manager

5. Once there, download and import the package

6. Once imported, you will have the following folder hierarchy in your Project view

Then, go to the Assets → Barking_Dog → 3D Free Modular Kit → Test_Map, select the Test_Map scene and open it. You should be able to have the same scene as shown in Figure 11.3.

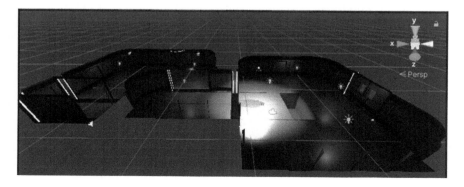

FIGURE 11.3   The asset scene.

11.2 STEP 2: INSERTING THE ROBOT ASSET

Next, you need to download the robot named Industrial robot arm **Free 3D Models** (Figure 11.4). The model can download from the following link:

https://free3d.com/3d-model/industrial-robot-arm-53669.html

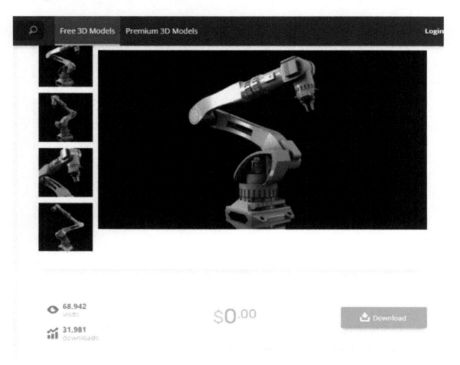

FIGURE 11.4   Industrial robot arm.

Click the Download part and take the zip file. Once you downloaded it, unzip the file and move it to the projects Assets folder (Figure 11.5).

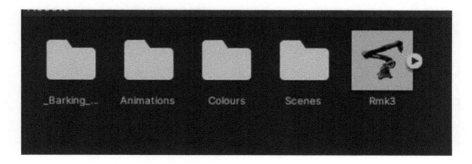

FIGURE 11.5   Move the robot arm to the Asset folder.

Then drag it into the scene; Unpack the Prefab by right-clicking it on the: Hierarchy window → Prefab → Unpack Completely (Figure 11.6)

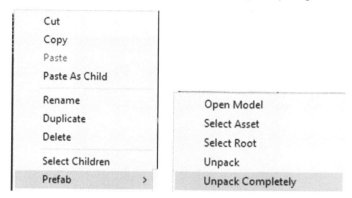

FIGURE 11.6   Unpack the asset.

Once it's on the scene, you need to scale and position it to the coordinates (Figure 11.7) based on the following table:

Transform	X	Y	Z
Position	−22	0	4
Rotation	0	0	0
Scale	0.003	0.003	0.003

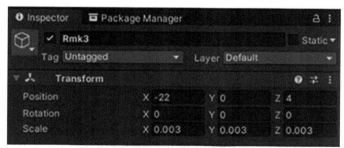

FIGURE 11.7   Positioning the robot arm.

11.3 STEP 3: ROBOT COLOUR

Add colour to the robot by using materials. You can use any colour you want. We select the red colour (Figure 11.8).

FIGURE 11.8 Changing the colour for robot arm.

11.4 STEP 4: ROBOT PARTS POSITION SETTING

Next, you should create a new game object named KUKA, move all the components in Rmk3 into it, and position based on Figure 11.9.

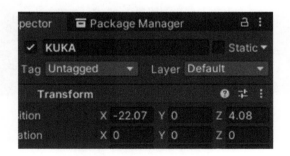

FIGURE 11.9 Robot position settings.

Next, make a change in components name and rename to their relevant function (Figure 11.10).

FIGURE 11.10   Change in components.

Create an empty object, then name it to **Rotate**, position according to the following coordinates and then organise it to the hierarchy (Figure 11.11):

Transform	X	Y	Z
Position	−0.12	0	−0.16
Rotation	0	0	0
Scale	1	1	1

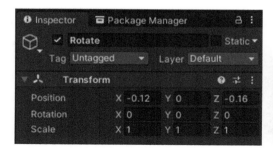

FIGURE 11.11   Create Rotate object.

Make an empty object named **MiddleArmJoint** and set it as the following table coordinates and hierarchy (Figure 11.12).

Transform	X	Y	Z
Position	−383	197	33
Rotation	−3.47	48.69	−3.69
Scale	333.33	333.33	333.33

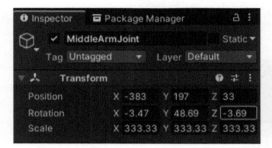

FIGURE 11.12   Create MiddleArmJoint object.

Form an empty object named **ArmTopJoint**, and set it like the following table coordinates and hierarchy (Figure 11.13).

Transform	X	Y	Z
Position	−21.427	1.267	3.384
Rotation	0	40.46	0
Scale	1	1	1

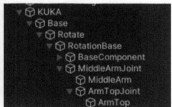

FIGURE 11.13   Create ArmTopJoint object.

Create an empty object named **GripGearJoint**, and set it like the following table coordinates and hierarchy (Figure 11.14).

Transform	X	Y	Z
Position	−22.657	1.717	4.425
Rotation	0	43.17	0
Scale	1	1	1

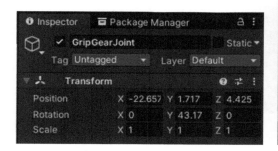
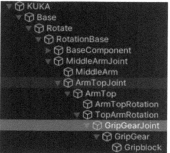

FIGURE 11.14   Create GripGearJoint object.

Create an empty object named **GripControllerJoint**, and change its coordinates like the following table and hierarchy (Figure 11.15).

Transform	X	Y	Z
Position	−22.752	1.392	4.488
Rotation	0	30.5	18.01
Scale	1	1	1

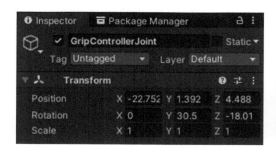

FIGURE 11.15   Create GripControllerJoint object.

After all changes, your final hierarchy should be like the hierarchy as shown in Figure 11.16.

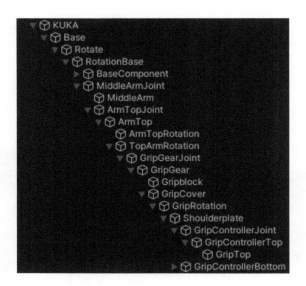

FIGURE 11.16   The final hierarchy view.

11.5 STEP 5: ROBOT IN AUTOMATIC MODE MOVEMENT

Follow the path: Window → Animation → Animation (Figure 11.17)

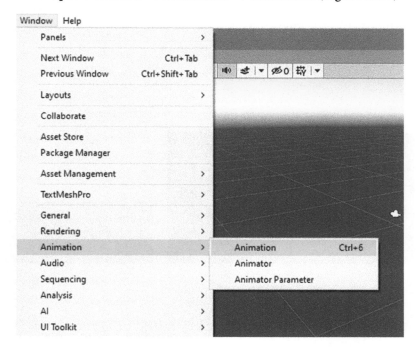

FIGURE 11.17   How to select Animation.

In the Animation window, select **Rotation**, then select Create (Figure 11.18), then create a new animation clip named **Movement**.

FIGURE 11.18 Make a rotation.

Next, you should press the red-record button in the Animation window and, after that, move the scrubber to 01:00. Move to the inspector and change the **Rotate** component rotation to the mentioned values as shown in Figure 11.19.

Transform	X	Y	Z
Rotation	0	360	0

FIGURE 11.19 Rotate the Rotate object.

Whereas the scrubber is at **01:00** from there, you must select **JointMidArm**, move to the inspector and change the rotation of the component according to the following table or Figure 11.20:

Transform	X	Y	Z
Rotation	0	42.765	76

FIGURE 11.20 Rotate the JointMidArm object.

While the scrubber is at **01:00**; from there, select **JointMidTopArm**. Then move to the inspector and change the rotation of the component according to the following table or Figure 11.21:

Transform	X	Y	Z
Rotation	0	42.765	−77.4

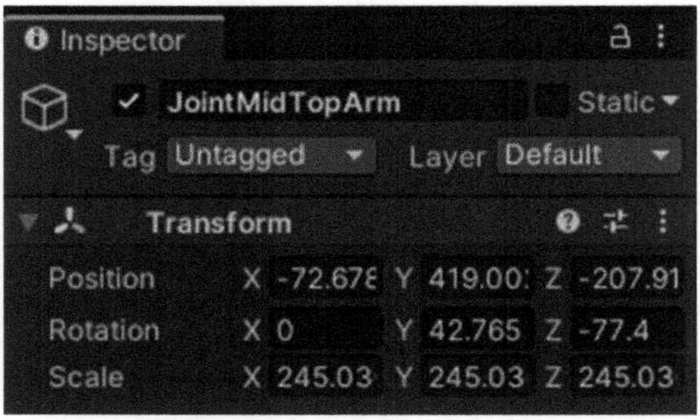

FIGURE 11.21 Rotate the JointMidTopArm object.

In the scrubber is at **01:00**, select **GripGearJoint** and move to the inspector and then change the rotation of the component according to the following table or Figure 11.22:

Transform	X	Y	Z
Rotation	0	42.765	51.3

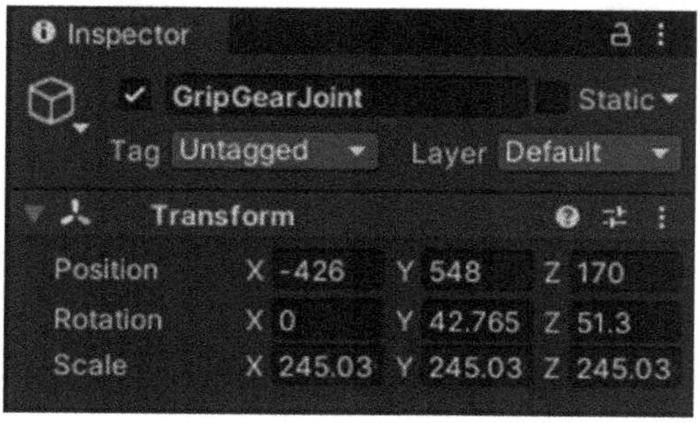

FIGURE 11.22   Rotate the GripGearJoint object.

While the scrubber is at **01:00**, select **GripTopJoint** and move to the inspector and then change the position of the component according to the following table or Figure 11.23:

Transform	X	Y	Z
Position	−468	452.3	208.1

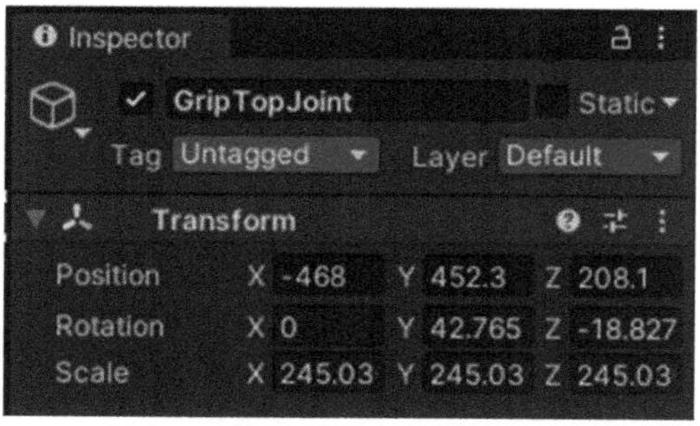

FIGURE 11.23   Rotate the GripTopJoint object.

After this step, by adding the scrips, you should be ready to animate the object.

11.6 STEP 6: MOVEMENT WITH KEYBOARD

First, you need to create the four scripts and name them as ArmTopJoint, GripGearJoint, MiddleArmJoint, and Rotation (Figure 11.24), which will be necessary to move the components.

ArmTopJoint
GripGearJoint
MiddleArmJoint
Rotation

FIGURE 11.24   **Scripts.**

Start with the first script and type the following code for the update block for the Rotation Script (Figure 11.25).

```
void Update()
{
float moveInput = Input.GetAxis("Horizontal");
    if (moveInput > 0f)
    {
        transform.rotation = Quaternion.Euler(0f, moveInput * 90f, 0f);
    }
else if (moveInput < 0f)
    {
        transform.rotation = Quaternion.Euler(0f, moveInput * 90f, 0f);
    }
else
    {
        transform.rotation = Quaternion.Euler(0f, 0f, 0f);
    }
}
```

```
// Update is called once per frame
void Update()
{
    float moveInput = Input.GetAxis("Horizontal");
    if (moveInput > 0f)
    {
        transform.rotation = Quaternion.Euler(0f, moveInput * 90f, 0f);
    }
    else if (moveInput < 0f)
    {
        transform.rotation = Quaternion.Euler(0f, moveInput * 90f, 0f);
    }
    else
    {
        transform.rotation = Quaternion.Euler(0f, 0f, 0f);
    }
}
```

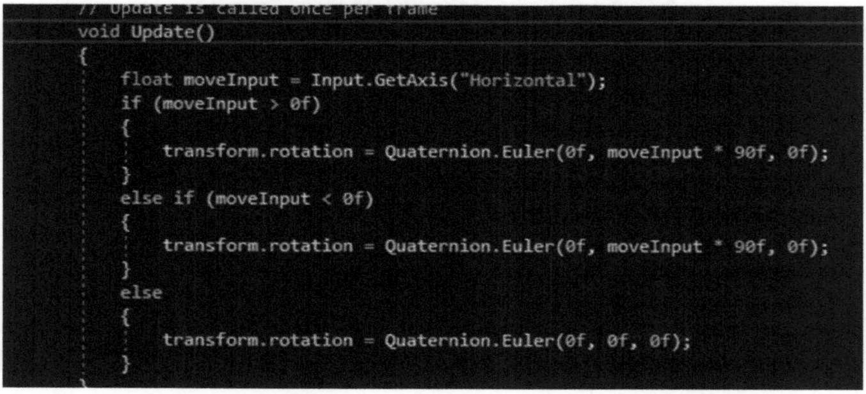

FIGURE 11.25   **The rotation script.**

Next, you need to enter the following code for the MiddleArmJoint (Figure 11.26):

```
void Update()
  {
    float moveInput = Input.GetAxis("Vertical");
    if (moveInput > 0f)
    {
      transform.rotation = Quaternion.Euler(0f, 42.765f, moveInput * 90f);
    }
    else if (moveInput < 0f)
    {
      transform.rotation = Quaternion.Euler(0f, 42.765f, moveInlut*30f);
    }
  }
```

```
void Update()
{
    float moveInput = Input.GetAxis("Vertical");
    if (moveInput > 0f)
    {
        transform.rotation = Quaternion.Euler(0f, 42.765f, moveInput * 90f);
    }
    else if (moveInput < 0f)
    {
        transform.rotation = Quaternion.Euler(0f, 42.765f, moveInput * 30f);
    }
}
```

FIGURE 11.26   The script for the rotation of the MiddleArmJoint.

Finally, you code the Top Arm Movement part (Figure 11.27).

```
void Update()
    {
      float moveInput = Input.GetAxis("Vertical");
      if (moveInput > 0f)
      {
        transform.rotation = Quaternion.Euler(0f,42.765f,  moveInput * 90f);
      }
      else if (moveInput < 0f)
      {
        transform.rotation = Quaternion.Euler(0f, 42.765f, moveInlut*30f);
      }
    }
```

```
void Update()
{
    float moveInput = Input.GetAxis("Vertical");
    if (moveInput > 0f)
    {
        transform.rotation = Quaternion.Euler(0f, 42.765f, moveInput * 90f);
    }
    else if (moveInput < 0f)
    {
        transform.rotation = Quaternion.Euler(0f, 42.765f, moveInput * 30f);
    }
}
```

FIGURE 11.27 The script for the rotation of the top arm.

Drag all the scripts to the joints' inspector windows, which share the same name, and now you can move your robot using a keyboard (Figure 11.28).

FIGURE 11.28 Final scene.

11.7 STEP 7: ALL KUKA SCRIPTS

Add the scripts based on the following part for the different movement:

GripTopMovement

```
using System.Collections;
using System.Collections.Generic;
using UnityEngine;
public class GripTopMovement : MonoBehaviour
{

private float movementSpeed = 5f;
// Update is called once per frame
void Update()
{

bool moveInput = Input.GetKey("2");
if (moveInput == true)
{
transform.position = transform.position + new Vector3(1f
* Time.deltaTime, 1f* Time.deltaTime, 0);
}
else
{
transform.position = transform.position + new Vector3( 0, 0,
0);
}
}
}
```

MidArmMovement

```
using System.Collections;
using System.Collections.Generic;
using UnityEngine;
public class MidArmMovement : MonoBehaviour
{

// Start is called before the first frame update
void Start()
{
}
void Update()
{

float moveInput = Input.GetAxis("Vertical");
if (moveInput > 0f)
{
transform.rotation = Quaternion.Euler(0f, 42.765f,
moveInput * 90f);
}
else if (moveInput < 0f)
{
transform.rotation = Quaternion.Euler(0f, 42.765f, moveInput * 30f);
}
}
}
```

MidTopArmMovement

```csharp
using System.Collections;
using System.Collections.Generic;
using UnityEngine;
public class MidTopArmMovement : MonoBehaviour
{
    // Start is called before the first frame update
    void Start()
    {
    }
    // Update is called once per frame
    void Update()
    {
        bool moveInput = Input.GetKey("1");
        if (moveInput == true)
        {
            transform.rotation = Quaternion.Euler(0f, 42.765f, 20f);
        }
        else
        {
            transform.rotation = Quaternion.Euler(0f, 42.765f, 0f);
        }
    }
}
```

Rotate

```csharp
using System.Collections;
using System.Collections.Generic;
using UnityEngine;
public class Rotate : MonoBehaviour
{
    // Start is called before the first frame update
    void Start()
    {
    }
    // Update is called once per frame
    void Update()
    {
        float moveInput = Input.GetAxis("Horizontal");
        if (moveInput > 0f)
        {
            transform.rotation = Quaternion.Euler(0f, moveInput * 90f, 0f);
        }
        else if (moveInput < 0f)
        {
            transform.rotation = Quaternion.Euler(0f, moveInput * 90f, 0f);
        }
        else
        {
            transform.rotation = Quaternion.Euler(0f, 0f, 0f);
        }
    }
}
```

UNITY IN EMBEDDED SYSTEM DESIGN AND ROBOTICS
A STEP-BY-STEP GUIDE

CHAPTER 12

Example 11: Communication between ARDUINO and UNITY

DOI: 10.1201/9781003268581-12

One of the exciting parts of Unity is interfacing the Unity design with the Arduino board is that it works as a bridge between Unity and the real world. Arduino is an open-source electronics platform invented based on easy-to-use hardware and software. Arduino permits users a simple pathway to create interactive objects that can take input from various accessories like switches, sensors, and control physical outputs like lights, motors, or actuators. These boards can easily read inputs and command your board what to do by sending a set of instructions to the microcontroller on the board. This chapter discusses the Arduino part and section and finally shows the step for interfacing with Unity design. In this chapter, some general definitions for Arduino are described then the project will be described.

12.1 INTRODUCTION OF ARDUINO

It is important for users to understand the three concepts of Arduino Hardware, Arduino Software, and Arduino Code in order to work with Arduino.

12.1.1 Arduino Hardware

Arduino boards are the physical components of an Arduino system. All Arduino boards have one thing in common: The microcontroller. The microcontroller as a small computer that enables us to read those different inputs and control those different outputs. When someone refers to an Arduino board, they are talking about a physical printed circuit board assembled with some electrical components. There are many kinds of Arduino boards, and, among all, the Arduino UNO is the most prevalent one.

12.1.2 Arduino Software

Arduino Integrated Development Environment (IDE) is the development environment on the Arduino board. You can write code into the computer and then use it to program the Arduino boards (Figure 12.1). This software is free and easy to use. The IDE can be downloaded from Arduino official website (https://www.arduino.cc/).

12.1.3 Arduino Code

With the help of Arduino IDE, you can load the code into the Arduino board's microcontroller. The Arduino code is called a sketch, and it is

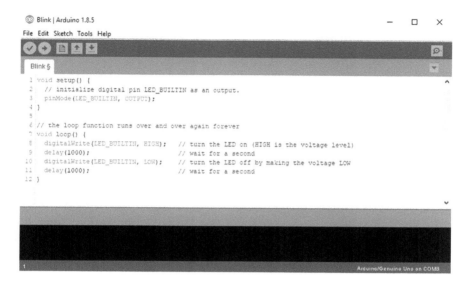

FIGURE 12.1   Arduino IDE.

mostly a derivative of the C and C++ programming languages, but with some Arduino-specific functions and structure.

12.2 CONNECTING ARDUINO TO UNITY

The Arduino board uses a port to communicate with a PC through serial communication and Unity interfacing. Serial communication is the process of sending/receiving data one bit at a time, and a serial port is an interface that allows a PC to transmit or receive data one bit at a time.

12.2.1 Unity to Arduino (ARDITY) Guide

There are various ways to connect Unity to Arduino. One of the easiest ways to link Unity and Arduino is using the ARDITY, which is recently introduced. ARDITY is open-source and free, which you can directly download from the link: https://ARDITY.dwilches.com/ or GitHub link: https://github.com/dwilches/ARDITY

As presented on the ARDITY web page, ARDITY connects your Arduino to Unity over a COM port. You can follow the following steps to have this bridge.

12.2.1.1 Step 1: Unity Installation

Install Unity from www.unity3d.com. Since this step was introduced in previous chapters, you can skip it.

12.2.1.2 Step 2: Download and Install the Arduino IDE

Install Arduino IDE from the link (https://www.arduino.cc/en/software). The Arduino IDE can download for the Windows, Mac, and Linux operating systems. For Windows, Mac, and Linux, you can directly download the Arduino IDE and follow the installation as shown in Figure 12.2.

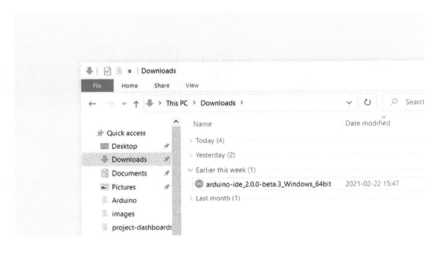

For Windows:

FIGURE 12.2   How to install Arduino IDE for Windows, Mac, and Linux. (*Continued*)

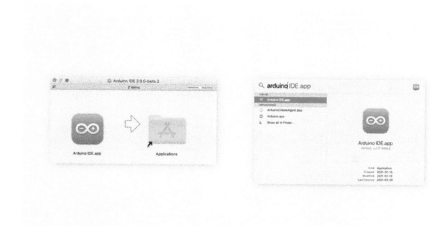

For Mac:

For Linux:

FIGURE 12.2 *(Continued)*

12.2.1.3 Step 3: Start Unity

Open Unity Hub and create a New Project (Figure 12.3).

12.2.1.4 Step 4: Download ARDITY

The ARDITY is free, and you can download ARDITY from https://ARDITY.dwilches.com (Figure 12.4).

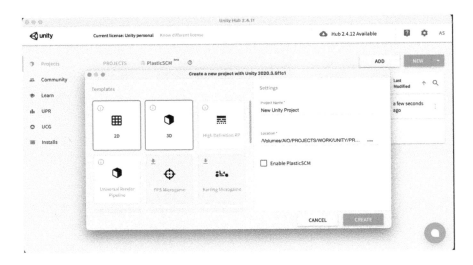

FIGURE 12.3   Open and create a new project.

FIGURE 12.4   Ardity.

12.2.1.5 Step 5: Import inside the Unity

To use the ARDITY, you should insert it inside the Unity and then import a custom package from path: Assets → Import Package → Custom Package. After that, browse and select **ARDITY.unitypackage** and then click Import in the following pop up dialogue (Figure 12.5).

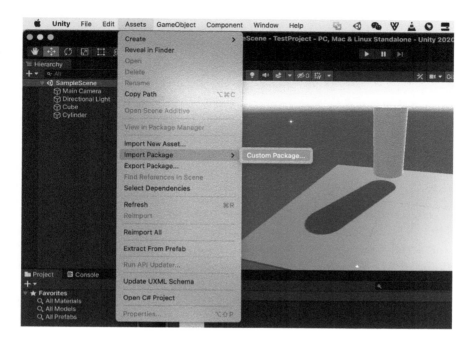

FIGURE 12.5 Import custom package.

12.2.1.6 Step 6: Error Resolving

After importing the package, you may get the following error:

Assets/Ardi/Scripts/Threds/AbstartcSerialThread.cs(13.17):error CS2034: … (Figure 12.6).

FIGURE 12.6   Error.

To fix the above-mentioned error, you should go to the following path: File → Build Settings → Player Settings, then click on Other Settings and scroll down to **API Compatibility Layer** and select .NET 4.x; After doing it, all errors should remove, and you can continue to the next step (Figure 12.7).

Another error you could encounter is, *"You are trying to replace or create a Prefab from the instance "SerialController_BinaryDelimited" that references a missing script. This is not allowed. Please change the script or remove it from the GameObject".*

To fix this error, navigate to Assets → ARDITY → Prefabs and click on SerialController_BinaryDelimited (Figure 12.8).

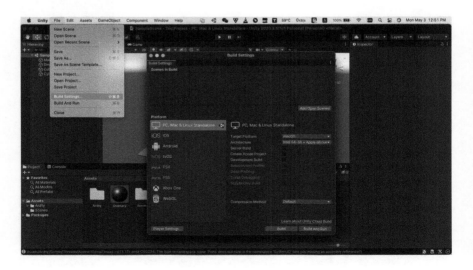

FIGURE 12.7   Select .NEX 4.x. (*Continued*)

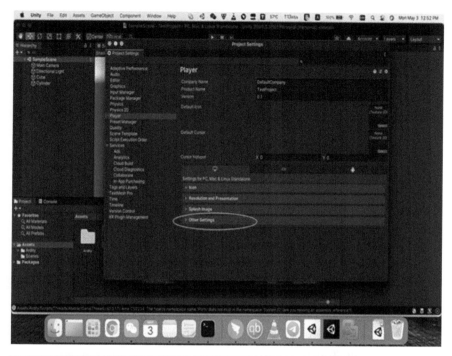

FIGURE 12.7 (*Continued*)

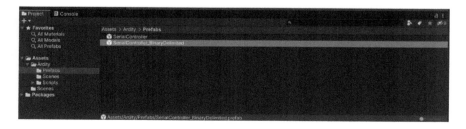

FIGURE 12.8 Fix second error.

Then, on the Inspector Window, click **Open Prefab** select script as shown in Figure 12.9.

FIGURE 12.9   Open prefab.

12.2.1.7 Step 7: Connect the Arduino Device via USB

To connect your Arduino device using a USB, you'll need to know which COM port your device is currently using. If you do not know your Arduino COM port concerning your operating system (OSO), you can find the COM port that is connected or not.

For Windows: Open Windows Search and type **Device Manager**, open it, look under **Ports (COM & LPT)** to find the device, and take note of the USB Serial Device's COM port.

For MacOS/Linux: Open terminal and run: ls/dev/tty.*

The naming should be obvious. Here our port is/dev/tty.usbserial-1410 [note it down or copy it] (Figure 12.10).

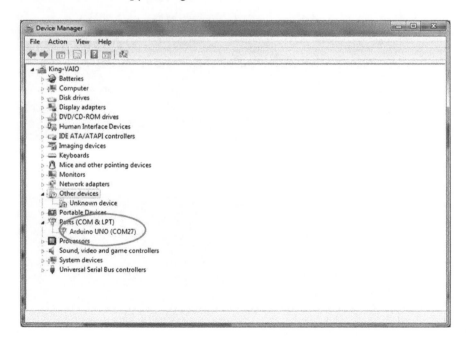

FIGURE 12.10   Find the name of the COM port. (*Continued*)

```
● ● ●                    roy — -zsh — 80×24
[roy@MacBook-Pro ~ % tty
/dev/ttys000
[roy@MacBook-Pro ~ % ls /dev/tty.*
/dev/tty.Bluetooth-Incoming-Port      /dev/tty.usbserial-1410
roy@MacBook-Pro ~ %
```

FIGURE 12.10   (*Continued*)

12.2.1.8 Step 8: Put the Port Name inside Unity

Click on SerialController from the Hierarchy Pane, and, on the inspector, put the port name from the previous step (Figure 12.11).

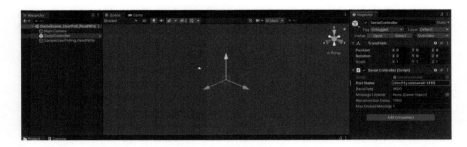

FIGURE 12.11 Add the port name to Unity.

12.2.1.9 Step 9: Upload the Code

Next, Open Arduino IDE, set up the Arduino Board, and make it ready for use:

Go to File → Examples → Basics and click on DigitalSerialRead and upload the following code (Figure 12.12).

```
bool lightOn = false;
// the setup routine runs once when you press reset:
void setup() {
  // initialize serial communication at 9600 bits per second:
  Serial.begin(9600);
  // make the pushbutton"s pin an input:
  pinMode(LED_BUILTIN, OUTPUT);
}
// the loop routine runs over and over again forever:
void loop() {
  // print out the state of the button:
  if(Serial.available())
  {
    char c = Serial.read();
    if (c)
    {
      if(c == "A")
      {
        lightOn = true;
      }
      else if(c == "Z")
      {
        lightOn = false;
      }
```

```
    c = NULL;
    }
 }
 if(lightOn)
 {
   digitalWrite(LED_BUILTIN, HIGH);
   Serial.println("on");
 }
 else
 {
   digitalWrite(LED_BUILTIN, LOW);
   Serial.println("off");
 }
 delay(1000);      // delay in between reads for stability
}
```

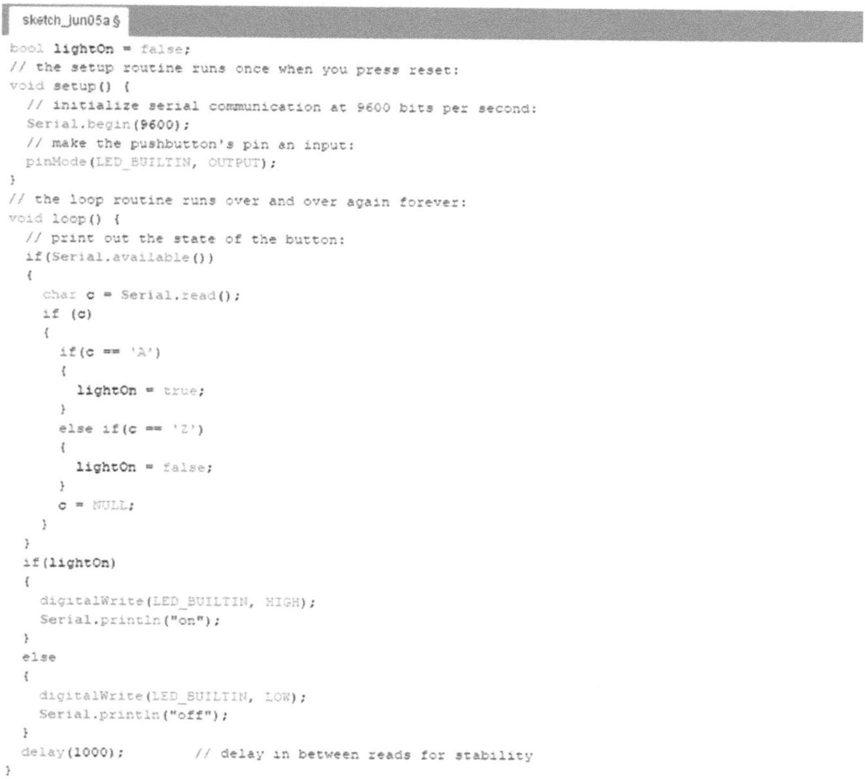

```
sketch_jun05a §
bool lightOn = false;
// the setup routine runs once when you press reset:
void setup() {
  // initialize serial communication at 9600 bits per second:
  Serial.begin(9600);
  // make the pushbutton's pin an input:
  pinMode(LED_BUILTIN, OUTPUT);
}
// the loop routine runs over and over again forever:
void loop() {
  // print out the state of the button:
  if(Serial.available())
  {
    char c = Serial.read();
    if (c)
    {
      if(c == 'A')
      {
        lightOn = true;
      }
      else if(c == 'Z')
      {
        lightOn = false;
      }
      c = NULL;
    }
  }
  if(lightOn)
  {
    digitalWrite(LED_BUILTIN, HIGH);
    Serial.println("on");
  }
  else
  {
    digitalWrite(LED_BUILTIN, LOW);
    Serial.println("off");
  }
  delay(1000);        // delay in between reads for stability
}
```

FIGURE 12.12   Arduino script.

12.2.1.10 Step 10: Run the Scene in Unity

Once the scene is running, you will see the information from the serial monitor in the Unity Console, as shown in Figure 12.13.

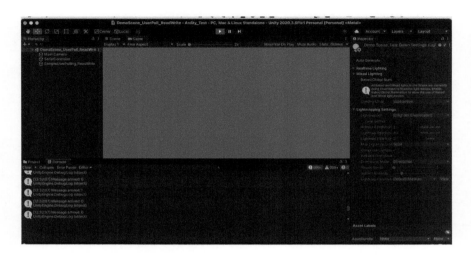

FIGURE 12.13   **Run the scene in Unity.**

12.2.2 Arduino to Unity (Control Unity Animation with Physical Buttons)

In this example, you will learn how to connect Arduino and Unity. You will send data from Arduino to Unity and an action will be performed based on your input data. This example aims to move the cube in Unity in the right and left direction by pressing the different buttons. The following steps will help you to acquire and process the data from Arduino in Unity.

12.2.2.1 Step 1: Unity Installation

Install Unity 3D (if you have already installed Unity 3D, you can ignore this step).

12.2.2.2 Step 2: Arduino COM Port

It is essential to know the Arduino serial port. This port can be found in the Mac or Linux Terminal or Device manager in Windows as shown in Figure 12.14.

For Windows: Search Device Manager and open it and look under Port to find the device. Take note of the Arduino COM Port.

For MacOS/Linux: Open Terminal and run: ls/dev/tty.*, please Note that the naming should be obvious. For example, in Figure (12.14, right), our port is shown/dev/tty.usbserial-1410 [note it down or copy it].

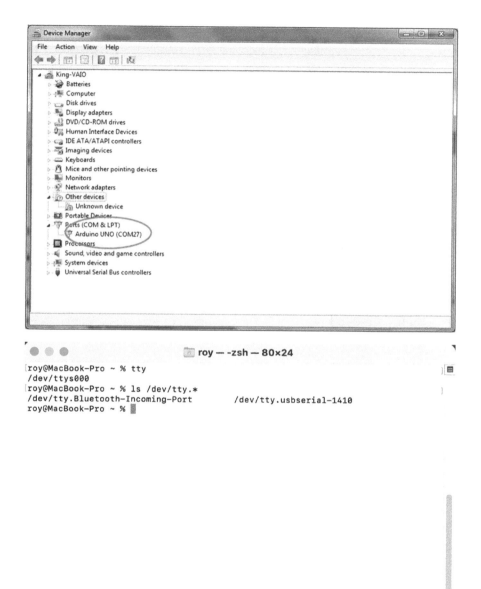

FIGURE 12.14   Serial comport over Windows and Mac.

12.2.2.3 Step 3: Hardware Assembly and Connection

For this example, we need two buttons, wires, and an Arduino UNO board (or any other Arduino board). Then, you can make the connections described in the following table and Figure 12.15 on the Arduino side. Schematics are shown in Figure 12.16.

No	Arduino Pin	Button
1	10	Right
2	11	Left
3	VCC	
4	GND	

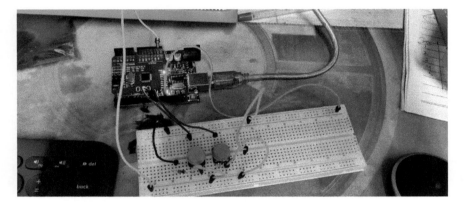

FIGURE 12.15   Arduino Buttons.

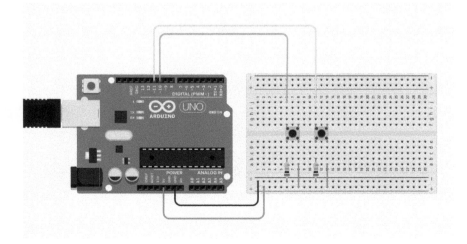

FIGURE 12.16   Arduino Buttons Schematic.

12.2.2.4 Step 4: Arduino Program Code Check

Debugging and compiling the Arduino code should be done before uploading the code, then write the following Arduino Buttons Sample code to test whether the buttons are working or not. In this code initially, the Digital pins of 10 (for left button) and 11 (for right button) are sets as the constant and serial communication established as the band rate for 9600 (Figure 12.17). The value of the Digital pin reads as the inputs of those buttons when pressed. Finally, serial communication is sent based on pressed keys, Right and Left word print by serial, and the values of 1 and 0.

```
const int buttonLeft = 10;    // the number of the pushbutton pin
const int buttonRight = 11;
int buttonLeftState = 0;      // variable for reading the pushbutton status
int buttonRightState = 0;
void setup() {
Serial.begin(9600);
 pinMode(buttonLeft, INPUT);
 // initialize the pushbutton pin as an input:
 pinMode(buttonRight, INPUT);
 // initialize the pushbutton pin as an input:
}
void loop(){
 buttonLeftState        =
digitalRead(buttonLeft);
 buttonRightState       =
digitalRead(buttonRight);

 if(buttonLeftState == HIGH){
       Serial.println("Left");
       Serial.write(1);
         delay(500);
         }
 if(buttonRightState == HIGH){
       Serial.println("Right");
       Serial.write(2);
         delay(500);
 }
}
```

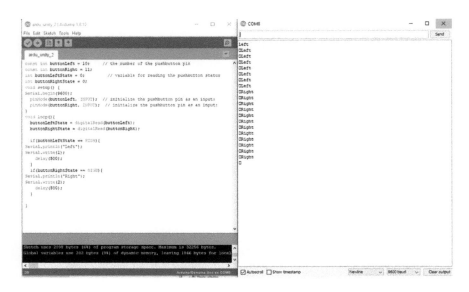

FIGURE 12.17   Arduino IDE program code check.

12.2.2.5 Step 5: Create a Cube Object

The next step focuses on the Unity aspect to create a sample scene with a cube from the following path: GameObject → 3D Object → Cube (Figure 12.18).

Click on the newly created game object on the left side of the screen (Hierarchy Pane) and put the values in the inspector pane (Right Side)

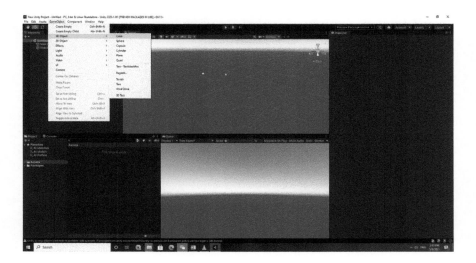

FIGURE 12.18   Create GameObject.

transform section, and change the values based on the following table (Figure 12.19).

Transform	X	Y	Z
Scale	2	2	2

FIGURE 12.19   Give attribute to the game object.

12.2.2.6 Step 6: Create a Ground

To improve the design, you can create a material that will make the cube green. We have created a plane with a green colour (Material Asset with Albedo **Green**). Click the asset section for new material and then double-click on that. Also, you can rename it to the Ground (Figure 12.20).

FIGURE 12.20   Create GameObject Plane.

To change the ground colour, you should create a plane with the colour green (Material Asset with Albedo **Green**) (Figures 12.21 and 12.22) and select the colour that you prefer. In this step, be cautious about the reference point and check the cube and plane (Figure 12.23).

FIGURE 12.21　Create Ground.

FIGURE 12.22　Create Ground rename.

FIGURE 12.23   Create colour material.

12.2.2.7 Step 7: Create a Tree Object

To add some life to the scene, we created a tree. Follow the path: **GameObject → 3D Object → Tree** (Figure 12.24) and add one Tree Asset to be a centre for the scene (Figure 12.25).

FIGURE 12.24   Create GameObject Tree.

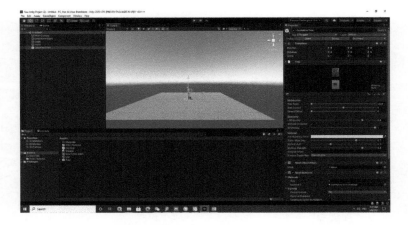

FIGURE 12.25   Add Tree's attributes.

Then click on the plane in the Hierarchy Pane and change the values on the inspector pane Scale section as shown in Figure 12.26 and in the following table.

Transform	X	Y	Z
Position	0	0	0
Rotation	0	0	0
Scale	10	10	10

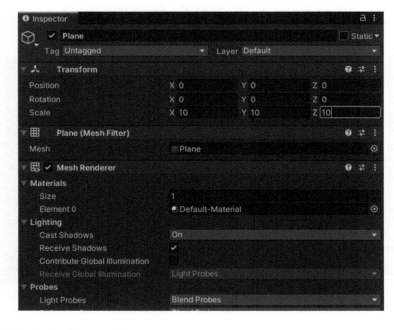

FIGURE 12.26   Tree attributes.

Next, right-click on the Project pane and create a new Material from path Create → Material (Figure 12.27).

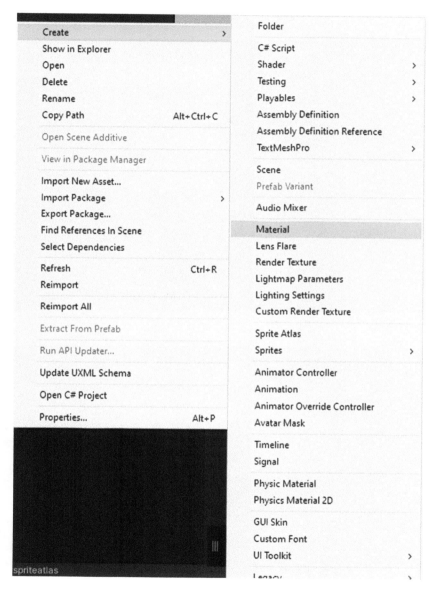

FIGURE 12.27   Material for tree.

Create a new folder, **Materials**, and move the new material to there. Right-click and rename it to Ground. Click on it to show its properties on the inspector pane. Drag the Ground onto the plane then, you should see the ground colour change to green (Figures 12.28 and 12.29).

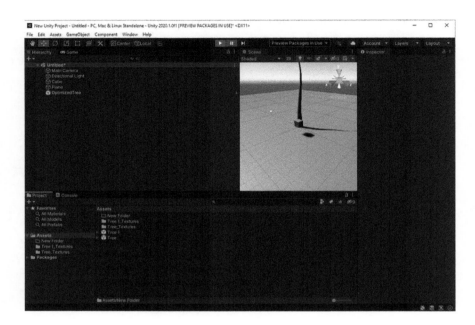

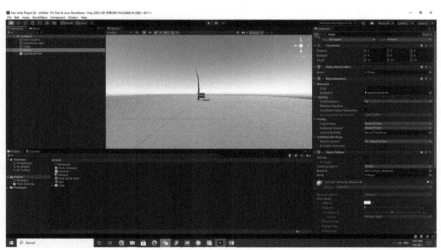

FIGURE 12.28　How to drag the Ground.

Click on the **Albedo** option and select any green colour of your choice from the colour picker (Figure 12.29).

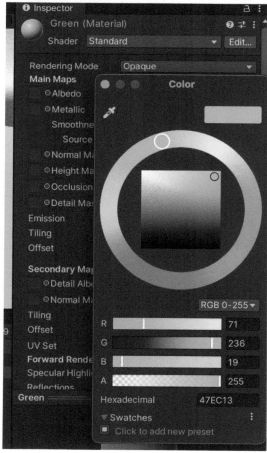

FIGURE 12.29   Add colour to Ground.

Select the Plane on the scene and drag the new Material on the Plane, then create new material called Brown and select a brown colour albedo like the earlier process (Figure 12.30).

FIGURE 12.30 Ground colour creation.

Next, select the brown colour in the inspector section (Figure 12.31).

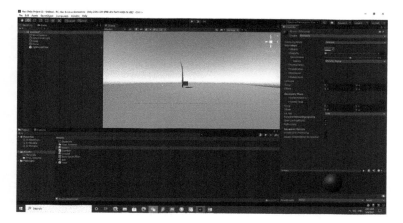

FIGURE 12.31   After adding colour to Ground.

Afterwards, create a new folder named **Materials** to keep things organised and drag and drop the Brown Material to optimise the tree game object (Figures 12.32 and 12.33).

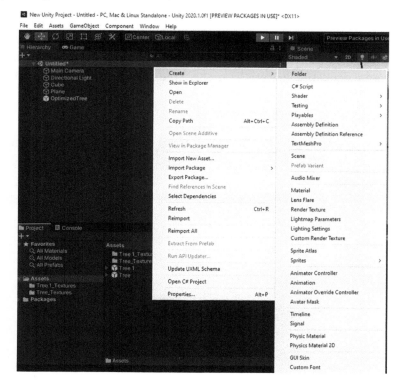

FIGURE 12.32   Create a new folder for organising.

FIGURE 12.33   Brown Material.

Select the Plane on the scene and drag the new Material on the Plane. Then drag and drop the material on the Tree object to change its colour. As the next stage to colour the object, create a new Material called Brown and select a brown colour albedo like the earlier process. Drag and drop the material on the Tree object to change its colour (Figure 12.34).

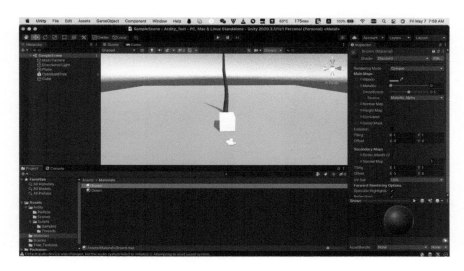

FIGURE 12.34   Tree colour changed.

12.2.2.8 Step 8: Check the Setting

To recheck your work so far done, setting for game objects based on inspector setting is shown in Figure 12.35.

CAMERA

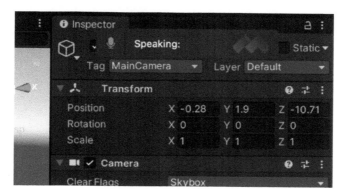

Transform	X	Y	Z
Position	−0.28	1.9	−10.71
Rotation	0	0	0
Scale	1	1	1

PLANE

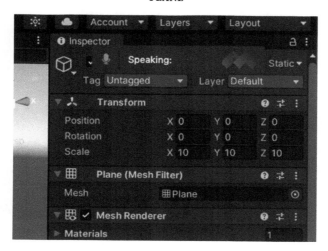

Transform	X	Y	Z
Position	0	0	0
Rotation	0	0	0
Scale	10	10	10

CUBE

Transform	X	Y	Z
Position	−0.23	1.08	−5.33
Rotation	0	0	0
Scale	2	2	2

TREE

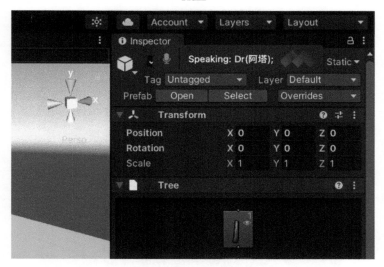

Transform	X	Y	Z
Position	0	0	0
Rotation	0	0	0
Scale	1	1	1

FIGURE 12.35 Attributes of different GameObjects.

12.2.2.9 Step 9: C# Script Code

To move the object, you need to create a C# Script inside the project pane and open it with Visual Studio. Then right-click on any free space in the projects pane and click on create → C# Script (Figure 12.36).

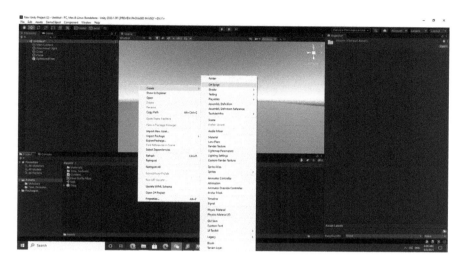

FIGURE 12.36 Creating C# Script.

12.2.2.10 Step 10: Script Name

By right-click on the inserted code and select the rename part, you can give a name to the script (Figure 12.37).

FIGURE 12.37 Rename Script. (*Continued*)

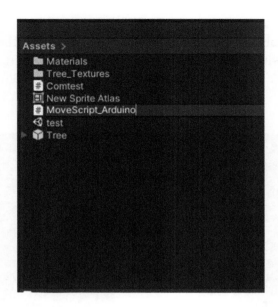

FIGURE 12.37 (*Continued*)

12.2.2.11 Step 11: External Script Editor Configuration

Unity is not pre-configured to use Visual Studio as its default editor. Changing it is done in the settings. Follow the path: Preferences from the top menu (Figure 12.38) → External Tools (Figure 12.39). Then, set the

FIGURE 12.38 Preferences.

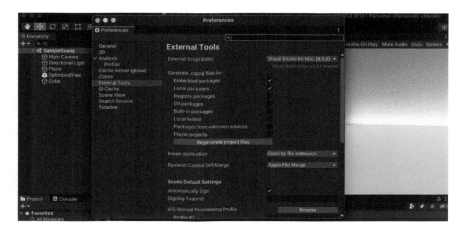

FIGURE 12.39   External tools settings.

External Script Editor to be Visual Studio besides checking the Embedded packages and a Local package check box.

Then check the Players Setting from: File → build Settings (Figures 12.40 and 12.41), and change the target platform to API compatibility Level to. NET 4.x (Figure 12.42).

New Unity Project (2) - test - PC, Mac & l

File	Edit	Assets	GameObject	Compo

New Scene	Ctrl+N
Open Scene	Ctrl+O
Save	Ctrl+S
Save As...	Ctrl+Shift+S
New Project...	
Open Project...	
Save Project	
Build Settings...	Ctrl+Shift+B
Build And Run	Ctrl+B
Exit	

FIGURE 12.40   Build Settings.

FIGURE 12.41   Nav to Player Settings.

FIGURE 12.42   API Compatibility Level.

12.2.2.12 Step 12: Attach the Script to the CUBE GameObject

Close the Preferences window. It will save automatically. Then double-click on the C# Script file from the projects pane for Visual Studio to open. The C# Code is as shown in Figure 12.43.

```csharp
using System.Collections;
using System.Collections.Generic;
using UnityEngine;
using System.IO.Ports;
public class MoveScript_Arduino : MonoBehaviour
{   // Start is called before the first frame update
   SerialPort sp = new SerialPort("/dev/tty.usbserial-1420", 9600);
   void Start()
   {
    sp.Open();
    sp.ReadTimeout = 1;
   }
   // Update is called once per frame
   void Update()
   {

    if(sp.IsOpen)
    {
      Debug.Log("SP IS OPEN");
      try
      {
        if (sp.ReadByte() == 1)
        {
            this.transform.Translate(Vector3.left * Time.deltaTime * 10);
            Debug.Log("LEFT");
        }
        if (sp.ReadByte() == 2)
        {
            this.transform.Translate(Vector3.right * Time.deltaTime * 10);
            Debug.Log("RIGHT");
        }
      }
      catch (System. Exception)
      {
      }
    }
   }
}
```

FIGURE 12.43　Code inside Visual Script.

Afterwards, drag or copy the script from the assets pane on the inspector of the GameObject, or you can add a script component from the inspector of the game object. After that, add the script from there too. Select the Cube GameObject from the Hierarchy Pane. Here the script's name is MoveScript_Arduino, and you should see the name from the imported Object section of the inspector (Figure 12.44).

FIGURE 12.44　Drag or attach script to CUBE GameObject.

12.2.2.13 *Step 13: Final Step and Cube Movement*

Now you can run the scene by pressing the play button and press the buttons to move the cube – simple drag the script from the assets pane on the inspector of the GameObject. Or, you can add a script component from the inspector of the game object and add the script from there too.

12.2.2.14 *Step 14: Drag Manually*

The fundamental goal to drag the script manually to the game object is the way. Unity and C# work in conjunction. The script will be applied to the game object. It will get the variables of that object and work with it. In short, to manipulate the game object, a script with code should be attached to it. To drag the task manually, you can select the Cube GameObject from the Hierarchy Pane (Figure 12.45) and then click on Add Component in the inspector pane (Figure 12.46). After that, click on Scripts and select the C# Script you just created. Here the name of the script is MoveScript_Arduino (Figure 12.47).

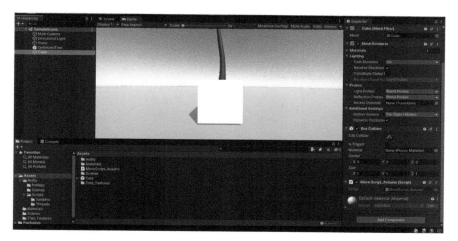

FIGURE 12.45   Add Component.

FIGURE 12.46   Add Script.

FIGURE 12.47 **Select Script.**

12.2.2.15 Step 15: Check the Camera

You can check the camera attributes and position as it is shown in Figures 12.48–12.50.

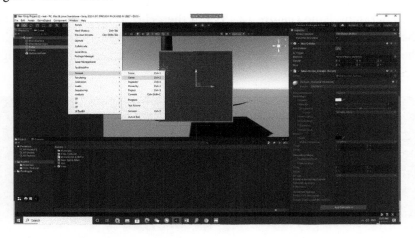

FIGURE 12.48 **Check camera.**

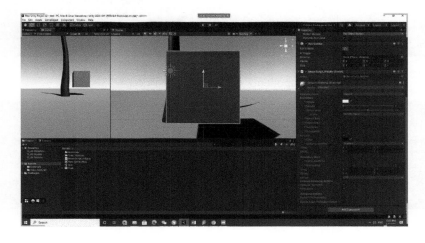

FIGURE 12.49 **Check camera attributes.**

FIGURE 12.50 Recheck camera.

12.2.2.16 Step 16: Run

Run the scene from the play button and press the buttons to move the cube. By pressing each button in Arduino, you should see the cube's movement to the right and left (Figure 12.51).

FIGURE 12.51 Run the scene.

UNITY IN EMBEDDED SYSTEM DESIGN AND ROBOTICS

A STEP-BY-STEP GUIDE

CHAPTER 13

Example 12: SpongeBob, Control Object by Keyboard and Arduino

DOI: 10.1201/9781003268581-13

In this example, we will review the character movement and control based on three methods: automatic movement, keyboard movement, and Arduino movement, once more. This example can be worked separately with the common initial steps for any mentioned methods. Besides, to have an interesting project, we used the SpongeBob character to navigate around the scene. The Character moves around using directional buttons and navigates the scene while the camera follows it. The camera can pan around the scene using mouse movement, and the Character will stay in the frame while panning. To achieve this, we will have to import two assets and use their scripts, prefabs, and scenes.

13.1 STEP 1: IMPORTING THE ASSET

This example consists of two assets, Jungle Set and SpongeBob, which you should initially add both.

13.1.1 Asset I: Casual Tiny Environment – Jungle Set

To have an excellent environment, you can use the Asset name Casual Tiny Environment – Jungle Set, representing the Jungle. The Casual Tiny Environment Asset can be downloaded from Unity by the following link:

https://assetstore.unity.com/packages/3d/environments/fantasy/casual-tiny-environment-jungle-set-169765 (Figure 13.1).

FIGURE 13.1 Download and import casual tiny environment.

Then go to your Unity project and download and import the asset in the package manager. Afterwards, go to Project → Assets → Casual Tiny Environment → Scene → Jungle 1. Then navigate to the Mesh GameObject from Hierarchy section under Jungle 1 (Figure 13.2).

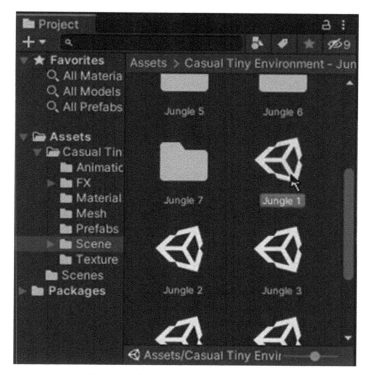

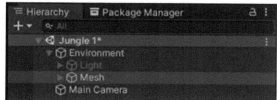

FIGURE 13.2   How to go to Jungle 1.

Afterwards, in the Mesh GameObject's inspector window, add Component → Mesh Collider and change the transform values based on the following table (Figure 13.3).

Transform	X	Y	Z
Position	0	0	0
Rotation	0	0	0
Scale	1	1	1

FIGURE 13.3   Change the values.

Then, select mesh_chapter_5_boss_wall in the Mesh property (Figure 13.4) and repeat before the stages with different meshes that start with **mesh_chapter_5**.

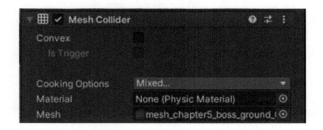

FIGURE 13.4   Change the mesh.

13.1.2 Asset II: SpongeBob 3D Model

Download the SpongeBob Blender 3D model from the following link:

https://free3d.com/3d-model/spongebob-71407.html (Figure 13.5).

Also, download and install Blender from their website using the following link:

https://www.blender.org/download/ (Figure 13.6).

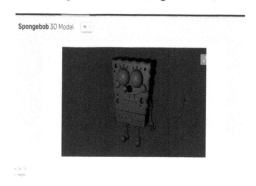

FIGURE 13.5 SpongeBob 3D model.

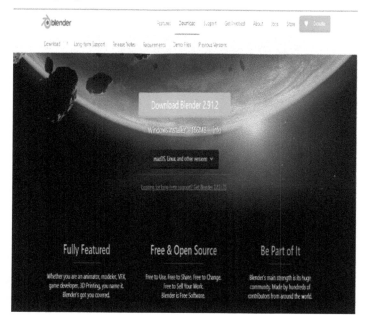

FIGURE 13.6 Blender.

Once installed, open the 3D model in Blender. You should see as shown in Figure 13.7.

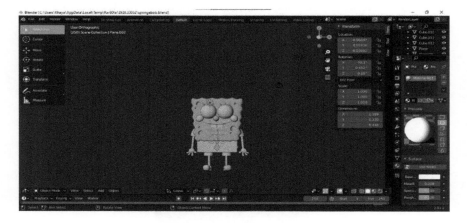

FIGURE 13.7   Install the Blender.

Then, click the select box in object mode and select the eyes, then, right-click and choose Duplicate objects (Figure 13.8).

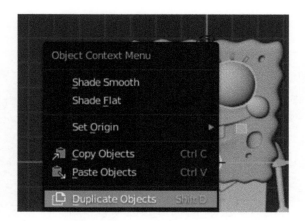

FIGURE 13.8   Duplicate object.

Once duplicated, change the position and the scale of the eyes to the following table coordinates (Figure 13.9). With the eyes selected, go to edit mode and press A to select all and press P and select by loose parts (Figure 13.10).

Transform	X	Y	Z
Location	0.07560	−0.55701	1.88799
Scale	0.383	0.383	0.383

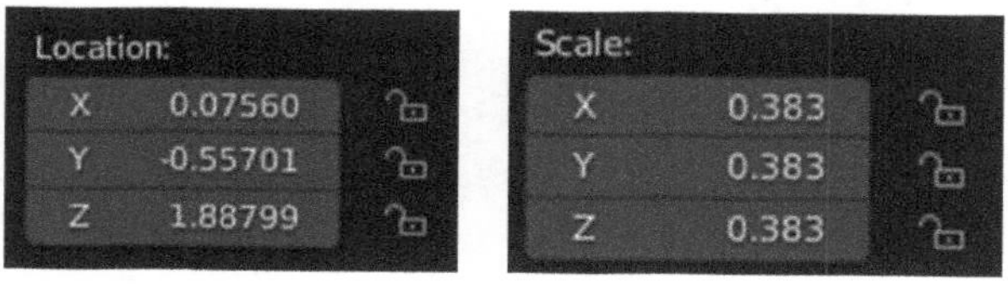

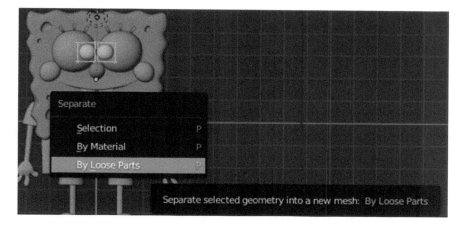

FIGURE 13.9   Change the eye values.

FIGURE 13.10   Edit mode by Loose Parts.

Then, go back to object mode and move the eyes to the following locations (Figure 13.11).

Transform	X	Y	Z
Location 1	0.51965	−0.55701	1.88799
Location 2	−0.62747	−0.55701	1.88799

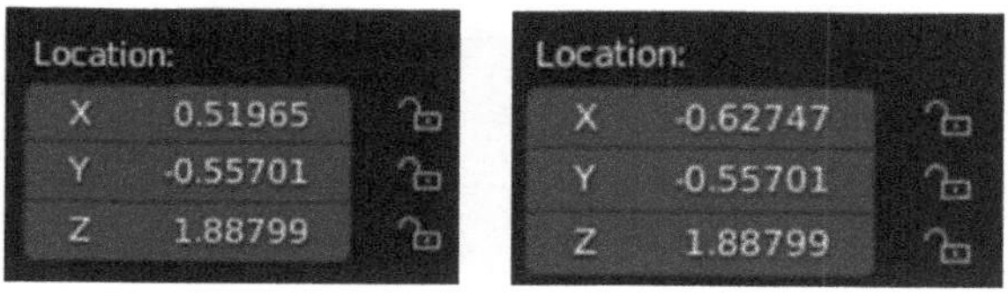

FIGURE 13.11   Change the other eye values.

Next, change the objects, which have mirrored Modifiers. Select Cube.003 and remove the mirrored modifier by right-clicking and deleting it (Figure 13.12).

FIGURE 13.12   Remove mirror modifier.

Duplicate Cube.003 and place it in the location where the previous mirrored object was placed. Mind the rotation of the object as well. Repeat for all mirrored objects. Next is colouring. To colour an object, change to Material Preview mode (Figure 13.13). Select the object you wish to change the colour. Once there, navigate to the Properties Editor and open Material Editor and remove the material that is currently there by clicking the minus button (Figure 13.14).

FIGURE 13.13   Change Material preview.

FIGURE 13.14   Remove the material.

Once the Material Slot is removed, add colour by pressing the plus button. Then press the new button that pops up and change the Base colour to your desired colour. Then, repeat this for all the objects to gain Figure 13.15.

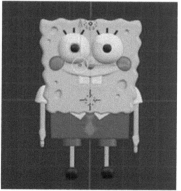

FIGURE 13.15   Add colours.

Next, export the model to the Unity project's Assets folder in the FBX format and select the Apply Transforms (Figure 13.16).

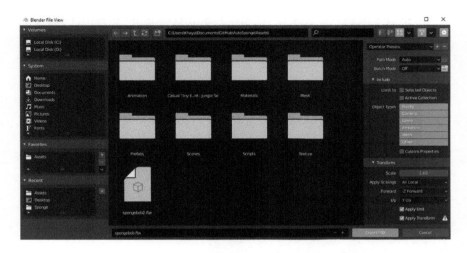

FIGURE 13.16   Import model to Unity by Apply Transforms.

13.2 STEP 2: REVIEW EXAMPLE 1 (AUTO SPONGE)

In this section, we review the process where the Character moves automatically. Then, after the Spongebob.fbx prefab has been imported, move it to the Hierarchy window and unpack it completely. Next, change its position and rotation to match the following (Figure 13.17).

Transform	X	Y	Z
Position	−2.75	14.71	−30.02
Rotation	0	141.506	0
Scale	0.30936	0.30936	0.30936

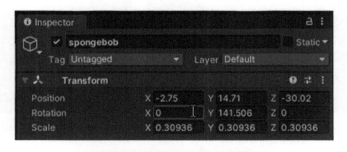

FIGURE 13.17   Change the movement values.

Then, rename the GameObjects to match the names as shown in Figure 13.18 and move the relevant objects' nest into the relevant parents as represented in this figure.

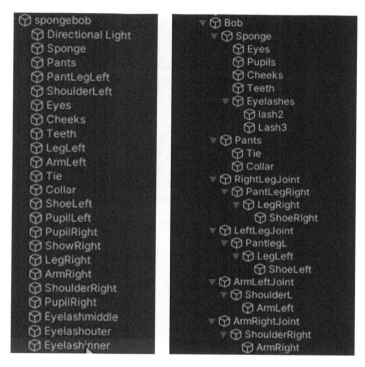

FIGURE 13.18   Rename and move the object.

Change the GameObject ArmLeft and ArmRight position, rotation, and according to the following tables' values in the inspector section (Figure 13.19).

ArmLeft			
Transform	**X**	**Y**	**Z**
Position	−3.45	3.29	2.5
Rotation	−6.805	−107.785	2.341
Scale	1	1	1
ArmRight			
Transform	**X**	**Y**	**Z**
Position	−5.2	4.59	−0.88
Rotation	2.417	345.826	−24.146
Scale	1	1	1

FIGURE 13.19   Change the values for the left and right arm.

Create two empty GameObjects, name them ArmLeftJoint and ArmRightJoint. Change the position, rotate, and scale of these objects according to the following tables' coordinates (Figure 13.20).

ArmLeftJoint			
Transform	**X**	**Y**	**Z**
Position	−3.25	0.46	0.12
Rotation	2.925	−75.84	0
Scale	2.07749	2.07749	2.07749
ArmRightJoint			
Transform	**X**	**Y**	**Z**
Position	−3.41	14.9	−30.52
Rotation	0	−53.66	0
Scale	1	1	1

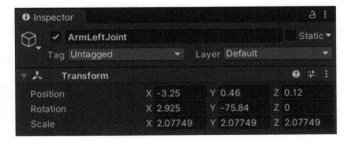

FIGURE 13.20   Change the values for the joints of the left and right arm. (*Continued*)

FIGURE 13.20   (*Continued*)

Nest the objects according to the following Hierarchy. Select the ArmRightJoint and navigation window and create a Waving animation clip (Figure 13.21).

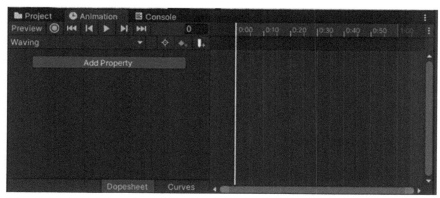

FIGURE 13.21   Create waving.

Press the red record button; keep the scrubber at 00:00 and the rotation values (Figure 13.22) to match the following table.

	ArmRightJoint		
Position	2.791802	0.03132875	0.4622436
Rotation	−105.166	−178.8	−90
Scale	3.23248	3.23248	3.23248

FIGURE 13.22   Values to the record of the first 30 seconds.

Then move the scrubber to 00:30 and change the rotation according to the following values (Figure 13.23).

	ArmRightJoint		
Position	2.791802	0.03132875	0.4622436
Rotation	−105.166	−231.3	−90
Scale	3.23248	3.23248	3.23248

FIGURE 13.23   Values to the record of the second 30 seconds.

Again, move the scrubber to 01:00 and change the rotation values to match the ones in the following table (Figure 13.24).

	ArmRightJoint		
Position	2.791802	0.03132875	0.4622436
Rotation	−105.166	−178.8	−90
Scale	3.23248	3.23248	3.23248

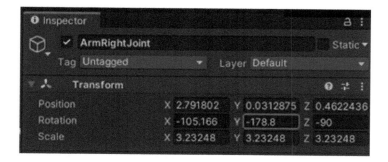

FIGURE 13.24   Values to the record of the third 30 seconds.

Then create LegJoints for both legs and position them appropriately. Nest them as shown in Figure 13.25.

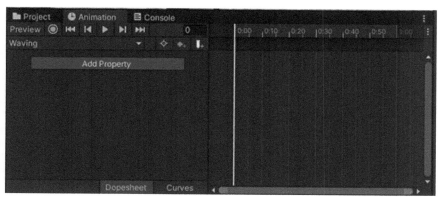

FIGURE 13.25   Create LegJoints.

Once created, you make a Walking animation; before steps alternating, put the X rotation values from –60 to 60 and back to –60 and the opposite for the other leg. Then, move the Orbiting Camera Script to the MainCamera GameObject and set SpongeBob as the target and play the scene (Figure 13.26).

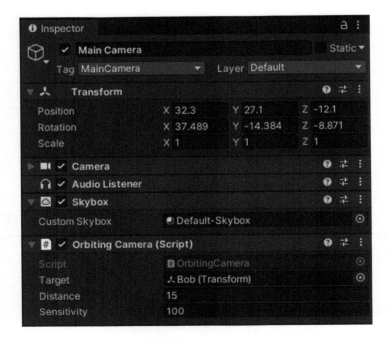

FIGURE 13.26   Move the camera.

13.3 STEP 3: REVIEW EXAMPLE 2: KEYBOARD MOVEMENT FOR SPONGEBOB

To create an Idle Animation in the Animation window, you can follow the following steps. First, select the Sponge GameObject and press the record button and then move the buffer to 00:30. Once there, change the scale (Figure 13.27) to the following values.

Transform			
Position	0	0	0
Rotation	0	0	0
Scale	1.04	1.04	1.04

▼ ⚲ Transform			? ⇄ ⋮
Position	X 0	Y 0	0
Rotation	X 0	Y 0	0
Scale	X 1.04	Y 1.04	1.04

FIGURE 13.27   Change the values for 30 seconds.

And then move the buffer to 00:00, set the Scale values back to 1. Next, go to the Animator window, create a bool parameter, name it **Waving**, and make a transition from Idle to Waving, then press the plus sign in the inspector window – conditions and set it to true. Next, make another transition from Waving to Idle and make a condition with its value being false (Figure 13.28).

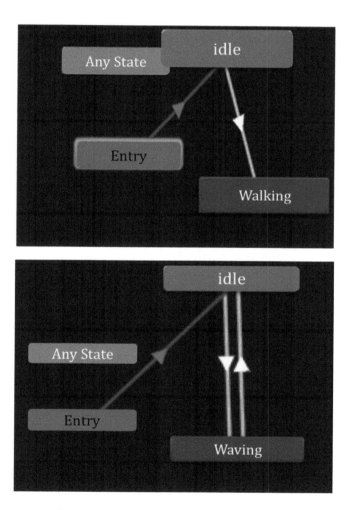

FIGURE 13.28   Make the transitions.

Then, add a script named the movement in the Project window Scripts folder and move it to the SpongeBob inspector window (Figure 13.29).

FIGURE 13.29   Add a script for SpongeBob.

Afterwards, you need to add the following C# script.

```csharp
using System.Collections;
using System.Collections.Generic;
using UnityEngine;
public class Movement : MonoBehaviour
{
    public Animator movementAnim;
    private Rigidbody rbody;
    private float moveSpeed;
    private bool onGround;
    public float jumpStrength;
    // Start is called before the first frame update
    void Start()
    {
        movementAnim = GetComponent<Animator>();
        rbody = GetComponent<Rigidbody>();
        moveSpeed = 4500f;
        onGround = false;
        jumpStrength = 100f;
    }
    // Update is called once per frame
    void Update()
    {
        float moveInput = Input.GetAxis("Horizontal");
        float vertInput = Input.GetAxis("Vertical");
        bool jumpInput = Input.GetKey("1");
        if (onGround)
        {
            if (jumpInput = true)
            {
                Jump();
            }
        }
        if (moveInput > 0f)
        {
            movementAnim.SetBool("Walking", true);
            transform.rotation = Quaternion.Euler(0f, moveInput * 90f, 0f);
            rbody.AddForce(moveSpeed * moveInput,  0f, 0f);
```

```
    }
    else if(moveInput < 0f)
    {
        movementAnim.SetBool("Walking", true);
        transform.rotation = Quaternion.Euler(0f, moveInput * 90f, 0f);
        rbody.AddForce(moveSpeed * moveInput,  0f, 0f);
    }
    else
    {
        movementAnim.SetBool("Walking", false);
        transform.rotation = Quaternion.Euler(0f,0f, 0f);
    }
}
void Jump()
{
    onGround = false;
    rbody.AddForce(0f, jumpStrength, 0f);
}

void OnCollisionEnter (Collision other)
{
    if(other.gameObject.CompareTag("ground"))
    {
        rbody.drag = 10f;
        onGround = true;
    }
}
}
```

13.4 STEP 4: REVIEW EXAMPLE 3: SPONGEBOB CONTROLLED BY ARDUINO

To fulfil Arduino communication, you need to prepare your environment from Unity and Arduino side both. Then you need to upload code to the Arduino and then move on to the game. For this aim, you need to be added with the following steps.

13.4.1 Step 1: Arduino Preparing

Open your Arduino IDE, copy the following script into your Arduino IDE sketch, and save the sketch as **Serial-Communication** or any other name. Once the sketch is saved, make sure that your Arduino board is connected by navigating to Tools-Port and selecting the port with the name of your Arduino board. As shown in code, initially, four-button initialised and then based on related Digital pin status, the specific word (here numbers) will print on the serial port.

```
//-------------------------------------------
//Prepare the game buttons
#define buttonA 2
#define buttonB 3
#define buttonC 4
#define buttonD 5
 void setup() {
 //Prepare the pins for the buttons
 pinMode(buttonA, INPUT);
 pinMode(buttonB, INPUT);
 pinMode(buttonC, INPUT);
 pinMode(buttonD, INPUT);
 pinMode(buttonE, INPUT);
 Serial.begin(9600);
 Serial.println("Serial: Ready");
 Serial.println("--------------------------------");
 }
void loop() {
 int readA = digitalRead(buttonA);
 int readB = digitalRead(buttonB);
 int readC = digitalRead(buttonC);
 int readD = digitalRead(buttonD);
 int readE = digitalRead(buttonE);
 if(readA == LOW) {
   Serial.println("one");
   Serial.flush();
   delay(10);
 }
 if(readB == LOW)
 {
   Serial.println("two");
   Serial.flush();
   delay(10);
 }
 if(readC == LOW)
 {
   Serial.println("three");
   Serial.flush();
   delay(10);
 }
 if(readD == LOW)
 {
   Serial.println("four");
   Serial.flush();
   delay(10);
 }
 if(readE == LOW)
 {
   Serial.println("five");
   Serial.flush();
   delay(10);
 }
 }
```

After selecting the board, upload the code onto the board by pressing the upload button (the button with an arrow) and then, once uploaded, open Unity. Please note that you should know your COMPORT name; here, we assume the COM8 used by Arduino to establish the Serial communication.

13.4.2 Step 2: Unity Settings

You need to create a new C# script on the Unity side and name it SpongeBob. Now you can facilitate movement in Unity by linking it to the Serial communication script using the following step and C# code. Then first, create a new folder named scripts, navigate to it, create a new C# script in Unity, and name it SpongeBob (Figure 13.30). Once created, open the file in your IDE and write the following code into it.

```
using System.Collections;
using System.Collections.Generic;
using UnityEngine;
using System.IO.Ports;
public class SpongeBob : MonoBehaviour
{
    public Animator movementAnim;
    public string movement;
    public Rigidbody _rigidbody;
    [SerializeField] private float _movementForce = 10f;
    [SerializeField] private double _maximumVelocity = 10f;
    private void Awake() => _rigidbody = GetComponent<Rigidbody>();
    void FixedUpdate()
    {
        StartCoroutine(updateInput());
        if (_rigidbody.velocity.magnitude >= _maximumVelocity)
            return;
        //move character forwards
        else if (movement == "one")
        {
            movementAnim.SetBool("Walking", true);
            transform.rotation = Quaternion.Euler(0f, 0f, 0f);
            _rigidbody.AddForce(_movementForce * transform.forward);
        }
        //move character backwards
        else if (movement == "two")
        {
            movementAnim.SetBool("Walking", true);
            transform.rotation = Quaternion.Euler(0f, 180f, 0f);
            _rigidbody.AddForce(_movementForce * transform.forward); // -forward
gives us back
        }
```

```
    //Character will move left arm
    else if (movement == "three")
    {
        movementAnim.SetBool("Waving Left", true);
    }
    //Character will wave right arm
    else if (movement == "four")
    {
        movementAnim.SetBool("Waving Right", true);
    }
    else
    {
        movementAnim.SetBool("Waving Right", false);
        movementAnim.SetBool("Waving Left", false);
        movementAnim.SetBool("Walking", false);
    }
  }
  IEnumerator updateInput()
  {
    yield return new WaitForEndOfFrame();
    movement = COM.input;
  }
}
```

All the C# scripts that you need are mentioned as follows:

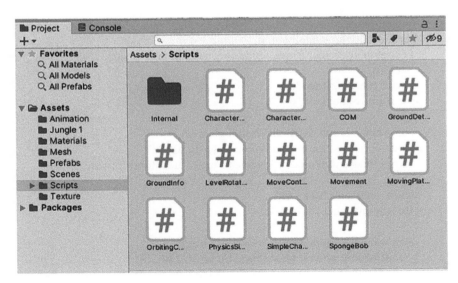

FIGURE 13.30   All C# scripts.

CharacterCapsule

```csharp
using UnityEngine;
usingMenteBacata.ScivoloCharacterController.Internal;
namespace MenteBacata.ScivoloCharacterController

    public class CharacterCapsule : MonoBehaviour
    {
        [SerializeField]
        [Tooltip("Vertical offset from the game object position to the bottom of the capsule.")]
        private float verticalOffset = 0f;
        [SerializeField]
        private float height = 2f;
        [SerializeField]
        private float radius = 0.5f;

        /// <summary>
        /// Vertical offset from the game object position to the bottom of the capsule.
        /// </summary>
        public float VerticalOffset
        {
            get => verticalOffset;
            set => verticalOffset = value;
        }

        /// <summary>
        /// Height of the capsule.
        /// </summary>
        public float Height
```

```
    {
        get => height;
        set => height = Mathf.Max(2f * radius, value);
    }

    /// <summary>
    /// Radius of the capsule.
    /// </summary>
    public float Radius
    {
        get => radius;
        set => radius = Mathf.Max(0f, value);
    }

    /// <summary>
    /// Capsule up direction.
    /// </summary>
    public Vector3 UpDirection
    {
        get => transform.up;
        set => transform.up = value;
    }

    /// <summary>
    /// Rotation of the capsule.
    /// </summary>
    public Quaternion Rotation
    {
        get => transform.rotation;
        set => transform.rotation = value;
```

```
    }
    /// <summary>
    /// World space center of the capsule.
    /// </summary>
    public Vector3 Center => transform.position + transform.TransformVector(LocalCenter);
    /// <summary>
    /// World space center of the capsule lower hemisphere.
    /// </summary>
    public Vector3 LowerHemisphereCenter => transform.position + ToLowerHemisphereCenter;
    /// <summary>
    /// World space center of the capsule upper hemisphere.
    /// </summary>
    public Vector3 UpperHemisphereCenter => transform.position + ToUpperHemisphereCenter;

    /// <summary>
    /// World space vector from game object position to the center of the capsule lower hemisphere.
    /// </summary>
    internal Vector3 ToLowerHemisphereCenter => transform.TransformVector(0f, verticalOffset + radius, 0f);
    /// <summary>
    /// World space vector from game object position to the center of the capsule upper hemisphere.
    /// </summary>
    internal Vector3 ToUpperHemisphereCenter => transform.TransformVector(0f, verticalOffset + height - radius, 0f);

    internal CapsuleCollider Collider { get; private set; }
    internal Rigidbody Rigidbody { get; private set; }
    private Vector3 LocalCenter => new Vector3(0f, verticalOffset + 0.5f * height, 0f);
```

```csharp
private void Awake()
{
    DoPreliminaryCheck();
    InstantiateComponents();
}

private void DoPreliminaryCheck()
{
    if (!Mathf.Approximately(transform.lossyScale.x, 1f) ||
        !Mathf.Approximately(transform.lossyScale.y, 1f) ||
        !Mathf.Approximately(transform.lossyScale.z, 1f))
    {
        Debug.LogWarning($"{nameof(CharacterCapsule)}: Object scale is not (1, 1, 1).");
    }

    foreach (var col in gameObject.GetComponentsInChildren<Collider>(true))
    {
        if (col != Collider && !col.isTrigger && !Physics.GetIgnoreLayerCollision(gameObject.layer, col.
gameObject.layer))
        {
            Debug.LogWarning($"{nameof(CharacterCapsule)}: Found other colliders on this gameobject or in
its childrens.");
            break;
        }
    }
}

private void InstantiateComponents()
{
```

```
            Collider = gameObject.AddComponent<CapsuleCollider>();
            Collider.center = LocalCenter;
            Collider.height = height;
            Collider.radius = radius;
            Collider.direction = 1; // Asse Y
            Rigidbody = gameObject.AddComponent<Rigidbody>();
            Rigidbody.isKinematic = true;
        }

        private void OnValidate()
        {
            Height = height;
            Radius = radius;
            if (Collider != null)
            {
                Collider.center = LocalCenter;
                Collider.height = height;
                Collider.radius = radius;
            }
        }

        private void OnDrawGizmosSelected()
        {
            Gizmos.color = GizmosUtility.defaultColliderColor;
            GizmosUtility.DrawWireCapsule(LowerHemisphereCenter, UpperHemisphereCenter, radius);
        }
    }
}
```

CharacterMover

```csharp
using UnityEngine;
using MenteBacata.ScivoloCharacterController.Internal;
namespace MenteBacata.ScivoloCharacterController
{

    public class CharacterCapsule : MonoBehaviour
    {

        [SerializeField]
        [Tooltip("Vertical offset from the game object position to the bottom of the capsule.")]
        private float verticalOffset = 0f;
        [SerializeField]
        private float height = 2f;
        [SerializeField]
        private float radius = 0.5f;

        /// <summary>
        /// Vertical offset from the game object position to the bottom of the capsule.
        /// </summary>
        public float VerticalOffset
        {

            get => verticalOffset;
            set => verticalOffset = value;

        }
        /// <summary>
        /// Height of the capsule.
        /// </summary>
        public float Height
        {
```

```
        get => height;
        set => height = Mathf.Max(2f * radius, value);
    }

    /// <summary>
    /// Radius of the capsule.
    /// </summary>
    public float Radius
    {
        get => radius;
        set => radius = Mathf.Max(0f, value);
    }

    /// <summary>
    /// Capsule up direction.
    /// </summary>
    public Vector3 UpDirection
    {
        get => transform.up;
        set => transform.up = value;
    }

    /// <summary>
    /// Rotation of the capsule.
    /// </summary>
    public Quaternion Rotation
    {
        get => transform.rotation;
        set => transform.rotation = value;
    }
```

```
/// <summary>
/// World space center of the capsule.
/// </summary>
public Vector3 Center => transform.position + transform.TransformVector(LocalCenter);
/// <summary>
/// World space center of the capsule lower hemisphere.
/// </summary>
public Vector3 LowerHemisphereCenter => transform.position + ToLowerHemisphereCenter;
/// <summary>
/// World space center of the capsule upper hemisphere.
/// </summary>
public Vector3 UpperHemisphereCenter => transform.position + ToUpperHemisphereCenter;
/// <summary>
/// World space vector from game object position to the center of the capsule lower hemisphere.
/// </summary>
internal Vector3 ToLowerHemisphereCenter => transform.TransformVector(0f, verticalOffset + radius, 0f);
/// <summary>
/// World space vector from game object position to the center of the capsule upper hemisphere.
/// </summary>
internal Vector3 ToUpperHemisphereCenter => transform.TransformVector(0f, verticalOffset + height - radius, 0f);

internal CapsuleCollider Collider { get; private set; }
internal Rigidbody Rigidbody { get; private set; }
private Vector3 LocalCenter => new Vector3(0f, verticalOffset + 0.5f * height, 0f);
private void Awake()
{
    DoPreliminaryCheck();
```

```
        InstantiateComponents();
    }

    private void DoPreliminaryCheck()
    {
        if (!Mathf.Approximately(transform.lossyScale.x, 1f) ||
            !Mathf.Approximately(transform.lossyScale.y, 1f) ||
            !Mathf.Approximately(transform.lossyScale.z, 1f))
        {
            Debug.LogWarning($"{nameof(CharacterCapsule)}: Object scale is not (1, 1, 1).");
        }

        foreach (var col in gameObject.GetComponentsInChildren<Collider>(true))
        {
            if (col != Collider && !col.isTrigger && !Physics.GetIgnoreLayerCollision(gameObject.layer, col.
gameObject.layer))
            {
                Debug.LogWarning($"{nameof(CharacterCapsule)}: Found other colliders on this gameobject or in
its childrens.");

                break;
            }
        }
    }

    private void InstantiateComponents()
    {
        Collider = gameObject.AddComponent<CapsuleCollider>();
        Collider.center = LocalCenter;
        Collider.height = height;
```

```
        Collider.radius = radius;
        Collider.direction = 1; // Asse Y
        Rigidbody = gameObject.AddComponent<Rigidbody>();
        Rigidbody.isKinematic = true;
    }

    private void OnValidate()
    {
        Height = height;
        Radius = radius;
        if (Collider != null)
        {
            Collider.center = LocalCenter;
            Collider.height = height;
            Collider.radius = radius;
        }
    }

    private void OnDrawGizmosSelected()
    {
        Gizmos.color = GizmosUtility.defaultColliderColor;
        GizmosUtility.DrawWireCapsule(LowerHemisphereCenter, UpperHemisphereCenter, radius);
    }
}
```

COM

```
using System.Collections;
using System.Collections.Generic;
using UnityEngine;
using System.IO.Ports;
using System;
public class COM : MonoBehaviour
{
    public bool debug = false;
    public static string input;
    public static int Baud = 9600;
    public static string userName;
    public static string userGender;
    public static string userWeight;
    public static string userHeight;
    public static string BMI;
    public static string comPort = "COM8";
    SerialPort myData;
    void Start()
    {
        openConnection();
        logDebug("Initialised");
    }
    //Get the selected COM Port Name from User
    public void HandleInputData(int val)
    {
        if (val == 1)
        {
            comPort = "COM3";
            openConnection();
        }
        else if (val == 2)
        {
            comPort = "COM4";
            openConnection();
        }
        else if (val == 3)
        {
            comPort = "COM5";
            openConnection();
        }
        else if (val == 4)
        {
            comPort = "COM6";
            openConnection();
        }   else if (val == 5)
        {
            comPort = "COM7";
            openConnection();
        }
```

```
      else if (val == 6)
      {
        comPort = "COM8";
        openConnection();
      }
    }
    void Update()
    {
      readInput();
    }
    void readInput()
    {
      try
      {
        input = myData.ReadLine();
        if (input.StartsWith("Name:"))
        {
          userName = input.Substring(5);
          print(userName);
        }
        else if (input.StartsWith("Gender:"))
        {
          userGender = input.Substring(7);
          print(userGender);
        }
        else if (input.StartsWith("Weight:"))
        {
          userWeight = input.Substring(7);
          print(userWeight);
        }
        else if (input.StartsWith("Height:"))
        {
          userHeight = input.Substring(7);
          print(userHeight);
        }
        else if (input.StartsWith("BMI:"))
        {
          BMI = input.Substring(4);
          print(BMI);
        }
        else
        {
          logDebug(input);
        }
      }
      catch (TimeoutException)
      {
        logDebug("No data read.");
        input = "Waiting";
      }
    }
```

```
//Start Serial Connection
void openConnection()
{
    print("Hey, I made it here!" + comPort);
    myData = new SerialPort(comPort, Baud);
    if (myData != null)
    {
        if (myData.IsOpen)
        {
            myData.Close();
            logDebug("Already open, closing...");
        }
        else
        {
            myData.Open();
            myData.ReadTimeout = 100;
            logDebug("Connection open");
            StartCoroutine(handshake(2));
        }
    }
    else
    {
        if (myData.IsOpen)
        {
            logDebug("Already Open");
        }
        else
        {
            logDebug("Setup is NULL - Check Settings");
        }
    }
}
IEnumerator handshake(float waitTime)
{
    yield return new WaitForSeconds(waitTime);
}
void OnApplicationQuit()
{
    myData.Close();
}
//Debug Messenger
void logDebug(string Msg)
{
    if (debug)
    {
        print(Msg);
    }
}
}
```

GroundDetector

```
//#define MB_DEBUG
using UnityEngine;
using MenteBacata.ScivoloCharacterController.Internal;
using static MenteBacata.ScivoloCharacterController.Internal.Math;
using static MenteBacata.ScivoloCharacterController.Internal.FloorAbovePointChecker;

namespace MenteBacata.ScivoloCharacterController
{
    [RequireComponent(typeof(CharacterCapsule), typeof(CharacterMover))]
    public class GroundDetector : MonoBehaviour
    {
        [SerializeField]
        [Tooltip("Small tolerance distance so that ground is detected even if the capsule is not directly touching it but just close enough.")]
        private float tolerance = 0.05f;
        [SerializeField]
        [Range(0f, 1f)]
        [Tooltip("Spacing between probe rays in relation to the capsule radius.")]
        private float raySpacing = 0.6f;
        [SerializeField]
        [Tooltip("Max distance for the rays used for probing ground.")]
        private float maxRayDistance = 1f;
        private LayerMask collisionMask;
        private CharacterMover mover;
        private CharacterCapsule capsule;
```

```
private void Awake()
{
    collisionMask = gameObject.CollisionMask();
    capsule = GetComponent<CharacterCapsule>();
    mover = GetComponent<CharacterMover>();
}

/// <summary>
/// Detects ground below the capsule bottom and retrieves useful info.
/// </summary>
public bool DetectGround(out GroundInfo groundInfo)
{
    float radius = capsule.Radius;
    Vector3 sphereCastOrigin = capsule.Center;
    Vector3 upDirection = capsule.UpDirection;
    float minFloorUp = Mathf.Cos(Mathf.Deg2Rad * mover.maxFloorAngle);
    float maxFloorDistance = 0.5f * capsule.Height - radius + tolerance;
    float maxDistance = maxFloorDistance + tolerance;
    if (!Physics.SphereCast(sphereCastOrigin, radius, -upDirection, out RaycastHit hit, maxDistance,
collisionMask, QueryTriggerInteraction.Ignore))
    {
        groundInfo = new GroundInfo();
        return false;
    }
    // If it hits floor it has to be within max floor distance, this is because it uses extra tolerance only when it hits
    // ground that is not floor.
```

```
                if (Dot(hit.normal, upDirection) > minFloorUp)
                {
                    if (hit.distance < maxFloorDistance)
                    {
                        groundInfo = new GroundInfo(hit.point, hit.normal, hit.collider, true);
                        return true;
                    }
                    else
                    {
                        groundInfo = new GroundInfo();
                        return false;
                    }
                }

        // Set collider to trigger so it doesn't interfere with geometry queries. The previous sphere cast is not a problem
        // since it starts inside the collider so it's ignored.
        bool isTrigger = capsule.Collider.isTrigger;
        capsule.Collider.isTrigger = true;
        groundInfo = new GroundInfo(hit.point, hit.normal, hit.collider,
            CheckFloorWithRaycasts(sphereCastOrigin - hit.distance * upDirection, hit.point, hit.normal,
upDirection, minFloorUp));
        capsule.Collider.isTrigger = isTrigger;
        return true;
    }

    private static Vector3 NormalFromThreePoints(in Vector3 point1, in Vector3 point2, in Vector3 point3)
    {
        return Normalized(Cross(point1 - point2, point1 - point3));
    }
```

```
private static void ComputeTriangleVertices(in Vector3 center, in Vector3 forwardDirection, in Vector3
rightDirection, float size,
        out Vector3 a, out Vector3 b, out Vector3 c)
{
    const float cos60 = 0.5f;
    const float sen60 = 0.866f;
    a = size * (sen60 * rightDirection + -cos60 * forwardDirection) + center;
    b = size * (-sen60 * rightDirection + -cos60 * forwardDirection) + center;
    c = size * forwardDirection + center;
}

private bool CheckFloorWithRaycasts(in Vector3 origin, in Vector3 contactPosition, in Vector3
contactNormal, in Vector3 upDirection, float minFloorUp)
{
    float maxDistance = maxRayDistance + capsule.Radius;
    // It should be smaller than maxDistance, this because even if a point is not on floor could still be used for
    // further evaluations.
    float maxFloorDistance = GetMaxFloorDistance(contactPosition, origin, upDirection, minFloorUp);
    Vector3 forwardDirection = Normalized(ProjectOnPlane(contactNormal, upDirection));
    Vector3 rightDirection = Cross(upDirection, forwardDirection);
    bool oResult = Physics.Raycast(origin, -upDirection, out RaycastHit oHit, maxDistance, collisionMask,
QueryTriggerInteraction.Ignore);
    if (oHit.distance < maxFloorDistance && Dot(oHit.normal, upDirection) > minFloorUp)
    {
        return true;
    }

    ComputeTriangleVertices(origin, forwardDirection, rightDirection, raySpacing * capsule.Radius,
```

```
        out Vector3 a, out Vector3 b, out Vector3 c);
    bool aResult = Physics.Raycast(a, -upDirection, out RaycastHit aHit, maxDistance, collisionMask,
QueryTriggerInteraction.Ignore);
    if (aHit.distance < maxFloorDistance && Dot(aHit.normal, upDirection) > minFloorUp)
    {
        return true;
    }
    bool bResult = Physics.Raycast(b, -upDirection, out RaycastHit bHit, maxDistance, collisionMask,
QueryTriggerInteraction.Ignore);
    if (bHit.distance < maxFloorDistance && Dot(bHit.normal, upDirection) > minFloorUp)
    {
        return true;
    }
    bool cResult = Physics.Raycast(c, -upDirection, out RaycastHit cHit, maxDistance, collisionMask,
QueryTriggerInteraction.Ignore);
    if (cHit.distance < maxFloorDistance && Dot(cHit.normal, upDirection) > minFloorUp)
    {
        return true;
    }
    // If it didn't detect floor from single hit points, it groups them into triangles and check their normals.
    // ABC
    if (aResult && bResult && cResult)
    {
        if (aHit.distance < maxFloorDistance || bHit.distance < maxFloorDistance || cHit.distance < maxFloorDistance)
        {
            if (Dot(NormalFromThreePoints(aHit.point, bHit.point, cHit.point), upDirection) > minFloorUp)
```

```
            {
                return true;
            }
        }
    }
    // OAB
    if (oResult && aResult && bResult)
    {
        if (oHit.distance < maxFloorDistance || aHit.distance < maxFloorDistance || bHit.distance < maxFloorDistance)
        {
            if (Dot(NormalFromThreePoints(oHit.point, aHit.point, bHit.point), upDirection) > minFloorUp)
            {
                return true;
            }
        }
    }
    // OBC
    if (oResult && bResult && cResult)
    {
        if (oHit.distance < maxFloorDistance || bHit.distance < maxFloorDistance || cHit.distance < maxFloorDistance)
        {
            if (Dot(NormalFromThreePoints(oHit.point, bHit.point, cHit.point), upDirection) > minFloorUp)
            {
                return true;
```

```
        }
      }
    }
    // OCA
    if (oResult && cResult && aResult)
    {
        if (oHit.distance < maxFloorDistance || cHit.distance < maxFloorDistance || aHit.distance <
maxFloorDistance)
        {
            if (Dot(NormalFromThreePoints(oHit.point, cHit.point, aHit.point), upDirection) > minFloorUp)
            {
                return true;
            }
        }
    }
    return false;
}

/// <summary>
/// Maximum distance from the raycast origin within which a point can be considered on a floor.
/// </summary>
private float GetMaxFloorDistance(in Vector3 contactPosition, in Vector3 origin, in Vector3 upDirection,
float minFloorUp)
{
    float maxFloorDistance = capsule.Radius;
```

```
        if (CheckFloorAbovePoint(contactPosition, capsule.Radius, capsule.Height, minFloorUp, upDirection,
collisionMask, out _))
        {
            // It uses contactPosition because it's lower than point on floor so it will result in a greater distance and
            // more chances to detect something below it.
            float stepDistance = Dot(origin - contactPosition, upDirection) + mover.maxStepHeight;
            maxFloorDistance = stepDistance > maxFloorDistance?  stepDistance : maxFloorDistance;
        }

        return maxFloorDistance + tolerance;
    }

    private void OnValidate()
    {
        tolerance = Mathf.Max(0f, tolerance);
        maxRayDistance = Mathf.Max(tolerance, maxRayDistance);
    }
}
```

Ground info

```
using UnityEngine;
namespace MenteBacata.ScivoloCharacterController
{
    public struct GroundInfo
    {
        public readonly Vector3 point;
        public readonly Vector3 normal;
        public readonly Collider collider;
        public readonly bool isOnFloor;
        public GroundInfo(Vector3 point, Vector3 normal, Collider collider, bool isOnFloor)
        {
            this.point = point;
            this.normal = normal;
            this.collider = collider;
            this.isOnFloor = isOnFloor;
        }
    }
}
```

Levelrotator

```
using UnityEngine;
using UnityEngine.UI;
namespace MenteBacata.ScivoloCharacterControllerDemo
{
    [DefaultExecutionOrder(2000)]
    public class LevelRotator : MonoBehaviour
    {
        public GameObject menuPanel;
        public Text xRotText, yRotText, zRotText;
        public Slider xRotSlider, yRotSlider, zRotSlider;
        public KeyCode showHideMenuKey;
        private Vector3 originalGravity;
        private void Start()
        {
            SetRotationText();
            menuPanel.SetActive(false);
            originalGravity = Physics.gravity;
        }
        private void Update()
        {
            if (Input.GetKeyDown(showHideMenuKey))
                ShowHideMenu();
        }
        public void ShowHideMenu()
        {
```

```
        menuPanel.SetActive(!menuPanel.activeSelf);
        SetEnableComponents(!menuPanel.activeSelf);
        Time.timeScale = menuPanel.activeSelf? 0f : 1f;
    }

    public void HandleRotationChange()
    {
        SetRotationText();
        Quaternion newRot = Quaternion.Euler(xRotSlider.value, yRotSlider.value, zRotSlider.value);
        transform.rotation = newRot;
        Physics.gravity = newRot * originalGravity;
    }

    private void SetRotationText()
    {
        xRotText.text = $"X: {Mathf.RoundToInt(xRotSlider.value)}°";
        yRotText.text = $"Y: {Mathf.RoundToInt(yRotSlider.value)}°";
        zRotText.text = $"Z: {Mathf.RoundToInt(zRotSlider.value)}°";
    }

    private void SetEnableComponents(bool enabled)
    {
        Camera.main.GetComponent<OrbitingCamera>().enabled = enabled;
        FindObjectOfType<SimpleCharacterController>().enabled = enabled;
        foreach (var m in FindObjectsOfType<MovingPlatform>())
        {
            m.enabled = enabled;
        }
    }
```

MoveContact

```
using UnityEngine;
namespace MenteBacata.ScivoloCharacterController
{
  public struct MoveContact
  {
    public readonly Vector3 position;
    public readonly Vector3 normal;
    public readonly Collider collider;
    public MoveContact(Vector3 position, Vector3 normal, Collider collider)
    {
      this.position = position;
      this.normal = normal;
      this.collider = collider;
    }
  }
}
```

Movement

```
using System.Collections;
using System.Collections.Generic;
using UnityEngine;
public class Movement : MonoBehaviour
{
  public Animator movementAnim;
  // Start is called before the first frame update
  void Start()
  {
    movementAnim = GetComponent<Animator>();
  }
  // Update is called once per frame
  void Update()
  {
    float moveInput = Input.GetAxis("Horizontal");
    if(moveInput > 0f)
    {
      movementAnim.SetBool("Walking", true);
      transform.rotation = Quaternion.Euler(0f, moveInput *  90f, 0f);
    }
    else if(moveInput < 0f)
    {
      movementAnim.SetBool("Walking", true);
      transform.rotation = Quaternion.Euler(0f, moveInput * 90f, 0f);
    }
    else
    {
      movementAnim.SetBool("Walking", false); ;
      transform.rotation = Quaternion.Euler(0f,0f, 0f);
    }
  }
}
```

Moving platform

```
using UnityEngine;
namespace MenteBacata.ScivoloCharacterControllerDemo
{

    [DefaultExecutionOrder(1000)]
    public class MovingPlatform : MonoBehaviour
    {

        public float speed = 2f;
        public float angularSpeed = 1f;
        private Transform start;
        private Transform end;
        private Vector3 deltaPosition;
        private Quaternion deltaRotation;
        private bool isMovingForward = true;
        private bool isDisplacementUpdated = false;
        private Vector3 CurrentDestination => isMovingForward? end.position : start.position;
        private Vector3 UpDirection => transform.parent != null? transform.parent.up : transform.up;


        private void Start()
        {

            start = transform.GetChild(0);
            end = transform.GetChild(1);
```

```
        start.SetParent(transform.parent, true);
        end.SetParent(transform.parent, true);
    }

    private void Update()
    {
        if (!isDisplacementUpdated)
            UpdateDisplacement(Time.deltaTime);
        transform.SetPositionAndRotation(transform.position + deltaPosition, deltaRotation * transform.rotation);
        // Invert moving direction when it reaches the destination.
        if ((CurrentDestination - transform.position).sqrMagnitude < 1E-04f)
            isMovingForward = !isMovingForward;
        isDisplacementUpdated = false;
    }

    public void GetDisplacement(out Vector3 deltaPosition, out Quaternion deltaRotation)
    {
        if (!isDisplacementUpdated)
            UpdateDisplacement(Time.deltaTime);
        deltaPosition = this.deltaPosition;
        deltaRotation = this.deltaRotation;
    }

    private void UpdateDisplacement(float deltaTime)
    {
        deltaPosition = Vector3.MoveTowards(Vector3.zero, CurrentDestination - transform.position, speed * deltaTime);
        deltaRotation = Quaternion.AngleAxis(angularSpeed * deltaTime, UpDirection);
        isDisplacementUpdated = true;
    }
}
```

orbitingCamera

```csharp
using UnityEngine;
namespace MenteBacata.ScivoloCharacterControllerDemo
{
    public class OrbitingCamera : MonoBehaviour
    {
        public Transform target;
        public float distance = 5f;
        public float sensitivity = 100f;
        private float yRot = 0f;
        private float xRot = 20f;

        private void Start()
        {
#if UNITY_EDITOR
            // Somehow after updating to 2019.3, mouse axes sensitivity decreased, but only in the editor.
            sensitivity *= 10f;
#elif UNITY_WEBGL
            // To prevent the mouse axes not being detected when the cursor leaves the game window.
            Cursor.lockState = CursorLockMode.Locked;
```

```
#endif
    }

    private void LateUpdate()
    {
        yRot += Input.GetAxis("Mouse X") * sensitivity * Time.deltaTime;
        xRot -= Input.GetAxis("Mouse Y") * sensitivity * Time.deltaTime;
        xRot = Mathf.Clamp(xRot, 0f, 75f);
        Quaternion worldRotation = transform.parent != null? transform.parent.rotation : Quaternion.
FromToRotation(Vector3.up, target.up);
        Quaternion cameraRotation = worldRotation * Quaternion.Euler(xRot, yRot, 0f);
        Vector3 targetToCamera = cameraRotation * new Vector3(0f, 0f, -distance);
        transform.SetPositionAndRotation(target.position + targetToCamera, cameraRotation);
    }
}
```

PhysicsSimulationUpdater

```
using UnityEngine;
namespace MenteBacata.ScivoloCharacterControllerDemo
{
    [DefaultExecutionOrder(3000)]
    public class PhysicsSimulationUpdater : MonoBehaviour
    {
        // It can happen that deltaTime is 0 even if timeScale is not (for instance when in the same frame timeScale turns
from 0
        // to 1). Since Physics.Simulate throws an error when called with a step of 0, it guarantees that a minimum value
for
        // deltaTime is used.
        public float DeltaTime
#if UNITY_EDITOR
            => UnityEditor.EditorApplication.isPaused?  Time.fixedDeltaTime : Mathf.Max(Time.deltaTime, 1E-05f);
#else
            => Mathf.Max(Time.deltaTime, 1E-05f);
#endif
        void Update()
        {
            if (Physics.autoSimulation)
                return;

            if (Time.timeScale == 0f)
                return;
            Physics.Simulate(DeltaTime);
        }
    }
}
```

SimpleCharcyerController

```
//#define MB_DEBUG
using MenteBacata.ScivoloCharacterController;
using System.Collections.Generic;
using UnityEngine;
namespace MenteBacata.ScivoloCharacterControllerDemo
{
    public class SimpleCharacterController : MonoBehaviour
    {
        public float moveSpeed = 5f;
        public float jumpSpeed = 8f;
        public float rotationSpeed = 720f;
        public float gravity = -25f;
        public CharacterMover mover;
        public GroundDetector groundDetector;
        public MeshRenderer groundedIndicator;
        private const float minVerticalSpeed = -12f;
        // Allowed time before the Character is set to ungrounded from the last time he was safely grounded.
        private const float timeBeforeUngrounded = 0.1f;
        // Speed along the character local up direction.
        private float verticalSpeed = 0f;
        // Time after which the character should be considered ungrounded.
        private float nextUngroundedTime = -1f;
        private Transform cameraTransform;
        private List<MoveContact> moveContacts = new List<MoveContact>(10);
```

```
private float GroundClampSpeed => -Mathf.Tan(Mathf.Deg2Rad * mover.maxFloorAngle) * moveSpeed;
private void Start()
{
    cameraTransform = Camera.main.transform;
}
private void Update()
{
    float horizontalInput = Input.GetAxis("Horizontal");
    float verticalInput = Input.GetAxis("Vertical");
    Vector3 moveDirection = CameraRelativeVectorFromInput(horizontalInput, verticalInput);
    UpdateMovement(moveDirection, Time.deltaTime);
}

private void UpdateMovement(Vector3 moveDirection, float deltaTime)
{
    Vector3 velocity = moveSpeed * moveDirection;
    PlatformDisplacement? platformDisplacement = null;
    bool groundDetected = groundDetector.DetectGround(out GroundInfo groundInfo);
    if (IsSafelyGrounded(groundDetected, groundInfo.isOnFloor))
        nextUngroundedTime = Time.time + timeBeforeUngrounded;
    bool isGrounded = Time.time < nextUngroundedTime;
    SetGroundedIndicatorColor(isGrounded);
    if (isGrounded && Input.GetButtonDown("Jump"))
    {
        verticalSpeed = jumpSpeed;
        nextUngroundedTime = -1f;
```

```
        isGrounded = false;
    }
    if (isGrounded)
    {
        mover.preventMovingUpSteepSlope = true;
        mover.canClimbSteps = true;
        verticalSpeed = 0f;
        velocity += GroundClampSpeed * transform.up;
        if (groundDetected && IsOnMovingPlatform(groundInfo.collider, out MovingPlatform movingPlatform))
            platformDisplacement = GetPlatformDisplacementAtPoint(movingPlatform, groundInfo.point);
    }
    else
    {
        mover.preventMovingUpSteepSlope = false;
        mover.canClimbSteps = false;
        BounceDownIfTouchedCeiling();
        verticalSpeed += gravity * deltaTime;
        if (verticalSpeed < minVerticalSpeed)
            verticalSpeed = minVerticalSpeed;
        velocity += verticalSpeed * transform.up;
    }
    RotateTowards(velocity);
    mover.Move(velocity * deltaTime, moveContacts);
    if (platformDisplacement.HasValue)
        ApplyPlatformDisplacement(platformDisplacement.Value);
}
```

```csharp
// Gets world space vector in respect of camera orientation from two axes input.
private Vector3 CameraRelativeVectorFromInput(float x, float y)
{
    Vector3 forward = Vector3.ProjectOnPlane(cameraTransform.forward, transform.up).normalized;
    Vector3 right = Vector3.Cross(transform.up, forward);
    return x * right + y * forward;
}

private bool IsSafelyGrounded(bool groundDetected, bool isOnFloor)
{
    return groundDetected && isOnFloor && verticalSpeed < 0.1f;
}

private void SetGroundedIndicatorColor(bool isGrounded)
{
    if (groundedIndicator != null)
        groundedIndicator.material.color = isGrounded ?  Color.green :  Color.blue;
}

private bool IsOnMovingPlatform(Collider groundCollider, out MovingPlatform platform)
{
    return groundCollider.TryGetComponent(out platform);
}

private void RotateTowards(Vector3 direction)
{
    Vector3 direzioneOrizz = Vector3.ProjectOnPlane(direction, transform.up);
    if (direzioneOrizz.sqrMagnitude < 1E-06f)
        return;
    Quaternion rotazioneObbiettivo = Quaternion.LookRotation(direzioneOrizz, transform.up);
```

```
            transform.rotation = Quaternion.RotateTowards(transform.rotation, rotazioneObbiettivo, rotationSpeed *
Time.deltaTime);
        }

    private PlatformDisplacement GetPlatformDisplacementAtPoint(MovingPlatform platform, Vector3 point)
    {
        platform.GetDisplacement(out Vector3 platformDeltaPosition, out Quaternion platformDeltaRotation);
        Vector3 localPosition = point - platform.transform.position;
        Vector3 deltaPosition = platformDeltaPosition + platformDeltaRotation * localPosition - localPosition;
        platformDeltaRotation.ToAngleAxis(out float angle, out Vector3 axis);
        angle *= Mathf.Sign(Vector3.Dot(axis, transform.up));
        return new PlatformDisplacement()
        {
            deltaPosition = deltaPosition,
            deltaUpRotation = angle
        };
    }

    private void BounceDownIfTouchedCeiling()
    {
        for (int i = 0; i < moveContacts.Count; i++)
        {
            if (Vector3.Dot(moveContacts[i].normal, transform.up) < -0.7f)
            {
```

```
            verticalSpeed = -0.25f * verticalSpeed;
            break;
        }
    }

    private void ApplyPlatformDisplacement(PlatformDisplacement platformDisplacement)
    {
        transform.Translate(platformDisplacement.deltaPosition, Space.World);
        transform.Rotate(0f, platformDisplacement.deltaUpRotation, 0f, Space.Self);
    }

    private struct PlatformDisplacement
    {
        public Vector3 deltaPosition;
        public float deltaUpRotation;
    }
}
```

SpongeBob Script

```
using System.Collections;
using System.Collections.Generic;
using UnityEngine;
using System.IO.Ports;
public class SpongeBob : MonoBehaviour
{
    public Animator movementAnim;
    public string movement;
    public Rigidbody _rigidbody;
    [SerializeField] private float _movementForce = 10f;
    [SerializeField] private double _maximumVelocity = 10f;
    private void Awake() => _rigidbody = GetComponent<Rigidbody>();
    void FixedUpdate()
    {
        StartCoroutine(updateInput());
        if (_rigidbody.velocity.magnitude >= _maximumVelocity)
            return;
        //move character forwards
        else if (movement == "one")
        {
            movementAnim.SetBool("Walking", true);
            transform.rotation = Quaternion.Euler(0f, 0f, 0f);
            _rigidbody.AddForce(_movementForce * transform.forward);
        }
        //move character backwards
```

```
    else if (movement == "two")
    {
        movementAnim.SetBool("Walking", true);
        transform.rotation = Quaternion.Euler(0f, 180f, 0f);
        _rigidbody.AddForce(_movementForce * transform.forward); // -forward gives us back
    }
    //Character will move left arm
    else if (movement == "three")
    {
        movementAnim.SetBool("Waving Left", true);
    }
    //Character will wave right arm
    else if (movement == "four")
    {
        movementAnim.SetBool("Waving Right", true);
    }
    else
    {
        movementAnim.SetBool("Waving Right", false);
        movementAnim.SetBool("Waving Left", false);
        movementAnim.SetBool("Walking", false);
    }
}

IEnumerator updateInput()
{
    yield return new WaitForEndOfFrame();
    movement = COM.input;
}
```

Afterwards, once the script is added, move it onto the Bob GameObject. Select the Bob (Animator) and Bob (Rigidbody). Ensure that your Adruino is connected and press the play button to start the game (Figure 13.31).

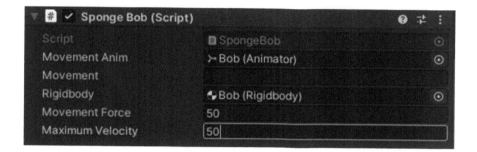

FIGURE 13.31   Adjust the speed.

Finally, SpongeBob should be able to move after clicking each button. SpongeBob will move forward. After clicking Button 1, it moves backwards by clicking Button 2. It waves its left arm by pressing Button 3; it waves the right arm after clicking Button 4 (Figure 13.32).

FIGURE 13.32   **All different movements.** (*Continued*)

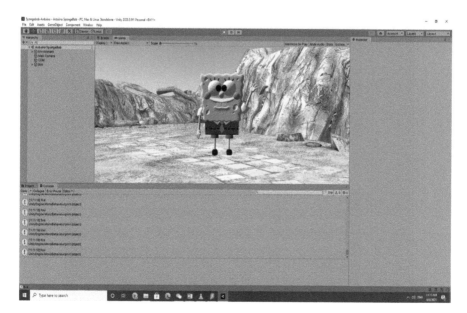

FIGURE 13.32 (*Continued*)

UNITY IN EMBEDDED SYSTEM DESIGN AND ROBOTICS
A STEP-BY-STEP GUIDE

CHAPTER 14

Example 13: Object Movement with Kinect

DOI: 10.1201/9781003268581-14

The Kinect is one of the famous sensors that have recently been employed in some applications. It has been used recently in various virtual reality (VR) applications. It is divided into two versions of v1 and v2. This chapter is going to present some information about the two types of Kinect structures. You will learn how to use both versions in Unity software. Both projects' aim is to detect the user using Kinect and show their movement in Unity.

14.1 BRIEF ABOUT KINECT

Kinect (codenamed Project Natal during development) is a motion-sensing input device produced by Microsoft. Based around a webcam-style add-on peripheral, it enables users to control and interact with their console/computer without the need for a game controller through a natural user interface using gestures and spoken commands. The Kinect technology was invented in 2005 by Zeev Zalevsky, Alexander Shpunt, Aviad Maizels, Javier Garcia, and Alex Kipman for Microsoft, and it was launched for the Xbox 360 on 11/4/2010. Even though the project's initial aim was to develop as a gaming tool/control, it was soon proven that its usage was far beyond gaming. The Kinect is an RGB-D sensor with synchronised colour and image depth. The depth-sensing technology extends the Kinect ability because of its lower cost than other traditional 3D cameras.

As mentioned above, the first-generation Kinect for Xbox 360 was introduced in November 2010. Microsoft announced a beta version of the Kinect software development kit for Windows 7 applications on June 16, 2011. The Beta SDK allowed developers to write Kinect apps in C++/CLI, C#, or Visual Basic. NET, but that was not for commercial purposes.

Version 1.0 of the Windows SDK, with the commercial applications, was released with and required the Kinect for Windows hardware. Finally, it was released in a new version with meaningfully extended hardware abilities. Kinect for Xbox One was released with the Xbox One platform in 2013. In 2014, Kinect for Windows v2 hardware was released with a supporting SDK. The 2.0 version of the Windows SDK supported the Kinect for Windows v2 and the Kinect for Xbox One hardware. In 2015, Microsoft announced the discontinuation of the first Kinect for Windows device, and the Kinect for Xbox 360 was discontinued along with the Console by April 2016. Besides, the Kinect for Windows v2 was also discontinued in 2015 and customers were encouraged to use the functionally identical Kinect for Xbox One hardware with an adapter for Windows machines instead. The Kinect for Xbox One was discontinued in October 2017. While Kinect as a primary gaming device has been discontinued, Microsoft continues to develop the platform for developers, with the most recent release being the Azure Kinect announced in February 2019.

Even though the original Kinect was removed from Microsoft Services, researchers have been trying to develop many applications like Depth sensor: Background removal, Object recognition, Skeletal tracking: Multi-user, Easy Gesture Recognition, Microphone array, Background removal, Object recognition, Sound source detection, and Speech recognition. Also, there are some recent products based on Kinect like Voice commands and Cortana, Webcams for Skype, Mixer and more, Quick Xbox One sign-in, and so on.

14.2 HOW DOES THE XBOX KINECT WORK?

Kinect infrared (IR) cameras are capable of processing data within a distance of 1–4 m.

The input grabbed is highly accurate, and data is captured at a rate of 30 fps. Kinect has the feature of automatic calibrating itself according to room conditions. For Kinect, we have two essential parts of software and hardware.

14.2.1 Software

The software is what makes the Kinect a breakthrough device. Developers for the Kinect gathered an incredible amount of data regarding the motion capture of moving things in real-life scenarios. Processing all of this data using a unique artificial intelligence machine-learning algorithm allows the Kinect to map the visual information it collects to models representing people of different backgrounds (age, height, gender, body type, clothing, and more). The Kinect's **brain** is the secret. Stored in the system is enough intelligence to analyse what it sees and aligns with the stored collection of skeletal structures to interpret your movements. Once the brain has enough data on your body parts, it outputs this reference data into a simplified 3D avatar shape. Beyond gauging player movements, the Kinect must also judge the distances of different points on your body throughout the entire game. To do this, it uses a host of sensors and analyses all this data 30 times a second.

14.2.2 Hardware

The Kinect contains three vital pieces that work together to detect your motion and create your physical image on the screen: an RGB colour VGA video camera, a depth sensor, and a multi-array microphone (Figure 14.1). The camera detects the red, green, and blue colour components and body type and facial features. It has a pixel resolution of 640×480 and a frame rate of 30 fps. This helps in facial recognition and body recognition. The depth sensor contains a monochrome CMOS sensor and IR projector that help create the 3D imagery throughout the room. It also measures the distance of each point of the player's body by transmitting invisible near-IR light and measuring its **time of flight** after it reflects off the objects. The microphone is an array of four microphones that can isolate the player's voices from other background noises allowing players to use their voices as an added control feature. These components come together to detect and track 48 different points on each player's body and repeat 30 times every second. Putting both hardware and software together give the Kinect the ability to generate 3D images and recognise human beings within its field of vision. It can analyse the person in front of it and go through multiple **filters** to try and determine which type of body structure matches with the correct type programmed in its system. Data is constantly being transferred back and forth between the Kinect and the objects in its field of vision while you enjoy the fun of being a character in a game without holding anything in your hands. As great as it sounds to play a game without the controller, it doesn't stop at just playing video games. There are tons of possible applications with the Kinect far from the gaming world.

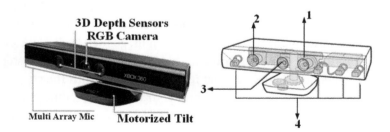

FIGURE 14.1   Kinect setup for different sensors: (1) infrared sensor, (2) infrared camera, (3) RGB (red green blue) camera, (4) microphone array.

14.3 KINECT XBOX 360 TO UNITY

14.3.1 Step 1: Unity 3D Installation

You can ignore if you have already installed it.
   Install Unity 3D from unity.com

14.3.2 Step 2: Kinect Software Requirement

To make Kinect ready for connection to Unity, you need to download and install the three programs from the following given link:

1. Kinect for Windows SDK v1.8

2. Kinect for Windows Runtime v1.8

3. Kinect for Windows Developer Toolkit v1.8

14.3.2.1 Install the Kinect for Windows SDK v1.8

Download the file from https://www.microsoft.com/en-us/download/details.aspx?id=40278 and install it to see the complete setup message (Figure 14.2).

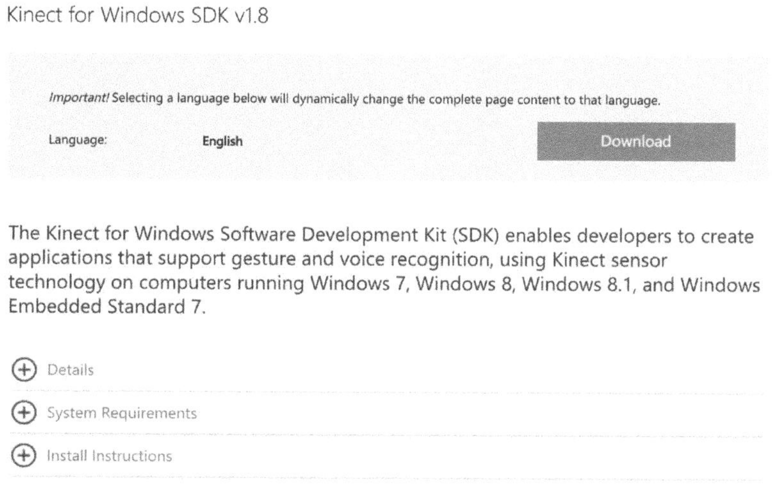

Kinect for Windows SDK v1.8

Important! Selecting a language below will dynamically change the complete page content to that language.

Language: **English**   Download

The Kinect for Windows Software Development Kit (SDK) enables developers to create applications that support gesture and voice recognition, using Kinect sensor technology on computers running Windows 7, Windows 8, Windows 8.1, and Windows Embedded Standard 7.

⊕ Details

⊕ System Requirements

⊕ Install Instructions

FIGURE 14.2   **Install the Kinect for Windows SDK. (*Continued*)**

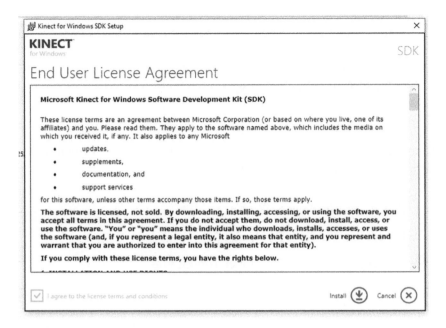

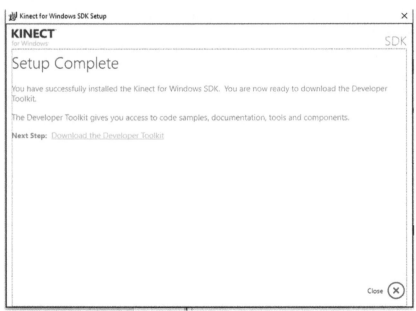

FIGURE 14.2 (*Continued*)

14.3.2.2 Kinect for Windows Runtime v1.8

Download the file from https://www.microsoft.com/en-us/download/details.aspx?id=40277 and install it to see the complete setup message (Figure 14.3).

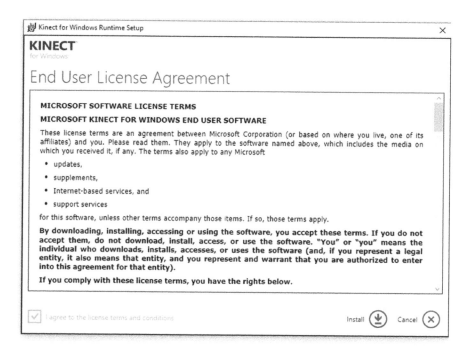

FIGURE 14.3   Install the Kinect for Windows runtime. (*Continued*)

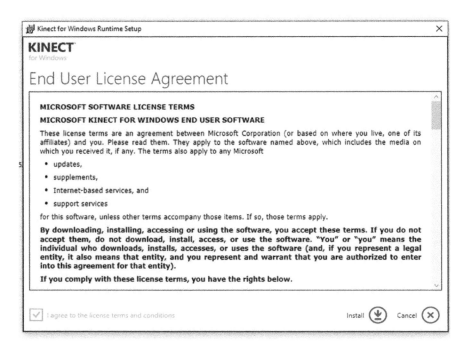

FIGURE 14.3   (*Continued*)

14.3.2.3 Kinect for Windows Developer Toolkit v1.8

Download the file from https://www.microsoft.com/en-us/download/details.aspx?id=40276 and install it to see the complete setup message (Figure 14.4).

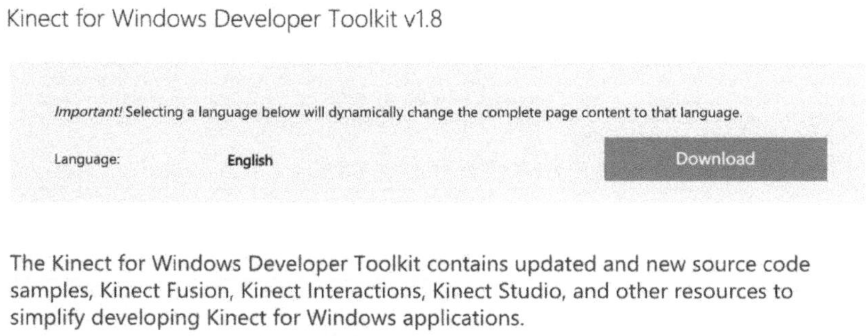

Kinect for Windows Developer Toolkit v1.8

Important! Selecting a language below will dynamically change the complete page content to that language.

Language: **English**

Download

The Kinect for Windows Developer Toolkit contains updated and new source code samples, Kinect Fusion, Kinect Interactions, Kinect Studio, and other resources to simplify developing Kinect for Windows applications.

FIGURE 14.4   **Install the Kinect for Windows Developer toolkit. (*Continued*)**

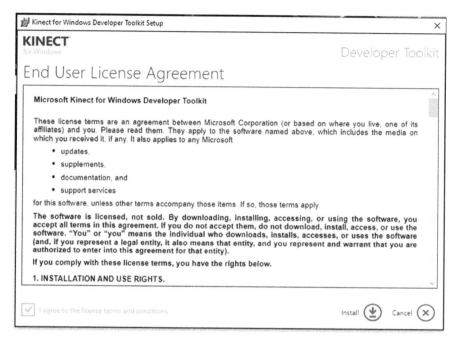

FIGURE 14.4 (*Continued*)

14.3.3 Step 3: Kinect Connect to Computer

Based on Figure 14.5, connect the Kinect to the computer (the USB cable and Kinect power supply).

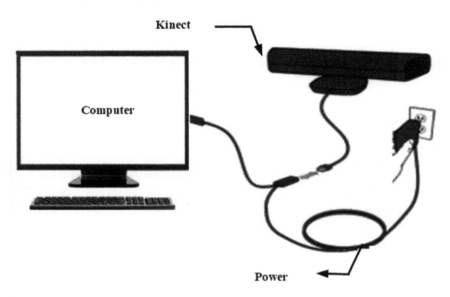

FIGURE 14.5   How to Kinect to computer.

14.3.4 Step 4: Unity Project

Open the unity Hub and start Unity, and create a new project (Figure 14.6).

FIGURE 14.6   Run Unity.

14.3.5 Step 5: Import the Asset

To insert the Asset, go to the Unity Asset store and add the following Asset to your Unity account. The Asset can be downloaded from the link (https://assetstore.unity.com/packages/tools/kinect-with-ms-sdk-7747), download and then import to Unity (Figure 14.7).

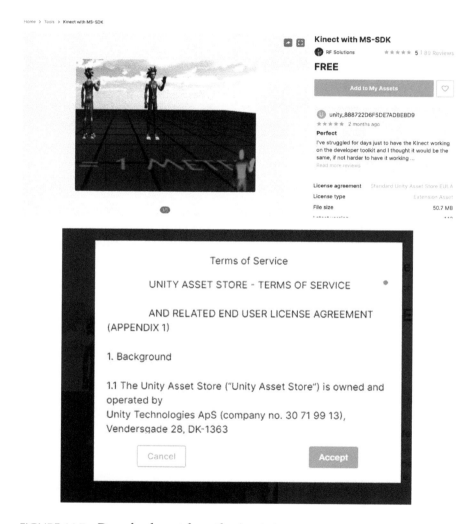

FIGURE 14.7   Download asset from the Asset store.

Then go to Window → Package Manager → select My Assets from Dropdown Menu (Figure 14.8).

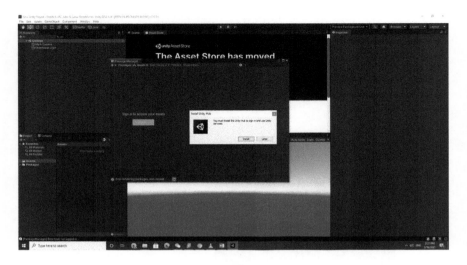

FIGURE 14.8   Import asset to Unity.

To check whether the assets are entered, you can see the files, but to ensure that the editor is okay, check the path: edit → preferences → external tools. Remember that in this box **visual studio Community** should select. Mainly its will occur when you reinstall the Unity. (Figure 14.9).

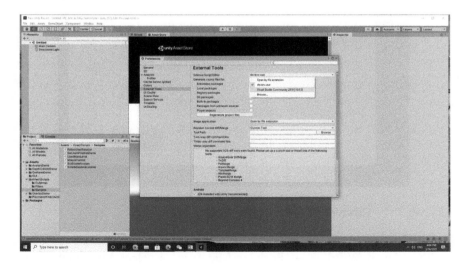

FIGURE 14.9   Double-check the entering assets correctly. (*Continued*)

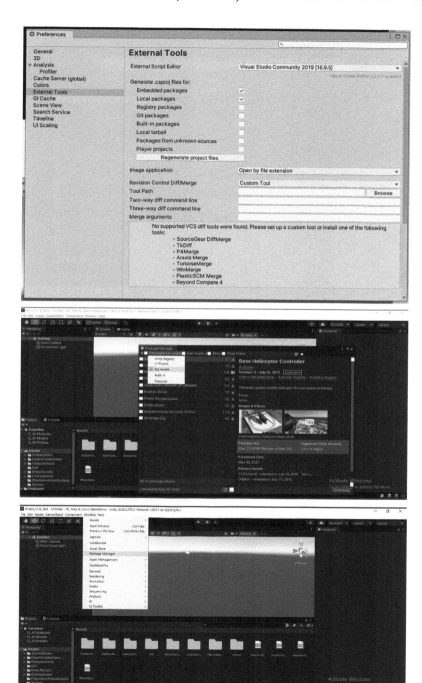

FIGURE 14.9 (*Continued*)

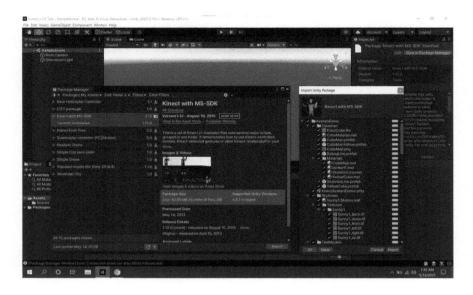

FIGURE 14.9   (*Continued*)

After import, you will see the screen as shown in Figure 14.10, which shows some errors.

14.3.6 Step 6: Fix Errors

It should notice that this Asset is originally for Unity v5. So we need to fix errors. Double-click on the Red Errors in the Console to open the

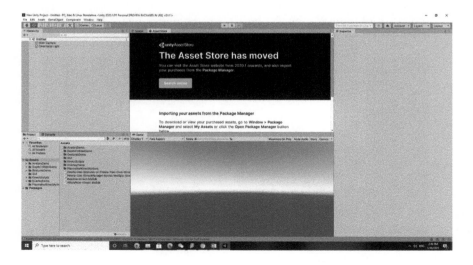

FIGURE 14.10   Error page after entering assets. (*Continued*)

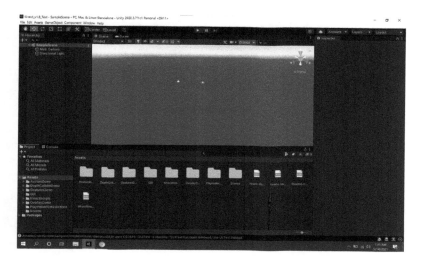

FIGURE 14.10 (*Continued*)

Visual Studio, and if the Visual Studio wants to enter, select the not now (Figure 14.11).

To solve the error:

A. Click Edit → Find and Replace → Replace in Files, now some replacement should follow in the file based on the following table:

No.	Find	Replace
1	GUIText	Text
2	GUITexture	Image
3	.guiText.text	.text
4	.guiTexture	

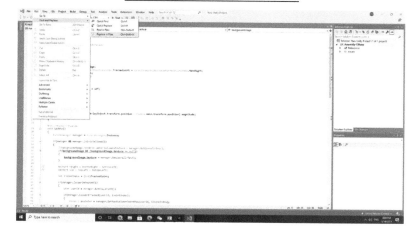

FIGURE 14.11 Solve the error. (*Continued*)

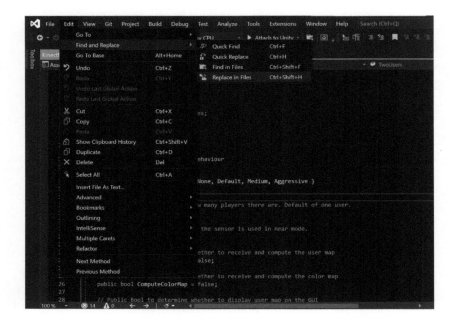

FIGURE 14.11   (*Continued*)

FIGURE 14.11 (*Continued*)

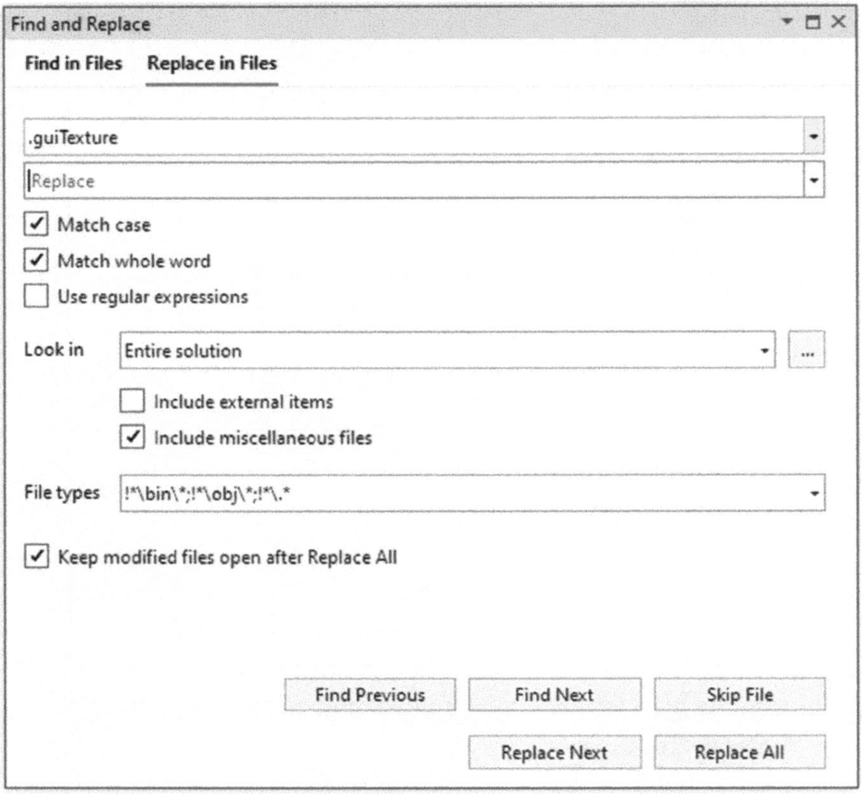

FIGURE 14.11   (*Continued*)

B. In the second part for each of the opened files, add the **using UnityEngine.UI;** in the line after the statement of **Using XXX;** and save all (Figure 14.12).

```
using UnityEngine;
using UnityEngine.UI;|
using System.Collections;
using System.Runtime.InteropServices;
using System;
```

FIGURE 14.12   Substitute **using UnityEngine.UI**. (*Continued*)

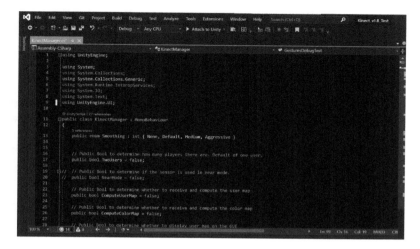

FIGURE 14.12 (*Continued*)

C. The last set of error is in the file **KinectOverlayer.cs**, then, after opening this file, replace lines 1–40 with the following code and then save
all files in Visual Studio and close it, then go back to Unity.

```
using UnityEngine;
using system.Collections;
using UnityEngine.UI;
public class KinectOverlayer: MonoBehaviour
{
//          public Vector3 TopLeft;
//          public Vector3 TopRight;
//          public Vector3 BottomRight;
//          public Vector3 BottomLeft;
Sprite mySprite;
public Image backgroundImage;
public KinectWrapper.NuiSkeletonPositionIndex TrackedJoint =
KinectWrapper.NuiSkeletonPositionIndex.HandRight;
public GameObject OverlayObject;
public float smoothFactor = 5f;
public Text debugText;
private float distanceToCamera = 10f;
void Start()
{
       if(OverlayObject)
       {
                distanceToCamera = (OverlayObject.transform.position -
Camera.main.transform.position).magnitude;
       }
```

```
}
void Update()
{
        KinectManager manager = KinectManager.Instance;
        if(manager && manager.IsInitialized())
        {
                mySprite = Sprite.Create(manager.GetUsersClrTex(), new Rect(0.0f,
0.0f, manager.GetUsersClrTex().width, manager.GetUsersClrTex().height), new
                Vector2(0.5f, 0.5f), 100.0f);
                //backgroundImage.renderer.material.mainTexture = manager.GetUsersClrTex();
                if(backgroundImage && (backgroundImage == null))
                {
                        backgroundImage.sprite = mySprite;
                }
```

14.3.7 Step 7: Open Scene

To open the scene **AvatarsDemo**, click on AvatarsDemo folder and double-click on the KinectAvatarsDemo scene (Figure 14.13). Then run the
scene and move your hands around in front of Kinect to see the effect.
After it works out, stop the scene.

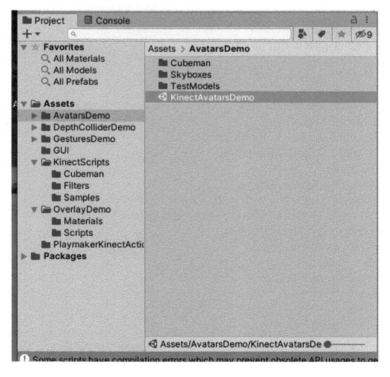

FIGURE 14.13   Run the scene. (*Continued*)

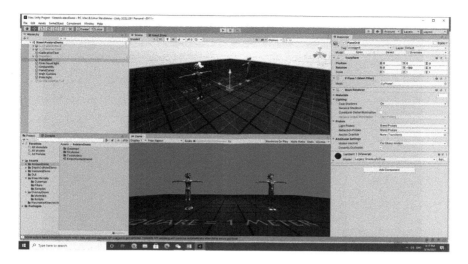

FIGURE 14.13 (*Continued*)

14.3.8 Step 8: Edit the Asset and Setup the Camera

Delete the Game Objects U_CharacaterBack and U_CharacterFront by right-clicking on the object in the Hierarchy Window. Then set the camera at the proper position by selecting the Main Camera in the Hierarchy Pane. Change the values in the Inspector Pane (Figure 14.14).

FIGURE 14.14 Set the camera. (*Continued*)

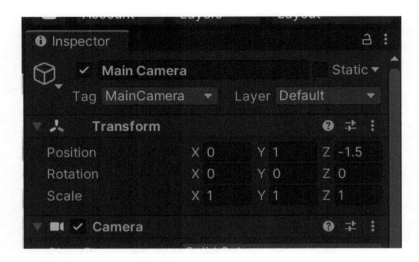

FIGURE 14.14   (*Continued*)

14.3.9 Step 9: Final Run

Run the scene again. This is the scene running without any subject in it. You should see the skeleton shape if you stand in front of Kinect and move the hand and leg (Figure 14.15).

FIGURE 14.15   Move the skeleton. (*Continued*)

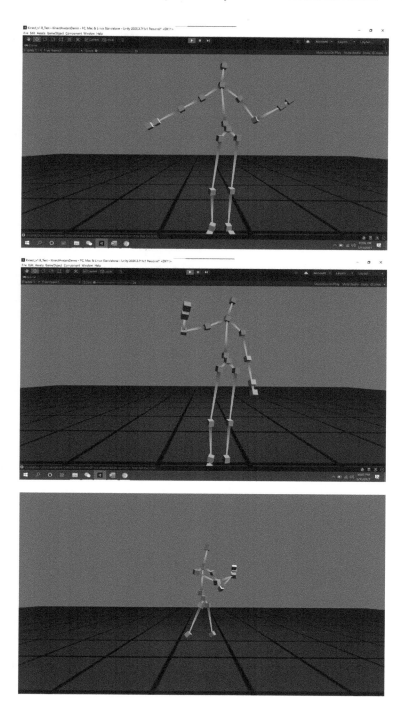

FIGURE 14.15   (*Continued*)

14.4 KINECT V2 TO UNITY

14.4.1 Kinect V2 Short Review

The most significant notable difference is the higher resolution capability of the Kinect v2 camera (Figure 14.16). Though the Kinect v1 device is a vast improvement over regular webcams, the Kinect v1 is restricted by its lower resolution output. Kinect v1 and Kinect v2 can be compared based on Table 14.1 from a pure technical spec standpoint.

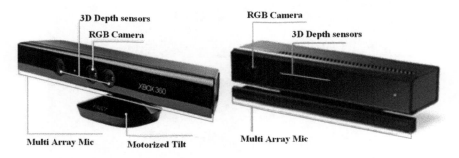

FIGURE 14.16   Kinect v2.

TABLE 14.1   Kinect v1 vs. Kinect v2 Spec Analysis

Feature	Kinect v1	Kinect v2
Colour camera	640×480@30 fps	1920×1080@30 fps
Depth camera	320×240	512×424
Max depth camera	4.5M	4.5M
Min depth camera	40 cm in near mode	50 cm
Horizontal field of view	57 degree	70 degree
Vertical field of view	43 degree	60 degree
Tilt motor	Yes	No
Skeleton joints defined	20 joints	26 joints
Full skeletons tracked	2	6
USB standard	2.0	3.0
Supported OS	Win 7, Win 8, Win 10	Win 8, Win 10

Experts claim that the Kinect v2 face recognition, motion tracking, and resolution are much more precise than the Kinect v1. Kinect v2 uses **time of flight** technology to determine the features and motion of particular objects. Kinect v2 can see just as well in a completely dark room as in a well-lit room, and the Kinect v2 has 1080 resolution (HD). Kinect v2 can process 2 gigabytes of data per second, USB 3 provides almost 10× faster broadband for the data transfer, 60% wider field of vision, and can detect and track 20 joints from 6 people's bodies, including thumbs. In comparison, the Kinect v1 could only track 20 joints from 2 people. On top of this, when using Kinect v2, users are capable of detecting heart rates, facial expressions, and weights on limbs, along with much more precious biometric data. The Kinect v1.0 device doesn't have the fidelity to track fingers and stretch and shrink with hands and arms, but the Kinect v2 has these capabilities. It's clear that this technology is undoubtedly much, much more powerful and complex than the first generation of Kinect.

14.4.2 Kinect V2 to Unity

As mentioned, Kinect has two types. By following the bellow step in this part, you will learn more.

14.4.2.1 *Step 1: Unity 3D Installation*

You can ignore if you already install it.

Install Unity 3D from unity.com (skip this step if you have already done it).

14.4.2.2 *Step 2: Kinect Software Requirement*

To make Kinect v2 ready for unity connection, you need to install these SDKs from the following link. Then download and install the following three software:

1. Kinect for Windows SDK 2

2. Kinect for Windows Runtime 2

3. Unity Pro

14.4.2.3 *Kinect for Windows SDK 2*

Download the file from https://www.microsoft.com/en-us/download/details.aspx?id=44561, and install it to see the complete setup message.

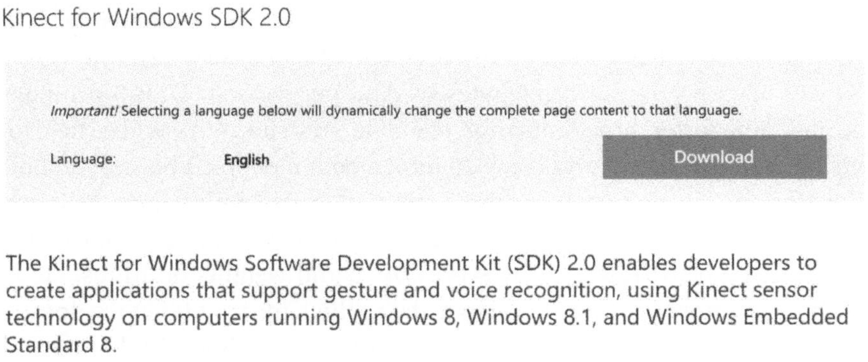
Kinect for Windows SDK 2.0
Important! Selecting a language below will dynamically change the complete page content to that language.
Language:
English
Download
The Kinect for Windows Software Development Kit (SDK) 2.0 enables developers to create applications that support gesture and voice recognition, using Kinect sensor technology on computers running Windows 8, Windows 8.1, and Windows Embedded Standard 8.

FIGURE 14.17 Kinect v2 for Windows SDK.

14.4.2.4 Kinect for Windows Runtime 2

Download the file from https://www.microsoft.com/en-us/download/details.aspx?id=44559 and install to see the complete setup message.

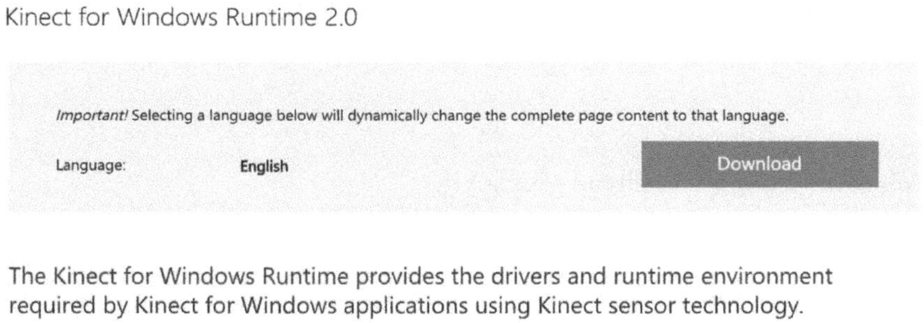
Kinect for Windows Runtime 2.0
Important! Selecting a language below will dynamically change the complete page content to that language.
Language:
English
Download
The Kinect for Windows Runtime provides the drivers and runtime environment required by Kinect for Windows applications using Kinect sensor technology.

FIGURE 14.18 Kinect v2 for Windows Runtime.

14.4.2.5 Unity Pro

Download the file from https://go.microsoft.com/fwlink/p/?LinkId=513177. This link downloads a zip file for Unity Pro. You need to extract them in a place to use them (Figure 14.19).

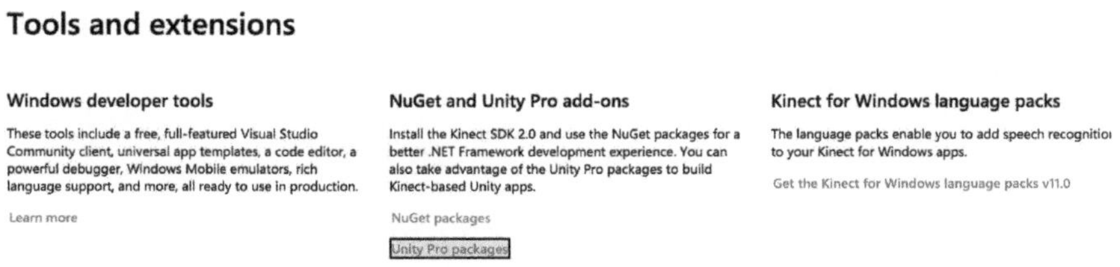
Tools and extensions
Windows developer tools
These tools include a free, full-featured Visual Studio Community client, universal app templates, a code editor, a powerful debugger, Windows Mobile emulators, rich language support, and more, all ready to use in production.
Learn more
NuGet and Unity Pro add-ons
Install the Kinect SDK 2.0 and use the NuGet packages for a better .NET Framework development experience. You can also take advantage of the Unity Pro packages to build Kinect-based Unity apps.
NuGet packages
Unity Pro packages
Kinect for Windows language packs
The language packs enable you to add speech recognitio
to your Kinect for Windows apps.
Get the Kinect for Windows language packs v11.0

FIGURE 14.19 Download Unity Pro.

14.4.2.6 Step 3: Unity Project

Open the unity Hub and start Unity, and create a new project (Figure 14.20).

FIGURE 14.20   **Start a new project.**

14.4.2.7 Step 4: Import the Unity Pro Package

As the next step, you should import the downloaded Unity Pro package into Unity by the following path: Click Assets → Import-Package → Custom Package (Figure 14.21).

FIGURE 14.21   **Import Unity Pro to Unity.**

The package that needs to be imported is Kinect.2.0.14100.19000.unity-package (Figures 14.22 and 14.23).

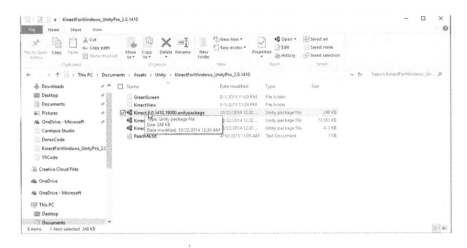

FIGURE 14.22 Find the relevant package.

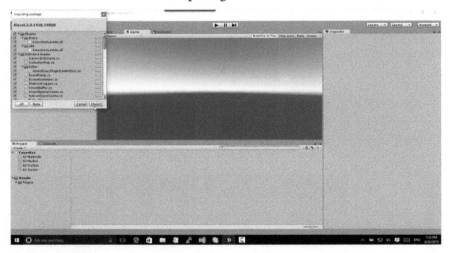

FIGURE 14.23 Import the package.

Next, a new folder appears on the project window parts, call Standard Assets (Figure 14.24).

FIGURE 14.24 Call assets.

Then drag and drop the Kinect view folder into the project window (Figure 14.25).

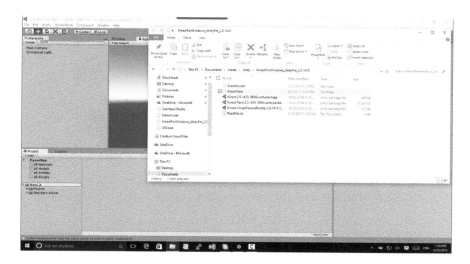

FIGURE 14.25   Import folder to the project window.

Click on **I Have Made a Backup, Go Ahead!** in the next prompt (Figure 14.26).

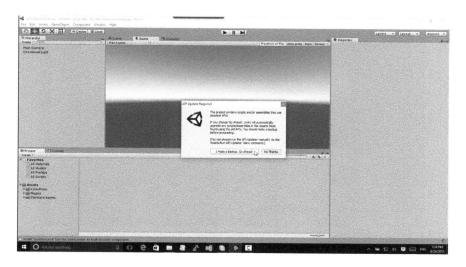

FIGURE 14.26   Make a backup.

14.4.2.8 Step 5: Kinect Connect to Computer

Based on Figure 14.27, connect the Kinect to the computer (the USB cable and Kinect power supply), connect the Kinect device and let windows install all the drivers for it.

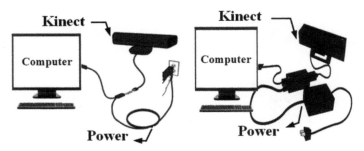

FIGURE 14.27   Connect Kinect v2 to computer.

14.4.2.9 Step 6: Back to Unity – Open Main Scene to Test

Select KinectView and then double-click on the MainScene scene contained inside it. This should open up your Kinect-enabled scene inside the game window. Click on the single arrow near the top centre of the IDE to see your application in action. The Kinect will automatically turn on, and you should see a colour image, an IR image, a rendering of any bodies in the scene, and, finally, a point cloud simulation. This scene has a few pre-made objects that connect to the Kinect device, get the data from it, and display it on the monitor. Then click on play to test (Figure 14.28).

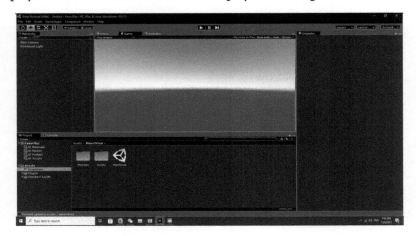

FIGURE 14.28   How to open the main scene to test. (*Continued*)

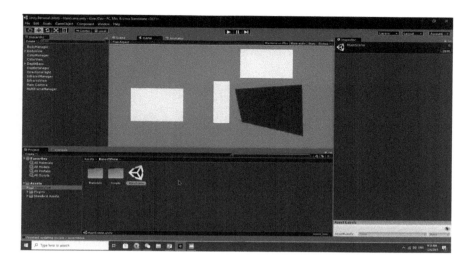

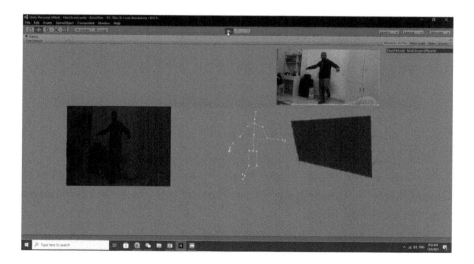

FIGURE 14.28 *(Continued)*

14.4.2.10 Step 7: Create a New Scene

As the next step, you should create a new scene, and you can name it Gestures (Figure 14.29).

FIGURE 14.29 Create a new scene.

Then create some Game Objects to interact with:

To create the new GameObject, you can follow by clicking **GameObject → Create Empty** then rename it to **BodySourceManager** (Figures 14.30 and 14.31).

FIGURE 14.30 Create a new object.

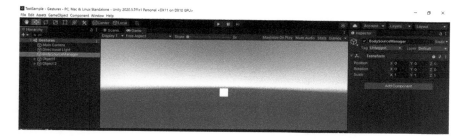

FIGURE 14.31   Rename the created object.

Then select it and add **Body Source Manager** as a component (Figure 14.32).

FIGURE 14.32   Add a component.

Again create a new GameObject by clicking **GameObject → Create Empty**, rename it to **Object1** (Figure 14.33).

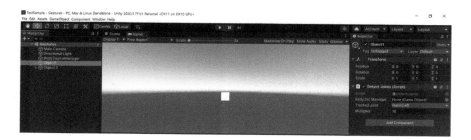

FIGURE 14.33   Rename the component.

In Assets, create a new folder and call it **Script** (Figure 14.34).

FIGURE 14.34   Create a folder.

In this folder, create a C# script and name it **DetectJoints** (Figure 14.35).

FIGURE 14.35   Create C# script.

Drag and drop it on Object1 → Add component and select script (Figure 14.36).

Right-click on the GameObject **Object1** and create a new 3D object called Cube (Figure 14.37). Click on Object1, and in the inspector window under the **Detect Joints Script** section, click on tracked joint and select the option **Hand Left** (Figure 14.38). Create another GameObject and name it **Object2** (Figure 14.39).

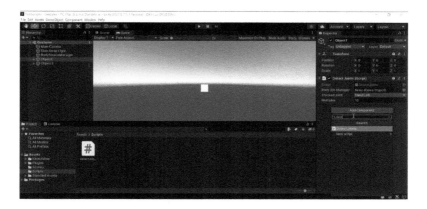

FIGURE 14.36   Add component and select script.

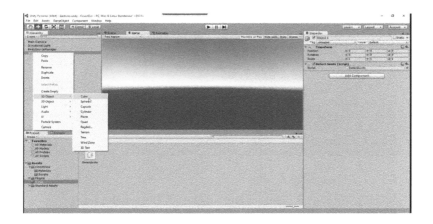

FIGURE 14.37   Create a cube.

FIGURE 14.38   Select Hand Left.

FIGURE 14.39 Create another object.

Drag the script **Detect Joints** to Object2 (Figure 14.40).

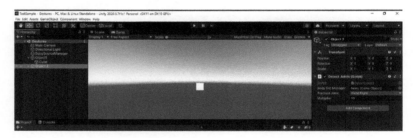

FIGURE 14.40 Drag script to object.

Right-click on it and create a particle system (Figure 14.41).

FIGURE 14.41 Create a particle system.

14.4.2.11 Step 8: Final Scene Screenshot

To have the final scene screenshot, you can follow the following process (Figure 14.42).

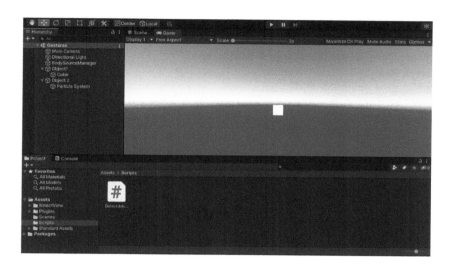

FIGURE 14.42   Final scene screenshot.

Double-click on the **Detect Joints** script to open Visual Studio and wait for it to start (Figure 14.43).

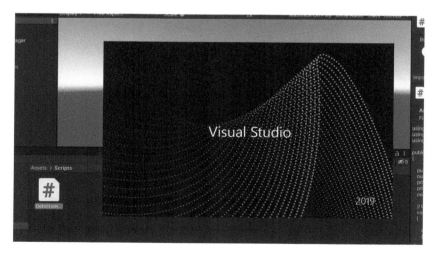

FIGURE 14.43   Open Visual Studio.

Then paste the following code to the file after removing the existing code:

```
using UnityEngine;
using system.Collections;
using Windows.Kinect;
public class DetectJoints : MonoBehaviour {
  public GameObject BodySrcManager;
  public JointType TrackedJoint;
  private BodySourceManager bodyManager;
  private Body[] bodies;
  public float multiplier = 10f;
    // Use this for initialization
    void Start () {
    if (BodySrcManager == null)
    {
      Debug.Log("Asign Game Object with Body Source Manager");
    }
    else
    {
      bodyManager = BodySrcManager.GetComponent<BodySourceManager>();
    }
      }
    // Update is called once per frame
    void Update () {
  if(BodySrcManager == null)
  {
    return;
  }

    bodies = bodyManager.GetData();
    if(bodies == null)
    {
     return;
    }
    for each (var body in bodies)
    {
     if(body == null)
     {
       continue;
      }
      if (body.IsTracked)
      {
       var pos = body.Joints[TrackedJoint].Position;
       gameObject.transform.position = new Vector3(pos.X * multiplier, pos.Y*multiplier);
      }
    }
      }
}
```

Now save the file in Visual Studio and close visual studio (Figure 14.44).

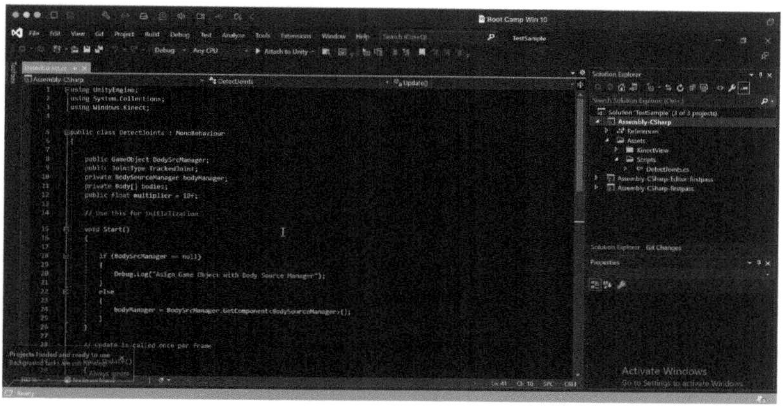

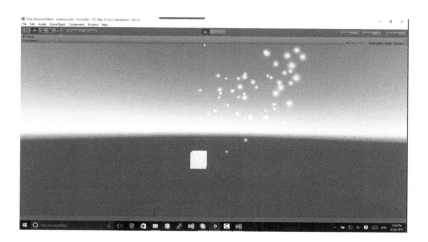

FIGURE 14.44   Add code to Visual Studio.

14.4.2.12 Step 9: Final Run

If you run the scene from Unity, you can observe the following action after moving them in front of Kinect (Figure 14.45).

FIGURE 14.45   Run final scene.

UNITY IN EMBEDDED SYSTEM DESIGN
AND ROBOTICS
A STEP-BY-STEP GUIDE

CHAPTER 15

Example 14: Log and Display Joint Coordinates with Kinect

DOI: 10.1201/9781003268581-15

In this example, you will learn how to log and display the data, log by Kinect in a Comma Separated Values (CSV) file and present them on your screen. The example design allows the user to log the Right-Hand Joint person movement data by pressing the stop/start button and storing them in a CSV format file. This example can help user to give an overview understanding of Robot Arm kinematic calculation in real applications.

15.1 STEP 1: INITIAL SETTING

As the primary steps, you should install and set up Prerequisites like Install Unity (you can ignore this step) and then create New Project. Afterwards, install three software for your Kinect interface and one Asset for your project as mentioned in the following table.

1	Kinect SDK 1.8	https://www.microsoft.com/en-us/download/details.aspx?id=40278
2	Kinect Developer Toolkit 1.8	https://www.microsoft.com/en-us/download/details.aspx?id=40276
3	Kinect Runtime for Windows 1.8	https://www.microsoft.com/en-us/download/details.aspx?id=40277
4	Import Asset	https://assetstore.unity.com/packages/tools/kinect-with-ms-sdk-7747

Please don't forget to Remove Extra GameObjects after importing, i.e., delete the Game Objects U_CharacaterBack and U_CharacterFront by right-clicking on the object in the Hierarchy Window. Then Connect Kinect for Xbox 360 and Run\Test the Project. This step is essential because you can ensure your Kinect and PC the software and hardware status.

15.2 STEP 2: UNITY INITIALIZATION

Create new GameObjects from the hierarchy pane, then Right-click and create an empty GameObject. Next, name it Canvas Group (Figure 15.1).

Then create a new Game Object by following right-click → UI → Text or Component → UI → Text paths as shown in Figure 15.2.

Create four text components in total and name them as RH_Coordinate, RH_X-Axis, RH_Y-Axis, and RH_Z-Axis. Then name the Canvas to

FIGURE 15.1   Create a new object.

FIGURE 15.2   Create a new UI text component.

RH_Canvas. Afterwards, click on RH_Canvas and set the settings of Canvas Scaler to scale with screen size and set Reference Resolution to Width: 1920 and Height: 1080 (Figure 15.3).

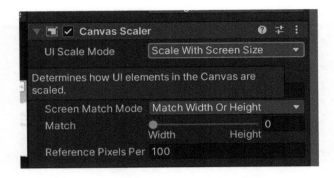

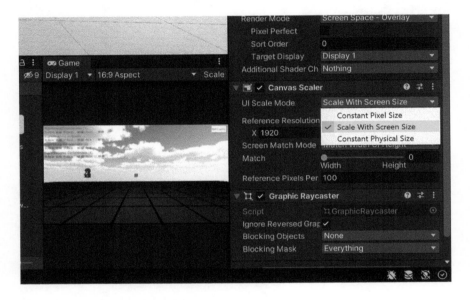

FIGURE 15.3   Set the scales.

15.3 STEP 3: OBJECTS SETTING

Follow the settings based on the following table and Figure 15.4 for each object parameter (RH_Coordinate, RH_X-Axis, RH_Y-Axis, and RH_Z-Axis). Follow and set its settings.

		POS X	POS Y	POS Z	Width	Height
1	RH_Coordinate	−469.999	346	0	960	360
2	RH_X-Axis	−643	455	0	360	50
3	RH_Y-Axis	−426	455	0	360	50
4	RH_Z-Axis	−210	458	0	360	50

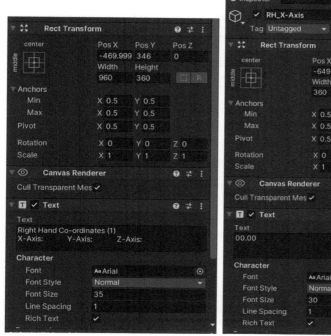

RH_Coordinate

RH_X-Axis

RH_Y-Axis

RH_Z-Axis

FIGURE 15.4 How to set the objects.

15.4 STEP 4: OBJECTS RENAME

Duplicate the RH_Canvas, three times for three more joints. Then right-click and copy and paste it in the same place. Once done. Rename them like Figure 15.5.

Name	Acronym	Index
Right Hand	RH	1
Right Wrist	RW	2
Right Elbow	RE	3
Right Shoulder	RS	4

FIGURE 15.5 Rename the object.

15.5 STEP 5: CREATE THE START/STOP LOGGING BUTTON

To have the Start/Stop Logging button, create the GameObject button from the component menu. Then right-click on RH_Canvas → UI → Button (Figure 15.6).

FIGURE 15.6 Create the start/stop logging button.

Set the properties of the button. Afterwards, change the name to **start-StopLogging Button** (Figure 15.7).

FIGURE 15.7 Change the name.

Next, expand the button and click on the **Text** component. Set the text property as shown in Figure 15.8.

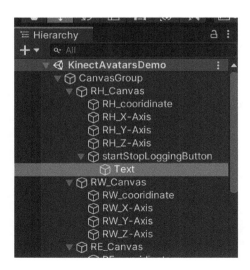

FIGURE 15.8 Set the text property. (*Continued*)

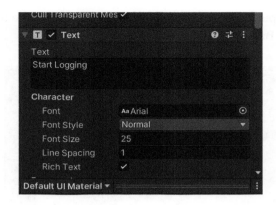

FIGURE 15.8   (*Continued*)

Then, right-click on the project pane → Create → Folder (Figure 15.9).

FIGURE 15.9   Create a folder.

In folder name: Custom Scripts, Enter Folder and create two new scripts as shown in Figure 15.10.

Script 1 Name: Right-Hand Joint

Script 2 Name: LabelFollow

FIGURE 15.10   Create C# script.

15.6 STEP 6: CODE SECTION

We need to focus on right-hand joint data. Then, open the Scripts and put the code for the right-hand joint and Label. Follow and save it.

RIGHT-HAND JOINT

```
using System;
using System.IO;
using UnityEngine;
using UnityEngine.UI;
public class RightHandJoint : MonoBehaviour
{
    // the joint we want to track
    public KinectWrapper.NuiSkeletonPositionIndex RHjoint =
KinectWrapper.NuiSkeletonPositionIndex.HandRight;
    public KinectWrapper.NuiSkeletonPositionIndex RWjoint =
KinectWrapper.NuiSkeletonPositionIndex.WristRight;
    public KinectWrapper.NuiSkeletonPositionIndex REjoint =
KinectWrapper.NuiSkeletonPositionIndex.ElbowRight;
    public KinectWrapper.NuiSkeletonPositionIndex RSjoint =
KinectWrapper.NuiSkeletonPositionIndex.ShoulderRight;
    public Text RH_X;
    public Text RH_Y;
    public Text RH_Z;
    public Text RW_X;
    public Text RW_Y;
    public Text RW_Z;
    public Text RE_X;
    public Text RE_Y;
    public Text RE_Z;
    public Text RS_X;
    public Text RS_Y;
    public Text RS_Z;
    Button loggingStartStop;
    Text loggingStartStopText;
    // joint position at the moment, in Kinect coordinates
    public Vector3 outputPosition;
    // if it is saving data to a csv file or not
    public bool isSaving = false;
    // how many seconds to save data into the csv file, or 0 to save non-stop
    public float secondsToSave = 0f;
    // path to the csv file (;-limited)
    public string RHsaveFilePath = "RH_joint_pos.csv";
    public string RWsaveFilePath = "RW_joint_pos.csv";
    public string REsaveFilePath = "RE_joint_pos.csv";
    public string RSsaveFilePath = "RS_joint_pos.csv";
```

```
// start time of data saving to csv file
private float saveStartTime = -1f;
private void Start()
{
    RH_X = GameObject.Find("RH_X-Axis").GetComponent<Text>();
    RH_Y = GameObject.Find("RH_Y-Axis").GetComponent<Text>();
    RH_Z = GameObject.Find("RH_Z-Axis").GetComponent<Text>();
    RW_X = GameObject.Find("RW_X-Axis").GetComponent<Text>();
    RW_Y = GameObject.Find("RW_Y-Axis").GetComponent<Text>();
    RW_Z = GameObject.Find("RW_Z-Axis").GetComponent<Text>();
    RE_X = GameObject.Find("RE_X-Axis").GetComponent<Text>();
    RE_Y = GameObject.Find("RE_Y-Axis").GetComponent<Text>();
    RE_Z = GameObject.Find("RE_Z-Axis").GetComponent<Text>();
    RS_X = GameObject.Find("RS_X-Axis").GetComponent<Text>();
    RS_Y = GameObject.Find("RS_Y-Axis").GetComponent<Text>();
    RS_Z = GameObject.Find("RS_Z-Axis").GetComponent<Text>();
    loggingStartStop = GameObject.Find("startStopLoggingButton").GetComponent<Button>();
    loggingStartStopText =
GameObject.Find("startStopLoggingButton").GetComponentInChildren<Text>();
    if (loggingStartStop != null)
        loggingStartStop.onClick.AddListener(buttonTask);
}
private void buttonTask()
{
    isSaving = !isSaving;
    if (isSaving)
    {
        loggingStartStopText.text = "Stop Logging";
    }
    if (!isSaving)
    {
        loggingStartStopText.text = "Start Logging";
    }
    throw new NotImplementedException();
}

void Update()
{
    if (isSaving)
    {
        // create the file, if needed
        if (!File.Exists(RHsaveFilePath))
        {
            using (StreamWriter writer = File.CreateText(RHsaveFilePath))
            {
```

```
          // csv file header
          string sLine = "time;joint;pos_x;pos_y;poz_z";
          writer.WriteLine(sLine);
        }
    }
    if (!File.Exists(RWsaveFilePath))
    {
        using (StreamWriter writer = File.CreateText(RWsaveFilePath))
        {
          // csv file header
          string sLine = "time;joint;pos_x;pos_y;poz_z";
          writer.WriteLine(sLine);
        }
    }
    if (!File.Exists(REsaveFilePath))
    {
        using (StreamWriter writer = File.CreateText(REsaveFilePath))
        {
          // csv file header
          string sLine = "time;joint;pos_x;pos_y;poz_z";
          writer.WriteLine(sLine);
        }
    }
    if (!File.Exists(RSsaveFilePath))
    {
        using (StreamWriter writer = File.CreateText(RSsaveFilePath))
        {
          // csv file header
          string sLine = "time;joint;pos_x;pos_y;poz_z";
          writer.WriteLine(sLine);
        }
    }

    // check the start time
    if (saveStartTime < 0f)
    {
        saveStartTime = Time.time;
    }
}
// get the joint position
KinectManager manager = KinectManager.Instance;

if (manager && manager.IsInitialized())
{
    if (manager.IsUserDetected())
    {
```

```
uint userId = manager.GetPlayer1ID();

if (manager.IsJointTracked(userId, (int)RHjoint))
{
  // output the joint position for easy tracking
  Vector3 RH_jointPos = manager.GetJointPosition(userId, (int)RHjoint);
  outputPosition = RH_jointPos;
  RH_X.text = string.Format("{0:F3}", RH_jointPos.x);
  //Debug.Log(RH_jointPos.x);
  RH_Y.text = string.Format("{0:F3}", RH_jointPos.y);
  RH_Z.text = string.Format("{0:F3}", RH_jointPos.z);
  if (isSaving)
  {
    if ((secondsToSave == 0f) || ((Time.time - saveStartTime) <= secondsToSave))
    {
      using (StreamWriter writer = File.AppendText(RHsaveFilePath))
      {
        string sLine = string.Format("{0:F3};{1};{2:F3};{3:F3};{4:F3}",
Time.time, (int)RHjoint, RH_jointPos.x, RH_jointPos.y, RH_jointPos.z);
        writer.WriteLine(sLine);
      }
    }
  }
}
if (manager.IsJointTracked(userId, (int)RWjoint))
{
  // output the joint position for easy tracking
  Vector3 RW_jointPos = manager.GetJointPosition(userId, (int)RWjoint);
  outputPosition = RW_jointPos;
  RW_X.text = string.Format("{0:F3}", RW_jointPos.x);
  //Debug.Log(RH_jointPos.x);
  RW_Y.text = string.Format("{0:F3}", RW_jointPos.y);
  RW_Z.text = string.Format("{0:F3}", RW_jointPos.z);
  if (isSaving)
  {
    if ((secondsToSave == 0f) || ((Time.time - saveStartTime) <= secondsToSave))
    {
      using (StreamWriter writer = File.AppendText(RWsaveFilePath))
      {
        string sLine = string.Format("{0:F3};{1};{2:F3};{3:F3};{4:F3}",
Time.time, (int)RHjoint, RW_jointPos.x, RW_jointPos.y, RW_jointPos.z);
        writer.WriteLine(sLine);
      }
    }
  }
}
```

```
        if (manager.IsJointTracked(userId, (int)REjoint))
        {
          // output the joint position for easy tracking
          Vector3 RE_jointPos = manager.GetJointPosition(userId, (int)REjoint);
          outputPosition = RE_jointPos;
          RE_X.text = string.Format("{0:F3}", RE_jointPos.x);
          //Debug.Log(RH_jointPos.x);
          RE_Y.text = string.Format("{0:F3}", RE_jointPos.y);
          RE_Z.text = string.Format("{0:F3}", RE_jointPos.z);
          if (isSaving)
          {
            if ((secondsToSave == 0f) || ((Time.time - saveStartTime) <= secondsToSave))
            {
              using (StreamWriter writer = File.AppendText(REsaveFilePath))
              {
                string sLine = string.Format("{0:F3};{1};{2:F3};{3:F3};{4:F3}",
Time.time, (int)RHjoint, RE_jointPos.x, RE_jointPos.y, RE_jointPos.z);
                writer.WriteLine(sLine);
              }
            }
          }
        }
        if (manager.IsJointTracked(userId, (int)RSjoint))
        {
          // output the joint position for easy tracking
          Vector3 RS_jointPos = manager.GetJointPosition(userId, (int)RSjoint);
          outputPosition = RS_jointPos;
          RS_X.text = string.Format("{0:F3}", RS_jointPos.x);
          //Debug.Log(RH_jointPos.x);
          RS_Y.text = string.Format("{0:F3}", RS_jointPos.y);
          RS_Z.text = string.Format("{0:F3}", RS_jointPos.z);
          if (isSaving)
          {
            if ((secondsToSave == 0f) || ((Time.time - saveStartTime) <= secondsToSave))
            {
              using (StreamWriter writer = File.AppendText(RSsaveFilePath))
              {
                string sLine = string.Format("{0:F3};{1};{2:F3};{3:F3};{4:F3}",
Time.time, (int)RHjoint, RS_jointPos.x, RS_jointPos.y, RS_jointPos.z);
                writer.WriteLine(sLine);
              }
            }
          }
        }
      }
    }
  }
}
```

LabelFollow Script Code

```
using System.Collections;
using System.Collections.Generic;
using UnityEngine;
using UnityEngine.UI;
public class LabelFollow : MonoBehaviour
{
    public Text RH_Label;
    // Start is called before the first frame update
    void Start()
    {
    }
    // Update is called once per frame
    void Update()
    {
        Vector3 RH_LabelPos = Camera.main.WorldToScreenPoint(this.transform.position);
        RH_Label.transform.position = RH_LabelPos;
    }
}
```

15.7 STEP 7: RIGHT-HAND JOINT SCRIPT

Drag and drop the Right-Hand Joint Script to CanvasGroup Object (Figure 15.11).

FIGURE 15.11   Right-hand joint script.

15.8 STEP 8: TEXT LABELS

Next, create text labels under CubeMan GameObject to follow around (Figure 15.12).

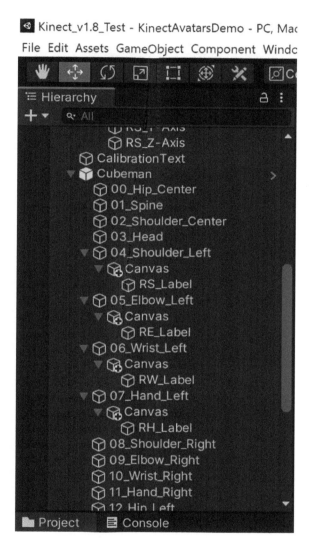

FIGURE 15.12 Text labels.

Then follow the path, create UI → Text under Shoulder_Left, Elbow_Left, Wrist_Left, and Hand_Left respectively and set the text of each text like Figure 15.13.

RS_Label

RE_Label

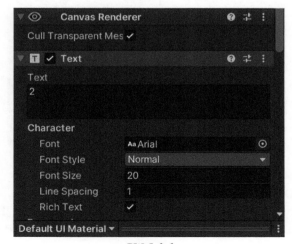

RW_Label

FIGURE 15.13   Set the text. (*Continued*)

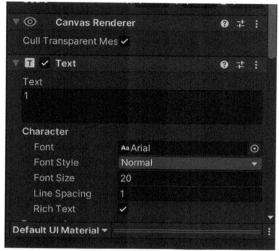

RH_Label

FIGURE 15.13 *(Continued)*

15.9 STEP 9: LABEL FOLLOW

Drag and drop LabelFollow on each text Canvas's parent (Shoulder_Left, Elbow_Left, Wrist_Left, and Hand_Left) as shown in Figure 15.14.

FIGURE 15.14 Label follow.

Next, drag and drop the Respective Text Label on the label section (RH_Label) (Figure 15.15).

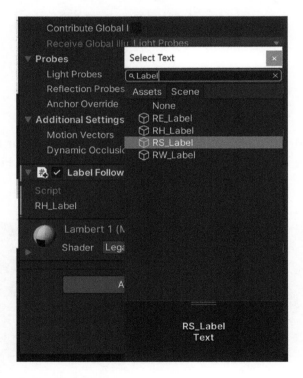

FIGURE 15.15 Select text label.

15.10 STEP 10: RUN THE PROJECT

After running the project, you should have the same environment as shown in Figure 15.16. You can click on Start Logging to start the Data Export to CSV.

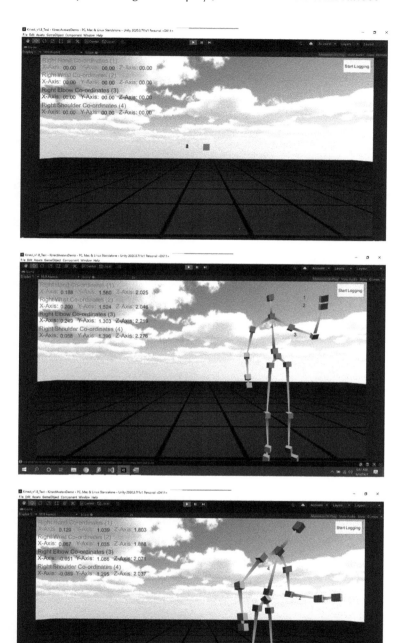

FIGURE 15.16 Data export to CSV.

15.11 STEP 11: PROJECT FOLDER

To browse the project folder, you should right-click on the Project Window and select **Show in Explorer.** In the Explorer window, you shall see the four CSV files (Figures 15.17 and 15.18).

FIGURE 15.17 Open explorer.

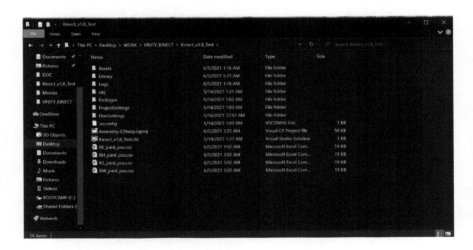

FIGURE 15.18 Explorer windows.

15.12 STEP 12: OPEN CSV FILES

To observe the data in your computer drive, you should double-click on the CSV files, and the files will be opened in Microsoft Excel. This will reveal the contents of the file (Figure 15.19).

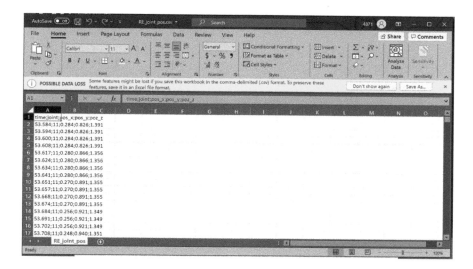

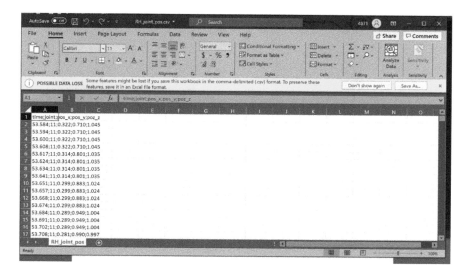

FIGURE 15.19 The CSV output files. (*Continued*)

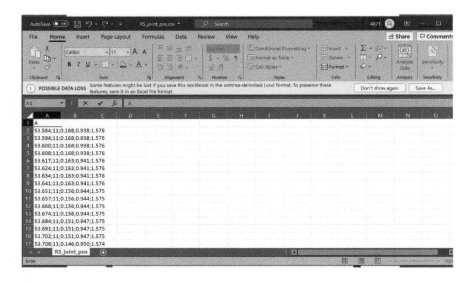

FIGURE 15.19 *(Continued)*

UNITY IN EMBEDDED SYSTEM DESIGN
AND ROBOTICS
A STEP-BY-STEP GUIDE

CHAPTER 16

Example 15:
Unity and Kinematics

DOI: 10.1201/9781003268581-16

Kinematics is the division of procedure that studies the motion of a body or a system of bodies without consideration given to its mass or the forces acting on it. Robot Kinematics refers to the analytical study of the motion of a robot manipulator. For Kinematics, we interfere with two words of Inverse Kinematics as well as forward Kinematics. The problem with **Inverse Kinematics** is that it can be seen as the one of finding the joint values corresponding to some specific position and/or orientation of a given body element (generally the end effector). In contrast, **Forward Kinematics** refers to the process of obtaining the position and velocity of the end effector, given the known joint angles and angular velocities. Formulating suitable kinematics models for a robot mechanism is crucial for analysing industrial manipulators' behaviour. More generally, it is a transformation from the task space coordinates into the joint space coordinates. In Unity, you can also consider the Inverse Kinematics for your character, because animation needs to work with the rotation of Angles of joints. In this chapter, we'll briefly look into how Inverse Kinematics is implemented in Unity. A Unity asset is an item that you can use in your game or project. An asset may come from a file created outside of Unity, such as a 3D model, an audio file, an image, or other file types that Unity supports. The main reason for using assets is to speed up development and ease of access. Assets are like templates. It can be a ready-made component that's downloaded and used or plug and play. It also provides users with a new and experienced introduction to new functions that are not readily available out of the box in Unity. The main goal of this example guide is to show how the concept of Inverse Kinematics can be applied in Unity with ready-made assets from the assets store of Unity. Users can learn how Inverse Kinematics can be implemented or at least get started in the direction of applying Inverse Kinematics in their game/project development.

16.1 INVERSE KINEMATICS

16.1.1 Step 1: Unity Installation and Preparation

Install Unity 3D from unity.com (Skip this step if you have already done so). Then create a new project from the unity hub (Figure 16.1).

16.1.2 Step 2: Asset Installation

Go to Asset store and add the following asset to your unity account from the link:

https://assetstore.unity.com/packages/tools/animation/inverse-kine-matics-1829 (Figure 16.2).

After installation, you can click Open in Unity here to open it in unity.

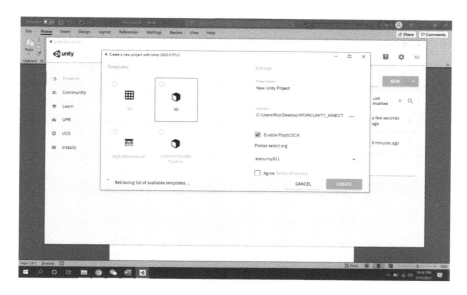

FIGURE 16.1 **Start Unity.**

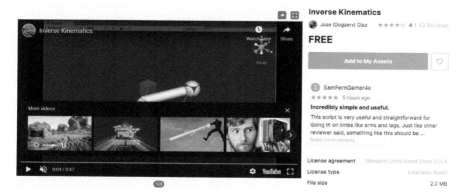

FIGURE 16.2 **Download and import Assets. (*Continued*)**

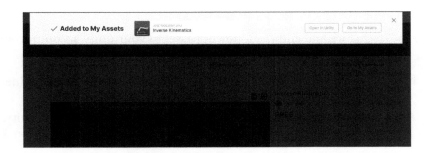

FIGURE 16.2 (*Continued*)

Then, inside Unity, go to the Window → Package Manager → Select My assets from the Packages dropdown menu (Figure 16.3). Download Inverse Kinematics from Packages manager and import it, then you will see the following scene, which you can get the IK section by download option (Figure 16.4).

FIGURE 16.3 Location of the imported package on Unity.

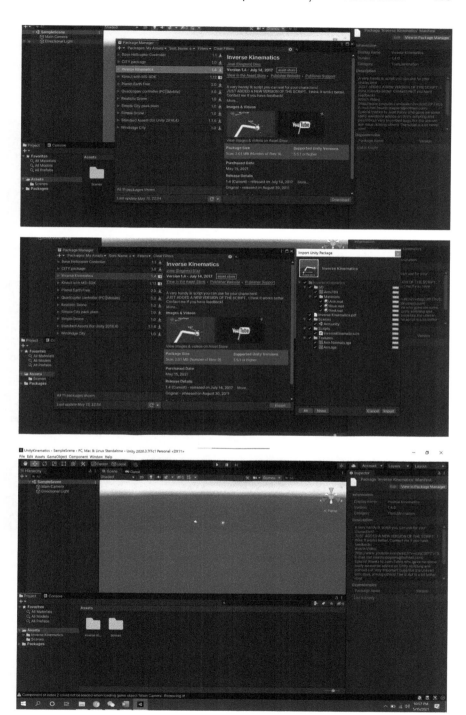

FIGURE 16.4   Import Inverse Kinematics on Unity.

16.1.3 Step 3: Open Default Scene

Go to Assets → Inverse Kinematics → Scenes and double-click on Arm. Then you will see the default scene (Figure 16.5).

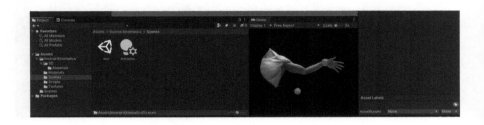

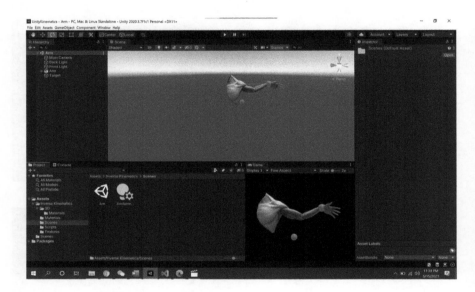

FIGURE 16.5   Open default scene.

16.2 FAST INVERSE KINEMATICS

16.2.1 Step 1: Unity Installation

Install Unity 3D from the unity website. You can ignore this step if you have already done it.

16.2.2 Step 2: Assent Installation

Go to the Unity Asset Store and download the asset from the following link:

https://assetstore.unity.com/packages/tools/animation/fast-ik-139972 (Figure 16.6).

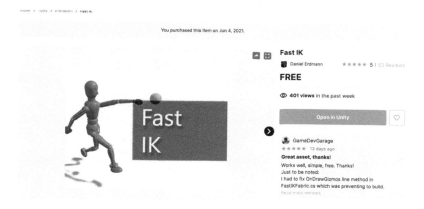

FIGURE 16.6 **Install asset.**

16.2.3 Step 3: Do the Project and Import the Asset

Create a new project in Unity and download Unity Asset, and import it to your project (Figure 16.7).

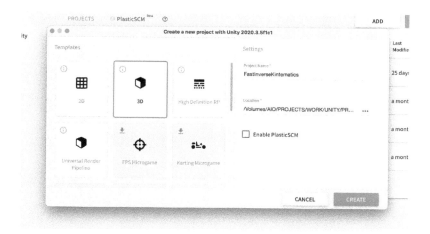

FIGURE 16.7 **Import asset to Unity.** (*Continued*)

FIGURE 16.7 (*Continued*)

16.2.4 Step 4: Import dialogue box

As Figure 16.8 shows, inside the package manager, refresh the list of assets. Then, click on fast IK and click on download. Once the download completes, click on Import and a new dialogue box will come up. Click Import on the importunity package dialogue to finish importing.

FIGURE 16.8 Set the defaults.

16.2.5 Step 5: Run Fast Inverse Kinematic Scene

Go inside the folder and follow the path Assets → FastIK → Scenes and double-click on FastIKSampleScene (Figure 16.9).

FIGURE 16.9   Run FIKS.

Now, you should see the Inverse Kinematics scene as shown in Figure 16.10. Then run the scene to see the Inverse Kinematics objects run.

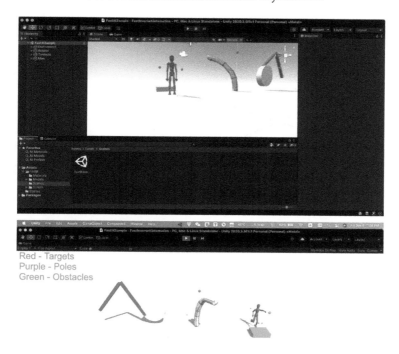

FIGURE 16.10   Inverse Kinematics scene.

UNITY IN EMBEDDED SYSTEM DESIGN
AND ROBOTICS
A STEP-BY-STEP GUIDE

CHAPTER 17

Running Unity Project on Raspberry Pi

DOI: 10.1201/9781003268581-17

The Raspberry Pi (RPi) computer is a small yet powerful device concerning its size and cost. But it is not an all-powerful device. Therefore running a Unity project on the RPi is not as good as running it on a laptop or desktop computer. Not only that, but this method is also not officially supported by Unity themselves; hence, it is unwise to rely on them for support if things go wrong while performing the steps mentioned here. It should be noted that the Unity app runs fine on its own in RPi but can be extremely slow if it has more graphics-intensive assets. Because the RPi's Broadcom GPU is not so powerful, the application doesn't render all graphics components.

This chapter states a detailed report on running a Unity-built program/project on the RPi. Unity is a cross-platform game engine initially released by Unity Technologies in 2005. The focus of Unity lies in the development of both 2D and 3D games and interactive content. Unity now supports over 20 different target platforms for deploying, while its most popular platforms are the PC, Android, and iOS systems. Unity does not provide any export method for arm-based processors with Linux OS. Hence, running Unity projects on RPi proves to be rather tricky. But, there is a glimmer of hope here as Unity does provide a way to run Unity exports as. apk or Android application. Meaning, one can run an Android application on Android devices. And luckily, there are Android ports for the RPi boards, and, as Android comes in both x86 and arm architectures, it becomes easy to run Unity games/programs on the RPi if those Android ports are installed. Another possible way to run Unity exports on RPi is through Unity's native WebGL export. WebGL applications run in browsers, so it should be rather easy to run it on an RPi will explore. The third potential way to run Unity games on the RPi is through an emulator, which will emulate an x86 environment over the on-board arm architecture. There is a software called Box86, which is explored in this document in detail too.

17.1 ANDROID METHOD

For this method to work, the required equipment hardware and software are mentioned in the following table.

Required Hardware	Required Software
Raspberry Pi 3/4	Android Flashable ZIP for raspberry pi (download from: https://konstakang.com/devices/rpi3/CM14.1)
Monitor	Unity 3D on a Laptop/Desktop (download from: https://unity3d.com/get-unity/download)
SD card	Balena Etcher (download from: https://www.balena.io/etcher/)
USB Card Reader	
Computer with Windows/Linux/Mac	Android Platform Tools (ADB TOOLS)

17.2 STEPS TO INSTALL THE UNITY

17.2.1 Step 1: Preparation

Insert the SD card into the computer with Windows/Mac/Linux, flash the Android flash zip with Balena Etcher, and initialise the RPi. Complete the setup and finish initialisation (Figure 17.1).

FIGURE 17.1 Android device setup.

17.2.2 Step 2: Unity 3D installation

Install Unity 3D on the Computer based on your OS Windows/Mac/Linux.

17.2.3 Step 3: Project Building

Build a Project with Unity (Figure 17.2).

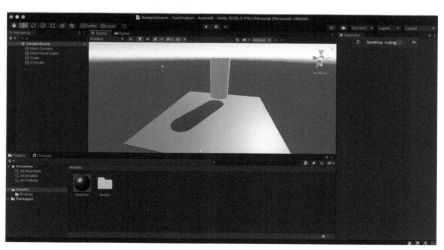

FIGURE 17.2 Make sample application.

17.2.4 Step 4: Temporary Close

Close the Project and follow the next project.

17.2.5 Step 5: Project Reopening

Reopen the project with Android custom settings (Figure 17.3).

FIGURE 17.3   Relaunch with Android.

Click on build settings under File (Figure 17.4).

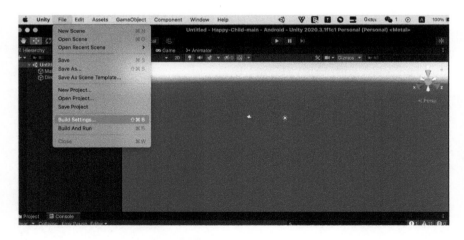

FIGURE 17.4   Unity Build Settings.

Replicate the settings as follows from the **Build settings** (Figure 17.5).

FIGURE 17.5 Android Player Build.

Click Build and generate an APK file and transfer the file to the RPi and install it.

You can install it via adb commands: adb installs <Apk Name> or transfer via pen drive. Then run the app from app drawer (Figure 17.6).

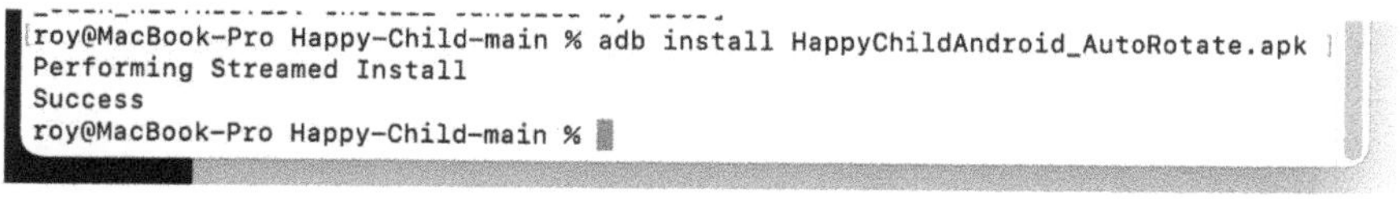

```
[roy@MacBook-Pro Happy-Child-main % adb install HappyChildAndroid_AutoRotate.apk ]
Performing Streamed Install
Success
roy@MacBook-Pro Happy-Child-main % ▋
```

FIGURE 17.6 Side Load Android APK via ADB.

17.2.6 Android Unity App Player Run Demo

Running the Unity on RPi consists of three steps depicted in Figures 17.7–17.9.

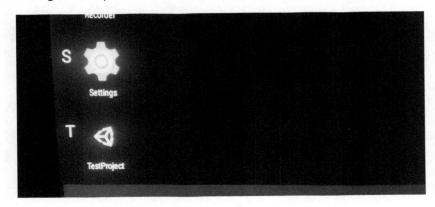

FIGURE 17.7   App installed and showing inside App drawer.

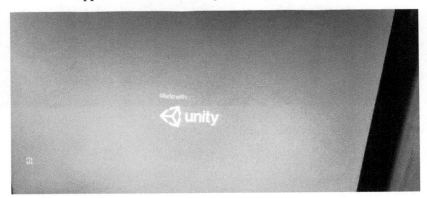

FIGURE 17.8   App starting in Android on RPi.

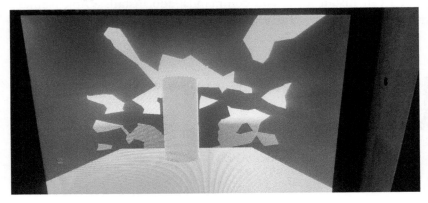

FIGURE 17.9   App running in Android on RPi.

17.3 WINDOWS 10 IoT CORE METHOD

This method does not by any means make the job better, but it does increase compatibility. Windows 10 IoT, as per Microsoft's developer website, is quoted as "Windows 10 IoT is a member of the Windows 10 product family that brings enterprise-class power, security, and manageability to the Internet of Things", which says that it is especially built for Windows IoT applications. One of the more significant advantages of using this OS for Unity app playing is that:

1. It is natively supported for the RPi hardware, unlike Android, which is ported from the x86 project, and

2. It supports UWP Application, which is Microsoft's Universal Windows Platform Application system.

The UWP Application system allows a single app to be built and run across all Windows devices across four major architectures, namely, x86, x64, ARM, and ARM64. The RPi 3b and 3b+ are ARM64 devices. But it should be mentioned here that in the testing, the ARM64 version of the application failed to install on the RPi even though both hardware and OS were 64-bit. So, the testing was done with the ARM version or the 32-bit version of arm architecture.

For this method to work, the required equipment, hardware, and software are mentioned in the following table.

Required Hardware	Required Software
Raspberry Pi ¾ Monitor SD card USB Card Reader Computer with Windows (Mac and Linux is not supported at all)	**Windows 10 IoT FFU Image** (download from: https://download.microsoft.com/download/9/6/2/9629C69B-02B8-4A82-A4C8-860D6E880C66/16299.15.170928-1534.rs3_release_amd64fre_IOTCORE_RPi.iso) **Unity 3D on a Laptop/Desktop** (download from: https://unity3d.com/get-unity/download) **Windows 10 IoT Dashboard** (download from: https://go.microsoft.com/fwlink/?LinkID=708576) **Android Platform Tools (ADB TOOLS)**

17.4 STEPS TO INSTALL THE UNITY

Insert MicroSD card to Windows Device using a card reader. Flash the FFU Image. There are two methods of installing the Unity: online and offline.

17.4.1 The Online Easy Method

Install Windows 10 IoT Dashboard and open it (Figure 17.10).

FIGURE 17.10   IoT Core Dashboard.

Then, select RPi 2/3 from the options menu, set username and password, and connect to an Internet connection. The software will automatically download the FFU Package and install it on the MicroSD card.

17.4.2 The Offline Method

In the scenario where the user is not eager to download the FFU package every time and install it, or the scenario where the Internet connection is not consistently good, this method is the one to follow.

1. Download and Mount the ISO file (16299.15.170928-1534.rs3_ release_amd64fre_IOTCORE_RPi.iso).

2. Open the mounted folder or extract and ISO using WinRAR or similar Unarchiving software and install the MSI Package inside the ISO.

3. After installation, the following figure will show up.

In step 3, as Figure 17.11 shows, the FFU Offline File will be under the location: C:\Program Files(x86)\Microsoft IoT. The user can then move the FFU File from there to another location for convenience.

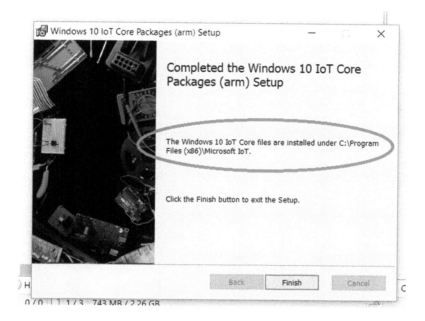

FIGURE 17.11   FFU Installation.

Install and open Windows 10 IoT Dashboard, select Custom FFU Package, and set the location of the FFU file as shown in Figure 17.12. Install the IoT Core OS on the SD card. The user will see the following progress window.

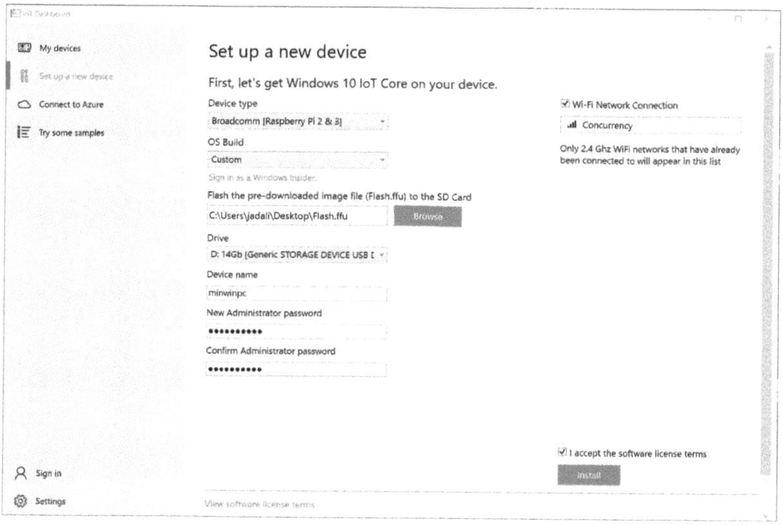

FIGURE 17.12   Custom FFU installation.

17.4.3 Deployment Steps

1. Insert the SD card inside RPi and power the device.

2. Please wait for it to boot (Figure 17.13).

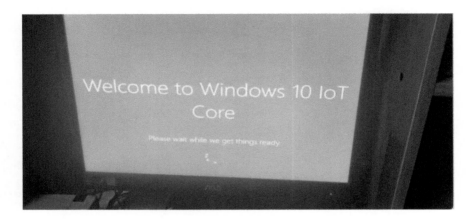

FIGURE 17.13   Windows 10 IoT Core Boot.

It's better to connect to a network while the setup is going on, or one can connect later via settings (Figure 17.14). Once the system is booted, the user will see as shown in Figure 17.15.

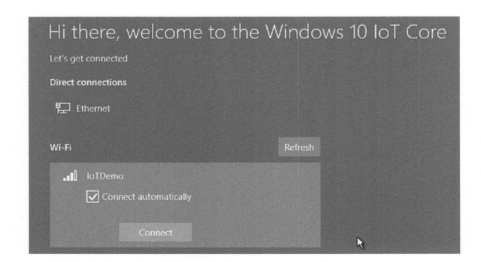

FIGURE 17.14   Setup Internet connection on First Boot.

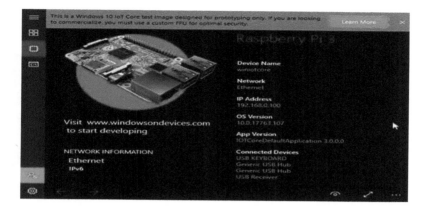

FIGURE 17.15   IoT Core Dashboard on RPi.

Note the IP address of the system after connecting it to an Ethernet or WiFi Connection while setting it up for the first time, or one can also do it from the settings menu and even from the device portal, which can be accessed from any computer on the same network using the IP address of the device with the port 8080 (if already connected to a network).

17.4.4 APPX Build Steps

On the Unity 3D editor side of things in a real windows machine, the user needs to build the UWP Application from the build settings (Figure 17.16).

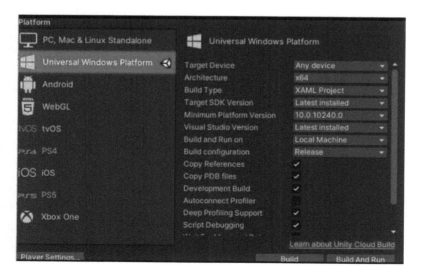

FIGURE 17.16   UWP Application Player Settings.

Application Player Settings should be as shown in Figures 17.17–17.20.

FIGURE 17.17 Supported Device Families.

FIGURE 17.18 Unity Player Quality Settings.

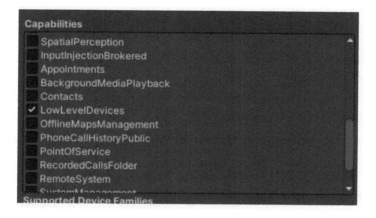

FIGURE 17.19 LowLevelDevices Settings.

FIGURE 17.20 Quality Settings for project.

After the application is built, Microsoft Visual Studio will open automatically. From there, the application needs to be imported and packaged into APPX files.

Pre-requirements for building UWP Application packages:

a. Windows 10 SDK (can be installed from inside the VS Installer).

b. Visual Studio C++ Development Tools (can be installed from inside the VS Installer).

c. UWP App Development Tools (can be installed from inside the Unity Hub/VS Installer).

Figure 17.21 shows the VS Installer Screenshots of installed components.

FIGURE 17.21 VS Installer.

Open or import the *.sln project file for VS, which was produced after building the Unity project in Unity 3D (Figure 17.22).

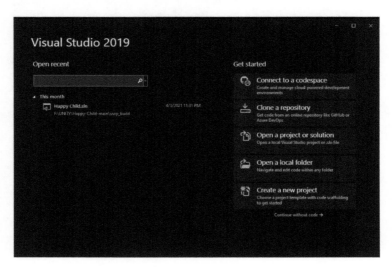

FIGURE 17.22 VS Project Selection Window.

Once the file is opened, the user will see as shown in Figure 17.23.

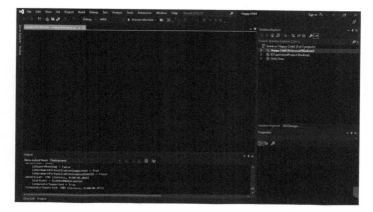

FIGURE 17.23   VS Project Workspace.

Build the solution as shown in Figure 17.24.

FIGURE 17.24   Build Solution.

After the build is completed, it is time to publish a package (Figure 17.25).

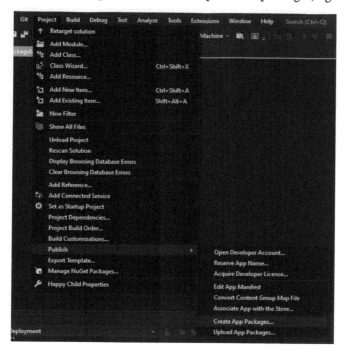

FIGURE 17.25   Create App Package.

Follow the steps as shown in Figure 17.26.

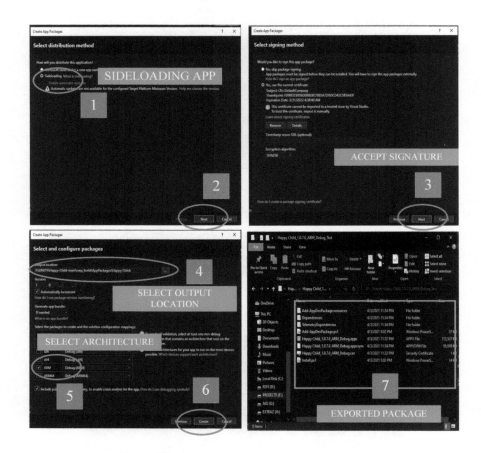

FIGURE 17.26   **Export APPX steps.**

Now the application can be installed on the RPi device.

17.4.4.1 APP Sideloading Steps

1. Open the browser on the main windows machine and go to the URL:
   <DEVICE IP ADDRESS>:<8080 (PORT)>

This will open the Device Portal for the RPi, as shown in Figure 17.27.

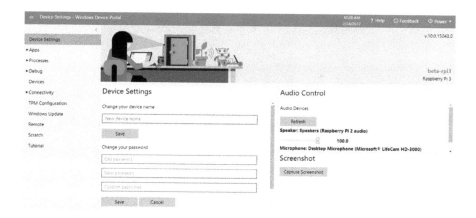

FIGURE 17.27   IoT Device Portal.

2. Select Apps → Apps manager and upload and install the appx file exported based on pervious step (Figure 17.28).

FIGURE 17.28   Sideload APPX.

For the sample app used to show the process, two apps need to be installed. First is the dependency application package. This file is inside the **Dependencies** folder of the exported folder from VS (Figure 17.29).

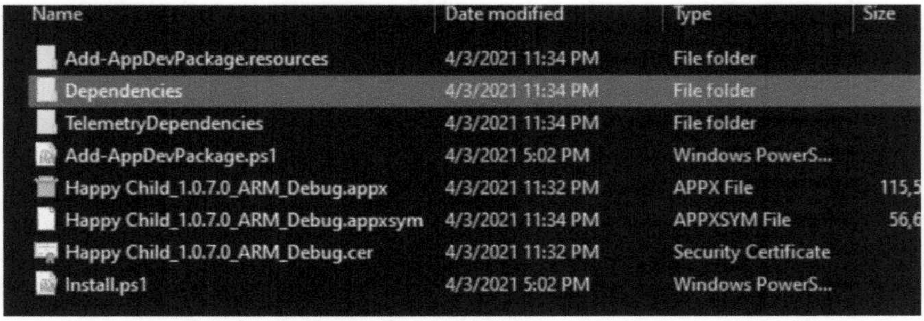

FIGURE 17.29   APP Dependency folder.

Inside the folder, there is an ARM folder (Figure 17.30).

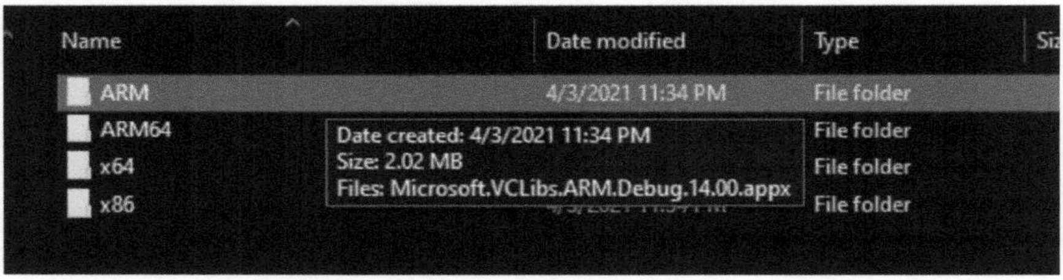

FIGURE 17.30   Dependency Architecture folder.

Inside the **ARM folder, the Microsoft.VCLibs.ARM.Debug.14.00.appx** file needs to be installed first. Please select the file and upload it (Figure 17.31).

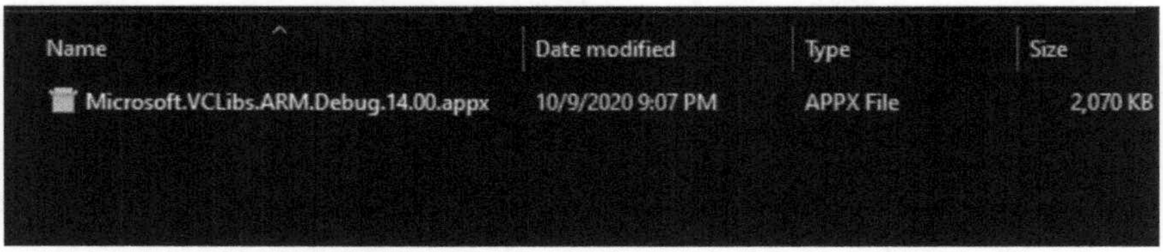

FIGURE 17.31   Dependency File APPX.

After this file is installed, the main app can be selected and installed (Figure 17.32).

FIGURE 17.32 Main Application APPX.

Once the installation commences, the user will be able to see its progress (Figure 17.33).

FIGURE 17.33 Appx sideload progress.

Once it is done, the message: **Package Successfully registered** will appear. This completes the appx sideload process (Figure 17.34).

FIGURE 17.34 Sideload Complete.

17.4.4.2 APP Running Steps

Start the application from the RPi using Mouse: Go to Start → Apps → **APP NAME** to run the newly installed application (Figure 17.35).

FIGURE 17.35 Windows IoT Start Menu.

Depending on the application's size and weight, it can take a bit of time to a significant amount of time. The application will crash if there were some things in the application the RPi could not handle. This did happen a few times in the testing procedure for this project. But once it deployed, it showed as in Figure 17.36.

FIGURE 17.36 Demo Application Running.

It should remind that the application runs better than Android, but still not commendable if it is graphics intensive. But, it shows how much the RPi is capable despite its size, shape, and cost.

UNITY IN EMBEDDED SYSTEM DESIGN AND ROBOTICS
AND ROBOTICS
A STEP-BY-STEP GUIDE

CHAPTER 18

Unity and ROS Bridge

DOI: 10.1201/9781003268581-18

The Robot Operating System (ROS) is an open-source, meta-operating system for any robot. It provides the services a user would expect from an operating system, including hardware abstraction, low-level device control, implementation of commonly-used functionality, message-passing between processes, and package management.

ROS is a flexible framework for writing robot software. It is a collection of tools, libraries, and conventions that aim to simplify creating complex and robust robot behaviour across a wide variety of robotic platforms. ROS is an open-source, meta-operating system for any robot. It provides the services users expect from an operating system, including hardware abstraction, low-level device control, commonly-used functionality, message-passing between processes, and package management. It also provides tools and libraries for obtaining, building, writing, and running code across multiple computers.

To work with this chapter, you should have some prior knowledge about ROS and install Linux, preferably Ubuntu, on your system. This chapter will be going into a Unity scene and creating a scene object that subscribes to that topic. Getting data from that topic will be doing fake odometry or post data, exciting or sitting manually. But once you do that, you should be able to apply it just about anything. This chapter can be an excellent key solution for users to start the Robot simulation in Unity.

18.1 STEP 1: CREATING ROS PACKAGE

To work with ROS, you should create your ROS package (Figure 18.1). To make the package work with Unity and ROS Bridge, you can follow the following steps.

Open a new terminal by pressing **Ctrl+Alt+T** and type the following four commands based on the following table.

No	Command
1	cd ~/catkin_ws/src
2	catkin_create_pkg beginner_tutorials std_msgs rospy roscpp
3	catkin_make
4	~/catkin_ws/devel/setup.bash

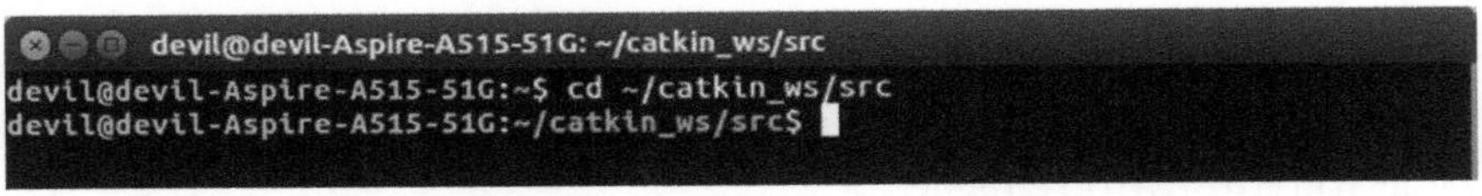

```
devil@devil-Aspire-A515-51G: ~/catkin_ws/src
devil@devil-Aspire-A515-51G:~$ cd ~/catkin_ws/src
devil@devil-Aspire-A515-51G:~/catkin_ws/src$
```

FIGURE 18.1 Create ROS package. (*Continued*)

```
devil@devil-Aspire-A515-51G: ~/catkin_ws/src
devil@devil-Aspire-A515-51G:~/catkin_ws/src$ catkin_create_pkg beginner_tutorial
s std_msgs rospy roscpp
```

```
devil@devil-Aspire-A515-51G: ~/catkin_ws
devil@devil-Aspire-A515-51G:~/catkin_ws$ catkin_make
```

```
devil@devil-Aspire-A515-51G: ~/catkin_ws
devil@devil-Aspire-A515-51G:~/catkin_ws$ . ~/catkin_ws/devel/setup.bash
```

FIGURE 18.1   (*Continued*)

After entering the commands, the package is ready for work. As the next step, you should create a publisher node to communicate with ROS.

18.2 STEP 2: WRITING PUBLISHER NODE

To communicate with ROS, you should create your publisher node to work with Unity and ROS Bridge. Then with this aim, follow the following steps.

Open a new terminal by pressing **Ctrl+Alt+T** and type the command **cd catkin_ws/src/beginner_tutorials**, and press Enter (Figure 18.2).

```
devil@devil-Aspire-A515-51G: ~
devil@devil-Aspire-A515-51G:~$ cd catkin_ws/src/beginner_tutorials
```

FIGURE 18.2   Open a new terminal.

Make a directory called scripts by typing the command **mkdir scripts** (Figure 18.3).

```
devil@devil-Aspire-A515-51G: ~/catkin_ws/src/beginner_tutorials
devil@devil-Aspire-A515-51G:~$ cd catkin_ws/src/beginner_tutorials
devil@devil-Aspire-A515-51G:~/catkin_ws/src/beginner_tutorials$ mkdir scripts
```

FIGURE 18.3   Make a directory.

Navigate to the scripts folder by typing the command **cd scripts** (Figure 18.4).

```
devil@devil-Aspire-A515-51G: ~/catkin_ws/src/beginner_tutorials
devil@devil-Aspire-A515-51G:~$ cd catkin_ws/src/beginner_tutorials
devil@devil-Aspire-A515-51G:~/catkin_ws/src/beginner_tutorials$ cd scripts
```

FIGURE 18.4   How to navigate to the scripts.

Download the file from the Internet by typing the following command: **wget   https://raw.github.com/ros/ros_tutorials/kinetic-devel/rospy_tutorials/001_talker_listener/talker.py** (Figure 18.5).

```
devil@devil-Aspire-A515-51G: ~/catkin_ws/src/beginner_tutorials/scripts
devil@devil-Aspire-A515-51G:~$ cd catkin_ws/src/beginner_tutorials
devil@devil-Aspire-A515-51G:~/catkin_ws/src/beginner_tutorials$ cd scripts
devil@devil-Aspire-A515-51G:~/catkin_ws/src/beginner_tutorials/scripts$ wget htt
ps://raw.github.com/ros/ros_tutorials/kinetic-devel/rospy_tutorials/001_talker_l
istener/talker.py
```

FIGURE 18.5   Download the file.

Then, make it executable by typing the command **chmod +x talker.py** (Figure 18.6).

```
devil@devil-Aspire-A515-51G: ~/catkin_ws/src/beginner_tutorials/scripts
devil@devil-Aspire-A515-51G:~$ cd catkin_ws/src/beginner_tutorials
devil@devil-Aspire-A515-51G:~/catkin_ws/src/beginner_tutorials$ cd scripts
devil@devil-Aspire-A515-51G:~/catkin_ws/src/beginner_tutorials/scripts$ chmod +x
 talker.py
```

FIGURE 18.6   How to have access.

Afterwards, open the script from the explorer (Figure 18.7).

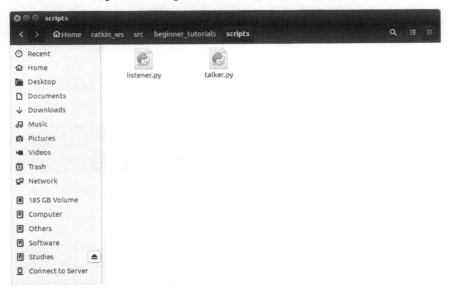

FIGURE 18.7   How to open the script from explorer.

Next, replace the source code inside with the code given below and save it.

```python
#!/usr/bin/env python
# Software License Agreement (BSD License)
#
# Copyright (c) 2008, Willow Garage, Inc.
# All rights reserved.
#
# Redistribution and use in source and binary forms, with or without
# modification, are permitted provided that the following conditions
# are met:
#
#  * Redistributions of source code must retain the above copyright
#    notice, this list of conditions and the following disclaimer.
#  * Redistributions in binary form must reproduce the above
#    copyright notice, this list of conditions and the following
#    disclaimer in the documentation and/or other materials provided
#    with the distribution.
#  * Neither the name of Willow Garage, Inc. nor the names of its
#    contributors may be used to endorse or promote products derived
#    from this software without specific prior written permission.
#
# THIS SOFTWARE IS PROVIDED BY THE COPYRIGHT HOLDERS AND CONTRIBUTORS
# "AS IS" AND ANY EXPRESS OR IMPLIED WARRANTIES, INCLUDING, BUT NOT
# LIMITED TO, THE IMPLIED WARRANTIES OF MERCHANTABILITY AND FITNESS
# FOR A PARTICULAR PURPOSE ARE DISCLAIMED. IN NO EVENT SHALL THE
# COPYRIGHT OWNER OR CONTRIBUTORS BE LIABLE FOR ANY DIRECT, INDIRECT,
# INCIDENTAL, SPECIAL, EXEMPLARY, OR CONSEQUENTIAL DAMAGES (INCLUDING,
# BUT NOT LIMITED TO, PROCUREMENT OF SUBSTITUTE GOODS OR SERVICES;
# LOSS OF USE, DATA, OR PROFITS; OR BUSINESS INTERRUPTION) HOWEVER
# CAUSED AND ON ANY THEORY OF LIABILITY, WHETHER IN CONTRACT, STRICT
# LIABILITY, OR TORT (INCLUDING NEGLIGENCE OR OTHERWISE) ARISING IN
# ANY WAY OUT OF THE USE OF THIS SOFTWARE, EVEN IF ADVISED OF THE
# POSSIBILITY OF SUCH DAMAGE.
#
# Revision $Id$
## Simple talker demo that published std_msgs/Strings messages
## to the 'chatter' topic
import rospy
#from std_msgs.msg import Float64 # from package.[msg/srv] import ["msg"/"srv"]
from geometry_msgs.msg import Pose
pose_msg = Pose()
pose_msg.orientation.x = 0
pose_msg.orientation.y = 0
pose_msg.orientation.z = 0
pose_msg.orientation.w = 1
def talker():
    #pub = rospy.Publisher('data_topic', Float64, queue_size=10) # TOPIC
    pub = rospy.Publisher('chatter_', Pose, queue_size=10) # TOPIC
```

```
        rospy.init_node('talker', anonymous=True)
        rate = rospy.Rate(10) # 10hz
        k=0.2
          while not rospy.is_shutdown():
            #hello_str = "hello world %s" % k
            variable = k
            #pub.publish(variable)
            pose_msg.position.x = -k/1.5
            pose_msg.position.y = k/2
            pose_msg.position.z = k/3
            pub.publish(pose_msg)
            #rospy.loginfo('Envio: %s', variable)
            rospy.loginfo('SEND DATA: \n%s', pose_msg)
            k=k+0.1
            rate.sleep()
if __name__ == '__main__':
  try:
    talker()
  except rospy.ROSInterruptException:
    pass
```

Until this step, almost everything is ready to work. Now you should work on Unity and ROS Bridge as the next target.

18.3 STEP 3: MAKING THE UNITY PROJECT

Initially, you should create a new 3D Unity project and open it (Figure 18.8). Then Type **ROS#** in the search box on the project tab below.

FIGURE 18.8 Create a new Unity project.

Next, find a button named **Open Asset Store** in the inspector tab and click on it (Figure 18.9).

FIGURE 18.9   Open asset store.

Afterwards, in the asset store tab, the asset will be shown., Scroll down, click on the import button, and import the asset (Figure 18.10).

FIGURE 18.10   Import asset.

Next, from the Hierarchy tab, create an empty game object and rename it as ROS CONNECTOR (Figure 18.11).

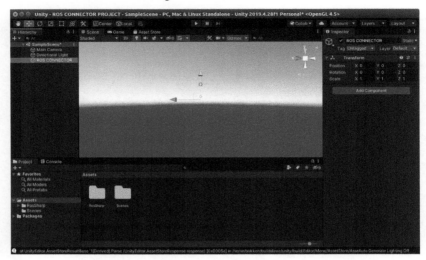

FIGURE 18.11   Create an object.

Then, in the inspector tab, add two components named **Ros Connector** and **Pose Stamped Subscriber** (Figure 18.12).

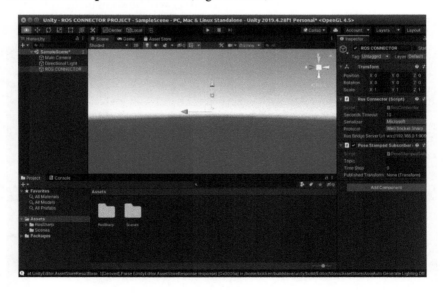

FIGURE 18.12   Inspector tab.

Next, open a terminal by clicking **Ctrl+Alt+T** and type the command **hostname -I** to check the host's IP address (Figure 18.13).

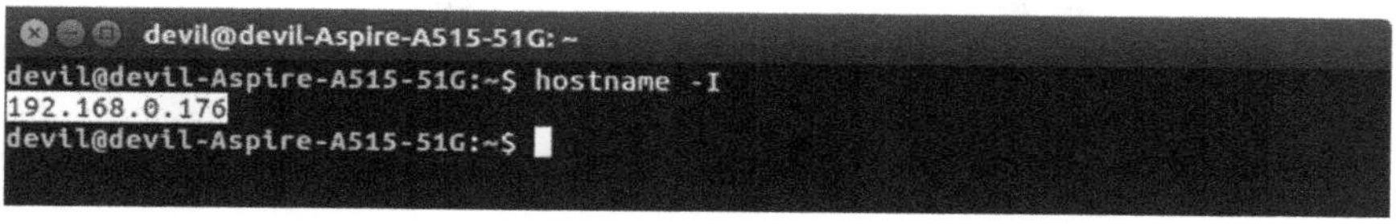

```
devil@devil-Aspire-A515-51G: ~
devil@devil-Aspire-A515-51G:~$ hostname -I
192.168.0.176
devil@devil-Aspire-A515-51G:~$
```

FIGURE 18.13   Open a terminal.

Afterwards, paste the IP address in the **Ros Connector (Script)** component's **Ros Bridge Server URL box** and rename the **Pose Stamped Subscriber's topic** as **chatter_** and change the **Serializer Newtonsoft_ JSON** in the **inspector** tab (Figure 18.14).

FIGURE 18.14   Unity inspector settings.

Next, open three-terminal by clicking **Ctrl+Alt+T** (Figure 18.15).

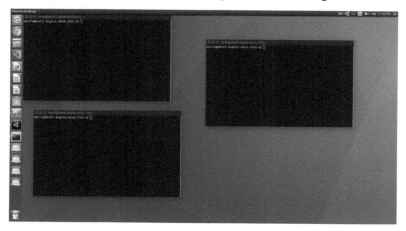

FIGURE 18.15   Open three terminals.

In terminal 1, type the command **roslaunch rosbridge_server rosbridge_websocket.launch** and click Enter (Figure 18.16).

```
⊗ ⊖ ⊡   devil@devil-Aspire-A515-51G: ~
devil@devil-Aspire-A515-51G:~$ roslaunch rosbridge_server rosbridge_websocket.la
unch█
```

FIGURE 18.16   Terminal 1 ROS Bridge command.

In terminal 2, types the command **cd ~/catkin_ws** (Figure 18.17).

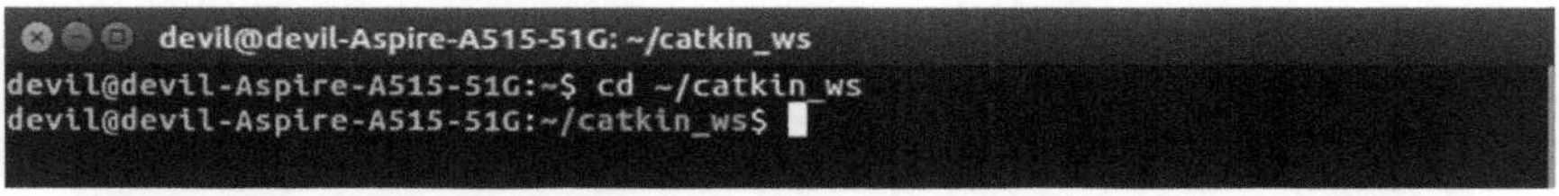

```
⊗ ⊖ ⊡   devil@devil-Aspire-A515-51G: ~/catkin_ws
devil@devil-Aspire-A515-51G:~$ cd ~/catkin_ws
devil@devil-Aspire-A515-51G:~/catkin_ws$ █
```

FIGURE 18.17   Terminal 2 Catkin command.

Then, in the same terminal, type the command **source. /devel/setup. bash** and click Enter (Figure 18.18).

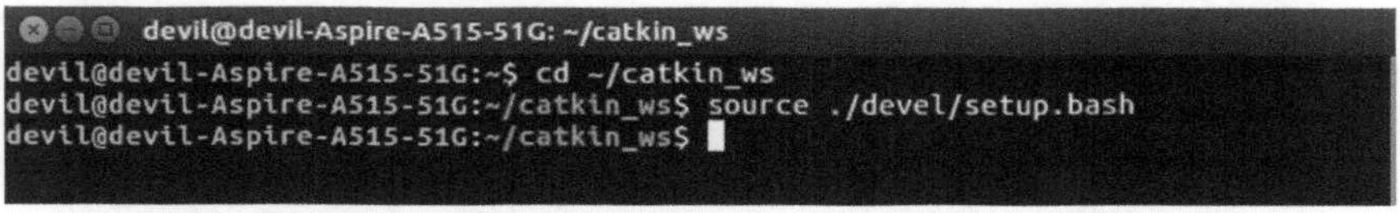

```
⊗ ⊖ ⊡   devil@devil-Aspire-A515-51G: ~/catkin_ws
devil@devil-Aspire-A515-51G:~$ cd ~/catkin_ws
devil@devil-Aspire-A515-51G:~/catkin_ws$ source ./devel/setup.bash
devil@devil-Aspire-A515-51G:~/catkin_ws$ █
```

FIGURE 18.18   Setup command in terminal 2.

Afterwards, in the same terminal, type the command **rosrun beginner_tutorials talker.py** (Figure 18.19).

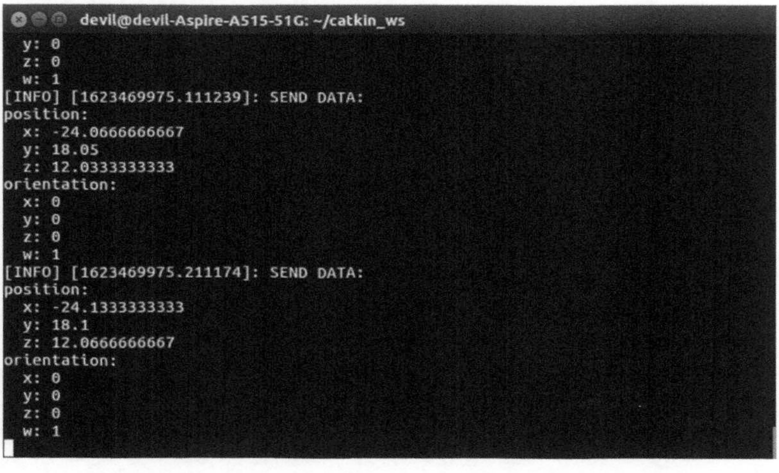

```
⊗ ⊖ ⊡   devil@devil-Aspire-A515-51G: ~/catkin_ws
  y: 0
  z: 0
  w: 1
[INFO] [1623469975.111239]: SEND DATA:
position:
  x: -24.0666666667
  y: 18.05
  z: 12.0333333333
orientation:
  x: 0
  y: 0
  z: 0
  w: 1
[INFO] [1623469975.211174]: SEND DATA:
position:
  x: -24.1333333333
  y: 18.1
  z: 12.0666666667
orientation:
  x: 0
  y: 0
  z: 0
  w: 1
```

FIGURE 18.19   Terminal 2 beginner_tutorials talker python program running.

Then, in terminal 3, type the command **rosrun rqt_graph rqt_graph** (Figure 18.20).

FIGURE 18.20   Terminal 3 rqt_graph command.

Now you will see the published nodes in the RQT Graph window (Figure 18.21).

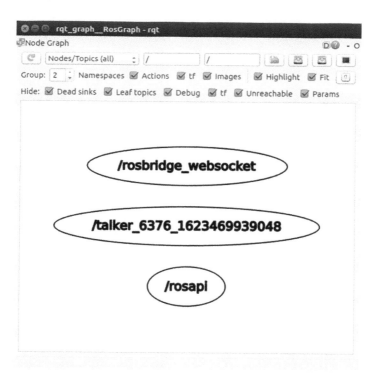

FIGURE 18.21   RQT Graph window.

Then return the **Unity Editor window** and click the **play button**. You will see that Unity is connected with ROS Bridge (Figure 18.22). Next, Open the RQT Graph window and see that the chatter connects to the talker and ROS Bridge WebSocket (Figure 18.23). You can observe that the talker script is published on chatter, and subscribed by ROS Bridge, and now it will get data, whenever you recall it.

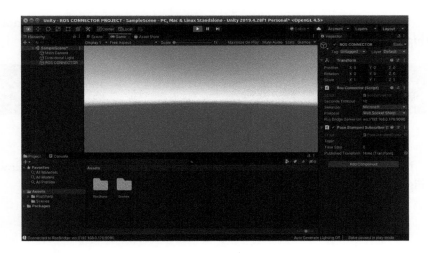

FIGURE 18.22 **Running Unity windows.**

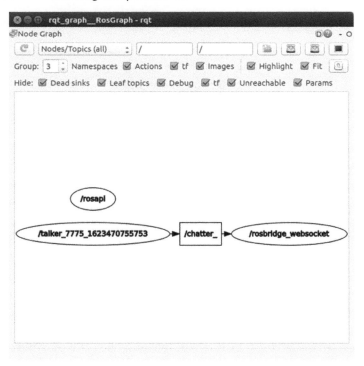

FIGURE 18.23 Unity ROS graph connection.

This example can be helpful in robot simulation as the virtual reality target. Now by this connection, you can navigate your simulated robot inside the Unity with the various virtual environments.

UNITY IN EMBEDDED SYSTEM DESIGN AND ROBOTICS

A STEP-BY-STEP GUIDE

CHAPTER 19

Example 16: Unity and Mobile Sensors Bond

DOI: 10.1201/9781003268581-19

Nowadays, making the game and running them on the mobile platform is more in demand. But, on the other hand, mobile is counted as an embedded system that can help acquire various data and even analyse these days. This chapter will learn how to interact with your mobile equipped with accelerometer and gyroscope, or gyro as short form, sensors. A gyroscope is a device that uses Earth's gravity to determine orientation. An accelerometer is a compact device designed to measure non-gravitational acceleration. For example, accelerometer sensors in mobile phones use to sense the phone's orientation. The gyroscope adds an extra dimension to the info supplied by the accelerometer by tracking rotation or twist. An accelerometer measures the linear acceleration of movement, while a gyro measures the angular rotational velocity. Both sensors measure the rate of change; they measure the rate of change for different things. In brief, an accelerometer will measure the directional movement. The gyroscope is a very sophisticated tiny mechanism that has found many diverse applications with accurate orientation measurements.

On the whole, a gyroscope is accountable for maintaining balance/orientation and resists change by correcting any angular movement, thereby providing stability control. The chief variance among the two devices is that one can sense rotation, whereas others cannot. **Accelerometers** are applicable in various applications like Compass/Map applications on your smartphone devices, tilt sensing; earthquake detection, fall sensing, medical devices, such as artificial body parts, fitness trackers/wearables, games/applications that require motion sensing, **Gyroscopes** are used in aircraft, space stations, stability in vehicles, motorcycles, ships, inertial guidance systems, etc. The comparison between Accelerometer and Gyroscope are listed in below table.

Function	Sensing linear movement; Worse for rotations; Good for tilt detection.	Measuring all types of rotation; Not suitable for detecting movements.
Signal to noise ratio	Lower	Higher
Measurement of angular velocity	It cannot measure rotation around its axis of movement.	It can measure angular velocity.

In this chapter, due to the common steps for both examples, Steps 1–5 described. Then based on your target, you can follow the other steps based on one sensor. In other words, after passing the initial steps, you can select the accelerometer or gyro sensor steps. The first example describes how to use the mobile accelerometer, and the next one describes how to use the gyroscope sensor.

19.1 INTRODUCTION TO UNITY REMOTE

To start the work with mobile sensors, you should learn what works with **Unity Remote**; Unity Remote is a downloadable app designed to help Android, iOS, and tvOS development. The app connects with Unity while you are running your project in Play Mode from the Unity Editor. The visual output from the Editor is sent to the device's screen, and the live inputs are sent back to the running project in Unity. This allows you to get a good impression of how your game looks and handles on the target device without the hassle of a complete build for each test. Unity Remote currently supports Android devices (on Windows and OS X via a USB connection) and iOS devices (iPhone, iPad, iPod touch, and Apple TV, through USB on OS X and Windows with iTunes). The Game View of the running Unity project is duplicated on the device screen but at a reduced frame rate.

The following input data from the device is also streamed back to the Editor: Touch and stylus input, Accelerometer, Gyroscope, Device camera, Streams, Compass, GPS, Joystick names and input. Note that the Remote app shows the visual output on the device and takes input from it. However, the Editor still does the game's actual processing on the desktop machine – so its performance is not a perfect reflection of the built app. To download the Unity Remote, you can follow the following links. The installation is shown in Figure 19.1.

Android Play Store	https://play.google.com/store/apps/details?id=com.unity3d.mobileremote
iOS App Store	https://itunes.apple.com/us/app/unity-remote-4/id871767552

FIGURE 19.1   Unity Remote installation.

19.1.1 Step 1 Common: Initial Setting

As the first step, you should install Unity 3D from **unity.com** and set it up accordingly with visual studio and Android Build Support for the SDK and NDK while installing from install options as shown in Figure 19.2.

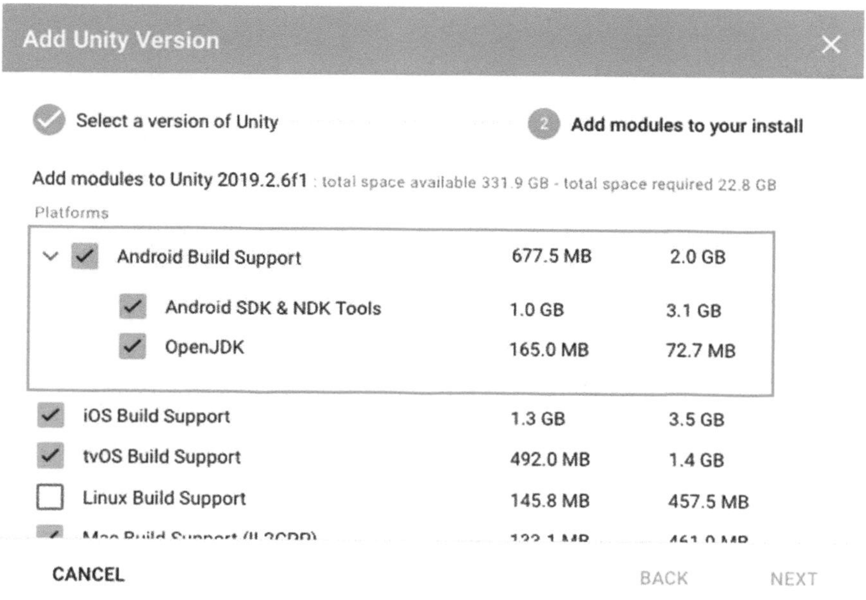

FIGURE 19.2   SDK and NDK item add Unity version.

You can ignore this step if you have done it before. Then install Unity Remote 5 on your Android or iOS device from the device's APP Store.

19.1.2 Step 2 Common: Configure Unity Remote

Once you have downloaded the app, install, and run it on your device, connect the device to your computer using a USB cable.

19.1.3 Step 3 Common: Create a New Unity Project and Setup Unity Remote

Start to create a new project from the Unity Hub (Figure 19.3).

FIGURE 19.3   Start the unity project.

Next, to enable Unity to work with your device, open the Editor settings in Unity from the following path:

Menu → Edit → Project Settings and select the Editor category (Figure 19.4).

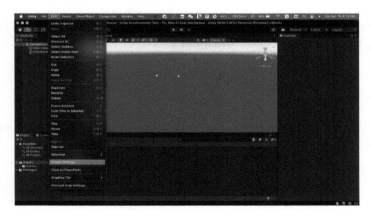

FIGURE 19.4   Project setting in windows.

Then select the device to use from the Unity Remote section. Afterwards, select any Android Device from the Device selection here (Figures 19.5 and 19.6).

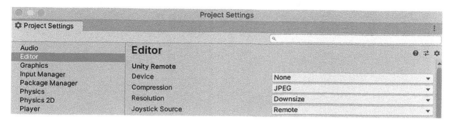

FIGURE 19.5 Project setting in Mac.

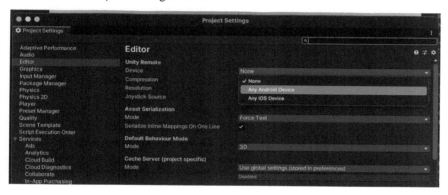

FIGURE 19.6 Project Setting and Any Android Device selection.

Note that to specify the location of your Android SDK, in windows, you should go to Edit → Preferences or in Mac, you should follow the path Unity → Preferences (Figure 19.7).

FIGURE 19.7 Preferences in Mac.

In the case that you finish the installation for Android SDK and NDK, you can see the windows as shown in Figure 19.8. Otherwise, you may need to install it manually and set the location or path of the SDK and NDK in the settings section. Please note that Unity Hub already does this for you if you select Android Support when installing Unity 3D.

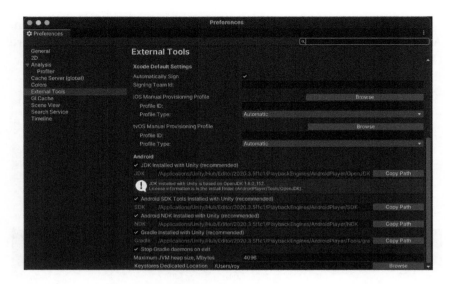

FIGURE 19.8 Create a plane on Unity.

19.1.4 Step 4 Common: Create the Sample Scene

If you open the new project, you can see that a sample scene is already ready for you to edit. We can edit it based on our requirements for the demo. To follow this task first, you should create a plane by following the path: GameObject → 3D Object → Plane (Figure 19.9).

FIGURE 19.9 Create a plane on Unity.

Then do the changes in the inspector → transform → scale section (Figure 19.10) based on the following table:

Property	X	Y	Z
Position	0	0	0
Rotation	0	0	0
Scale	100	100	100

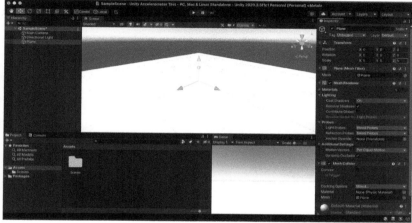

FIGURE 19.10   Inspector windows setting.

Then create a new folder, and after that, right-click on Assets Pane →
Create → Folder → Rename Folder to **Materials** (Figure 19.11).

FIGURE 19.11   Creating the folder.

Afterwards, double-click to enter the folder and create a new Material. Then right-click on Assets Pane → Create → Material → Rename Material to **SkyBlue** (Figure 19.12).

FIGURE 19.12   Material.

Next, click on the Material **SkyBlue** → Click on Albedo on Inspector → Select a suitable SkyBlue Color (Figure 19.13).

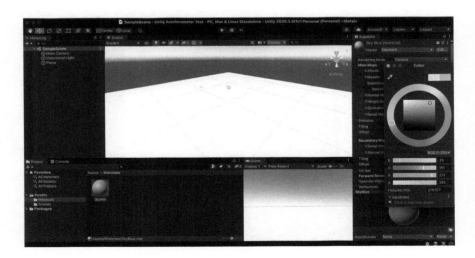

FIGURE 19.13   Color selection for material.

As the next stage, drag and drop the material onto the Plane and create two more materials named **Red** and **Light Green** in the same manner, then put albedos on them accordingly (Figure 19.14).

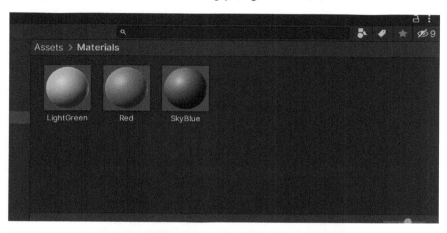

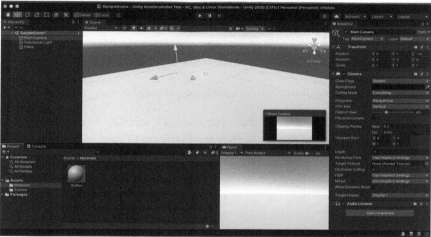

FIGURE 19.14   Creating the Material.

Next, create a new GameObject Sphere, from the menus GameObject → 3D Object → Sphere (Figure 19.15). Then, rename Sphere to **ControlObject** and change its Properties in inspector windows based on the following table.

Property	X	Y	Z
Position	0	2.27	−4.35
Rotation	0	0	0
Scale	3	3	3

FIGURE 19.15   GameObject Sphere and inspector setting.

Afterwards, create a Cube from the GameObject Options, rename it to **Platform**, and change the properties for Platform Object based on the following table (Figure 19.16).

Property	X	Y	Z
Position	0	0	−4.35
Rotation	0	0	0
Scale	20	1	15

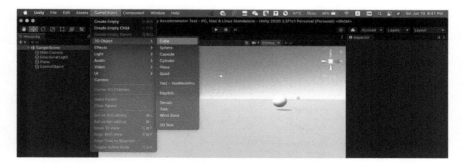

FIGURE 19.16   GameObject cube and inspector setting. (*Continued*)

FIGURE 19.16 (*Continued*)

Next, set the properties for the Main Camera according to the following table (Figure 19.17).

Property	X	Y	Z
Position	0	8.32	−18.26
Rotation	31.945	0	0
Scale	1	1	1

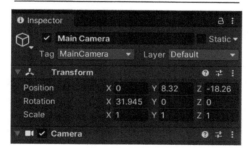

FIGURE 19.17 Main camera and inspector setting.

Till this step, the final scene will be as shown in Figure 19.18.

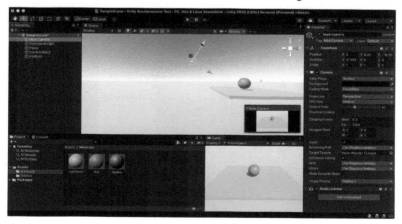

FIGURE 19.18 Final scene overview.

19.1.5 Step 5 Common: Further Modifications to the Scenes Game Objects

To get more modifications on the scene game object, you should select the sphere **ControlObject** and add a rigid body component to it from the **Add Component** option in the inspector pane (Figure 19.19).

FIGURE 19.19   Rigid body component.

19.2 EXAMPLE 1: USE MOBILE ACCELEROMETER IN UNITY

Now to make the accelerometer example, you can follow the following steps.

19.2.1 Step 1 _ Accelerometer: C# Script and GameObject Control

To control the object with accelerometer data as the next step, create a C# Script that controls the GameObject. Then, create a new folder called **Script** from the Assets pane, and inside the folder, create a new C# Script name it **Accelerometer** (Figure 19.20).

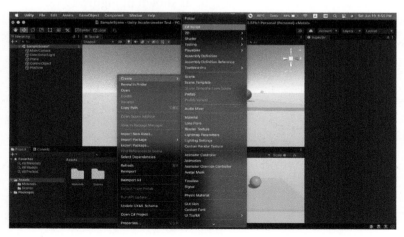

FIGURE 19.20   C# Script. (*Continued*)

FIGURE 19.20 (*Continued*)

Then, double-click on it to open Visual Studio, edit the script, and paste the following script and save it.

```
using System. Collections;
using System.Collections.Generic;
using UnityEngine;
public class Accelerometer: MonoBehaviour
{
    public bool isFlat = true;
    private Rigidbody rigid;
    // Start is called before the first frame update
    void Start()
    {
        rigid = GetComponent<Rigidbody>();
    }
    // Update is called once per frame
    void Update()
    {
        Vector3 tilt = Input.acceleration;
        if (isFlat)
        {
            tilt = Quaternion.Euler(90, 0, 0) * tilt;
        }
        rigid.AddForce(tilt);
        Debug.DrawRay(transform.position + Vector3.up, tilt, Color.magenta);
    }
}
```

The code is straightforward to understand, and the significant part is the Quaternion section. A quaternion rotation comprises four numbers, whose values all have a minimum of −1 and a maximum of 1, i.e., (0, 0, 0, 1) is a quaternion rotation equivalent to **no rotation** or a rotation of 0 around all axis. In the code, we set up Boolean value **isFlat** to determine if the surface is flat or not. If it is flat, we set the tilt of motion of the object towards the accelerometer's direction of acceleration hence the tilt angle. Then the force calculated with quaternion rotation is added to the rigid body property. Lastly, for debugging, a ray is added on top of the object with a different colour.

As the next stage, add the script to the Sphere by drag and drop (Figure 19.21).

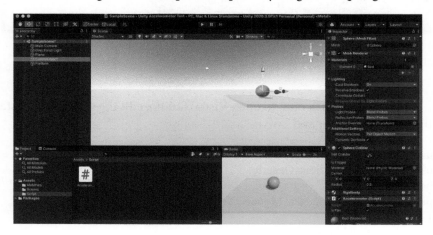

FIGURE 19.21   Add the Script to the Sphere.

19.2.2 Step 2 _ Accelerometer: Run the Project

Next, connect your phone to your computer with a USB cable. Please check for the Debugging enabled option in your mobile from the developer settings. Then, open the Unity Remote APP and run the project (Figure 19.22).

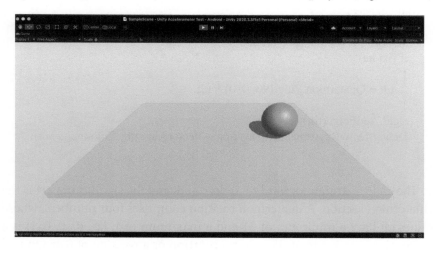

FIGURE 19.22   The Scene when Run the Project on Phone.

Note that if the project does not run or respond to the Phone Moving. Close the project and set the current platform of the project from **Current Platform** to Android from Unity Hub as shown in Figure 19.23.

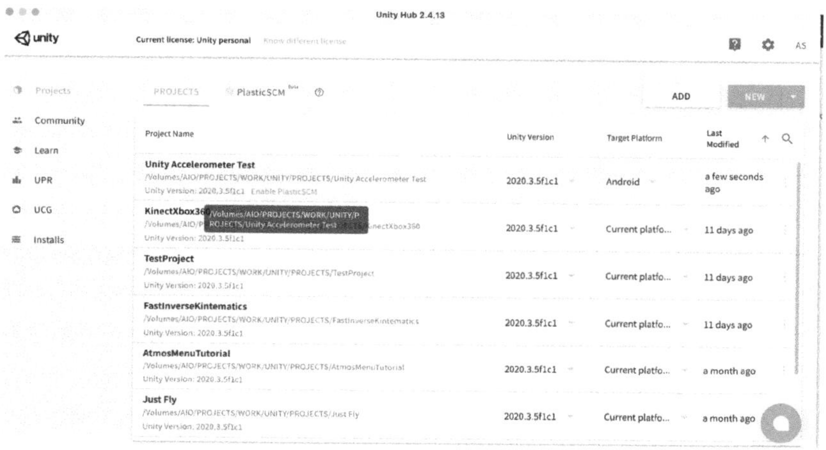

FIGURE 19.23   Unity Hub setting.

Finally, once the product demo is running, you can see that, when you move around your phone in different directions, the Unity 3D software gets the different angles in which the phone is tilted via the Unity Remote app. The project uses the data it gets from the Unity Remote app and uses it in the project (Figure 19.24).

FIGURE 19.24   Final project overview on mobile.

Please remember that you must export it in APK format from Unity Software if you want to run the project on your phone. You can do this from the Unity Hub by changing your build platform to Android.

19.3 EXAMPLE 2: USE MOBILE GYROSCOPE IN UNITY

As mentioned in Example 1, the first initial stage of this example is like the previous one. After completing the common initial steps, you can make your project touch the mobile gyroscope sensor.

19.3.1 Step 1 Gyroscope: Make a C# Script

You should select the MainCamera, click on Add Component on the inspector window, and select New Script. Next, give the name CamGyro (Figure 19.25) to the file, and after that, double-click on the Script to open visual studio and paste the following script.

FIGURE 19.25   CamGyro C# Script folder.

```
using System.Collections;
using System.Collections.Generic;
using UnityEngine;

public class CamGyro : MonoBehaviour
{
    GameObject camParent;
    // Start is called before the first frame update
    void Start()
    {
        camParent = new GameObject("camParent");
        camParent.transform.position = this.transform.position;
        this.transform.parent = camParent.transform;
        Input.gyro.enabled = true;
    }
    // Update is called once per frame
    void Update()
    {
        camParent.transform.Rotate(0, -Input.gyro.rotationRateUnbiased.y, 0);
        this.transform.Rotate(-Input.gyro.rotationRateUnbiased.x, 0, 0);
    }
}
```

Here, you are creating a parent object. So, this already doesn't exist in the scene and we should create it. So, you need to attach the code here to the camera and then in the start function, you should create the parent camera. It is better to position this parent camera in the same spot The next step is creating the parent and for that, you need to go to the new game object and set the cameras as transform dot parent.

Afterwards, you need to turn the Gyro ON, from the start function, then input Gyro and enable it. Also, the cameras can rotate around the up axis (the y-axis), and therefore camera is going to do the looking up and down. For the rotation around the x-axis, the camera is acting like bowing. In fact, you can see that, the rotation function is used in two directions. The value for looking left and right, rotating around the Y, will be 0 for the x- and z-axis. But the actual value we're going to use is the negative value of input, gyro rotation rate, unbiased dot Y. So, rotation rate, unbiased, gets you the unbiased rotation of the gyro as it's moving around, and the Y is the Y rotation. And then you do the same thing with the X, and you are using negative because the values reported back are inverted for the example purposes. So, if you wanted it to move differently, you might not need these negatives, but here we got them there (Figure 19.26).

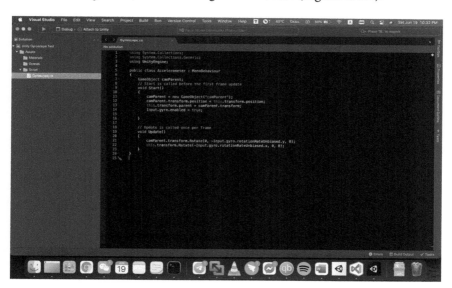

FIGURE 19.26 CamGyro C# Script code.

19.3.2 Step 2 Gyroscope: Run the Project

Afterwards, connect your phone to a computer with USB debugging enabled from the developer settings options in your mobile. Then, open the Unity Remote APP and run the project (Figure 19.27).

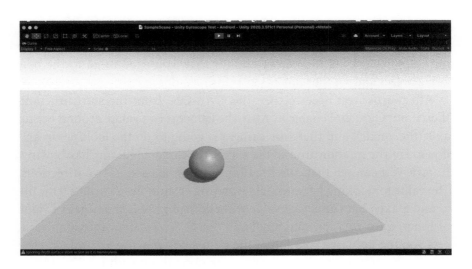

FIGURE 19.27   Gyro example demonstration.

Note: If the project does not run or respond to the Phone Moving, close the project and set the current platform of the project from "Current Platform" to Android from Unity Hub as shown in Figure 19.28.

Finally, you can test your program as shown in Figure 19.29.

When you move around your mobile device connected to your computer, you see that, due to the motion of the gyroscope changing when you move the device, the camera angle is also changing. It's showing different aspects of the scene.

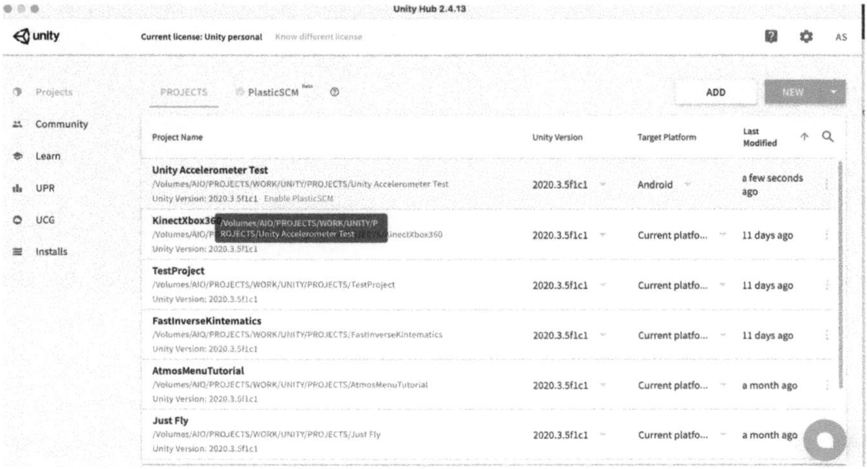

FIGURE 19.28   Gyro Unity program setting.

FIGURE 19.29   Gyro Unity program.

19.4 EXAMPLE 3: CAR GAME WITH ACCELEROMETER (UNITY)

To review the previous steps, in this example, you will learn the car game example for the accelerometer sensor; in this example, a simple car game designed with the help of stock assets and Unity.

19.4.1 Step 1: Initial Step: Inserting the Asset

First, you should create a new project in Unity Hub (Figure 19.30), and then go to the asset store and add the asset from the following link:

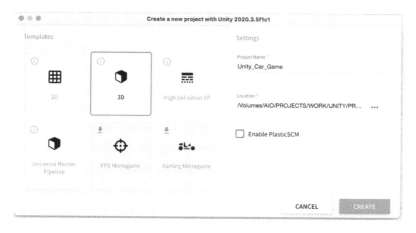

FIGURE 19.30   Car asset used in the example. (*Continued*)

FIGURE 19.30   (*Continued*)

https://assetstore.unity.com/packages/3d/vehicles/land/arcade-free-racing-car-161085#description

Then you should add the asset from the package manager inside Unity to your project (Figure 19.31).

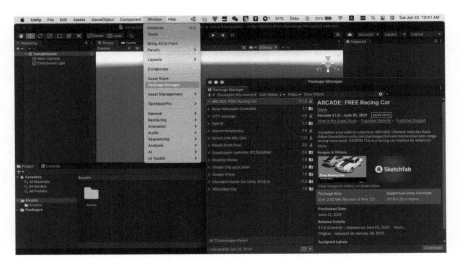

FIGURE 19.31   Package manager to insert the asset.

19.4.2 Step 2: Make the Scene

To work in this step, you must add the Road Prefab from the asset folder from the path ARCADE 8 → FREE Racing Car → Meshes, with drag and drop onto the Scene (Figure 19.32).

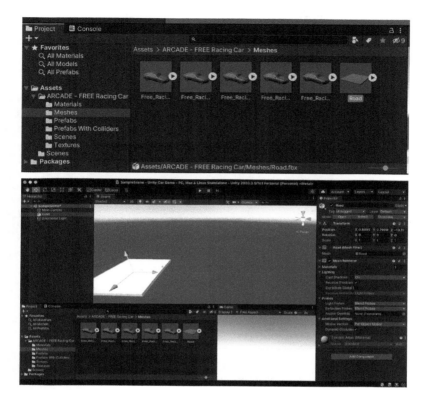

FIGURE 19.32   Make the Scene in assets.

Then, add the Road's Texture from the Materials folder of the Asset and drag and drop it on the Road in the Scene (Figure 19.33).

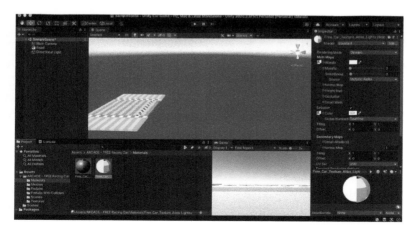

FIGURE 19.33   Road texture inserting.

Next, you should duplicate the Road from the hierarchy menu of the project and reposition it. The same work should repeat a couple of times to make the road longer (Figure 19.34).

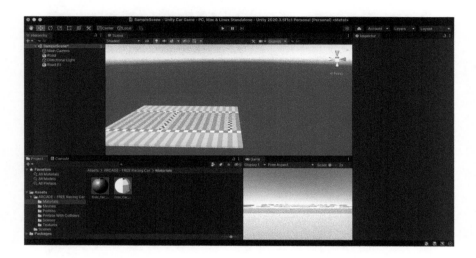

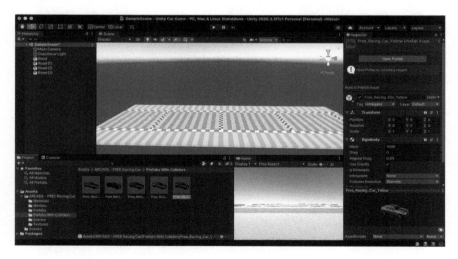

FIGURE 19.34   Road texture extension.

After that, drag and drop a car of your choice from the Prefabs with Colliders folder of the imported asset onto the scene (Figure 19.35). Then, put all the coordinates of the car to X:0, Y:0, Z:0 to reposition the car.

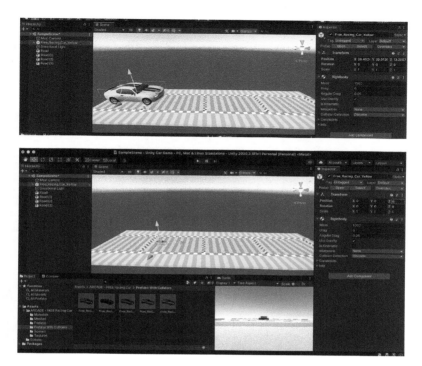

FIGURE 19.35   Inserting the car.

Now drag the car to the start of the road on the left side for better viewing (Figure 19.36). Note that position the Main Camera accordingly so that the car is in view for the user.

FIGURE 19.36   Inserting the car and camera view.

19.4.3 Step 3: Make the Scripts

To make the Scripts, first, create a new folder called scripts in the project root directory (Figure 19.37) and name it – **Scripts**. Then, inside the Scripts folder, create a new script called **CarController** (Figure 19.38).

FIGURE 19.37 Create a new folder called Scripts.

FIGURE 19.38 Create a new folder called CarController.

After that, double-click on it and open the Script in visual studio to edit and paste the following code there to use the accelerometer.

```csharp
using System;
using System.Collections;
using System.Collections.Generic;
using UnityEngine;
public class CarController : MonoBehaviour
{
    private const string HORIZONTAL = "Horizontal";
    private const string VERTICAL = "Vertical";
    private float horizontalInput;
    private float verticalInput;
    private float currentSteerAngle;
    private float currentbreakForce;
    private bool isBreaking;
    private Vector3 zeroAc;
    private Vector3 curAc;
    private float sensH = 10;
    private float sensV = 10;
    private float smooth = 10;
    private float GetAxisH = 0;
    private float GetAxisV = 0;
    [SerializeField] private float motorForce;
    [SerializeField] private float breakForce;
    [SerializeField] private float maxSteerAngle;
    [SerializeField] private WheelCollider frontLeftWheelCollider;
    [SerializeField] private WheelCollider frontRightWheelCollider;
    [SerializeField] private WheelCollider rearLeftWheelCollider;
    [SerializeField] private WheelCollider rearRightWheelCollider;
    [SerializeField] private Transform frontLeftWheelTransform;
    [SerializeField] private Transform frontRightWheeTransform;
    [SerializeField] private Transform rearLeftWheelTransform;
    [SerializeField] private Transform rearRightWheelTransform;
    private void ResetAxes()
    {
        zeroAc = Input.acceleration;
        curAc = Vector3.zero;
    }
    private void Start()
    {
        ResetAxes();
    }
    private void FixedUpdate()
    {
        GetInput();
        HandleMotor();
        HandleSteering();
        UpdateWheels();
    }
    private void GetInput()
    {
        Debug.Log(horizontalInput);
        curAc = Vector3.Lerp(curAc, Input.acceleration - zeroAc, Time.deltaTime / smooth);
```

```
        GetAxisV = Mathf.Clamp(curAc.y * sensV, -1, 1);
        GetAxisH = Mathf.Clamp(curAc.x * sensH, -1, 1);
        // now use GetAxisV and GetAxisH instead of Input.GetAxis vertical and horizontal
        // If the horizontal and vertical directions are swapped, swap curAc.y and curAc.x
        // in the above equations. If some axis is going in the wrong direction, invert the
        // signal (use -curAc.x or -curAc.y)
        horizontalInput = GetAxisH;
        verticalInput = GetAxisV;
        isBreaking = Input.GetKey(KeyCode.Space);
    }
    private void HandleMotor()
    {
        frontLeftWheelCollider.motorTorque = verticalInput * motorForce;
        frontRightWheelCollider.motorTorque = verticalInput * motorForce;
        currentbreakForce = isBreaking?  breakForce : 0f;
        ApplyBreaking();
    }
    private void ApplyBreaking()
    {
        frontRightWheelCollider.brakeTorque = currentbreakForce;
        frontLeftWheelCollider.brakeTorque = currentbreakForce;
        rearLeftWheelCollider.brakeTorque = currentbreakForce;
        rearRightWheelCollider.brakeTorque = currentbreakForce;
    }
    private void HandleSteering()
    {
        currentSteerAngle = maxSteerAngle * horizontalInput;
        frontLeftWheelCollider.steerAngle = currentSteerAngle;
        frontRightWheelCollider.steerAngle = currentSteerAngle;
    }
    private void UpdateWheels()
    {
        UpdateSingleWheel(frontLeftWheelCollider, frontLeftWheelTransform);
        UpdateSingleWheel(frontRightWheelCollider, frontRightWheeTransform);
        UpdateSingleWheel(rearRightWheelCollider, rearRightWheelTransform);
        UpdateSingleWheel(rearLeftWheelCollider, rearLeftWheelTransform);
    }
    private void UpdateSingleWheel(WheelCollider wheelCollider, Transform wheelTransform)
    {
        Vector3 pos;
        Quaternion rot
;  wheelCollider.GetWorldPose(out pos, out rot);  .
        wheelTransform.rotation = rot;
        wheelTransform.position = pos;
    }
}
```

Afterwards, drag and drop the Car Controller Script on the Car GameObject and edit the Script values on the inspector window based on options as shown in Figure 19.39. After selecting each option, a window will open with all available options to choose the corresponding variables. Figure 19.39 (last one) will show the completed option selection.

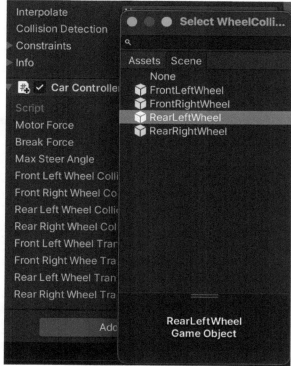

FIGURE 19.39   Options for the control of the car. (*Continued*)

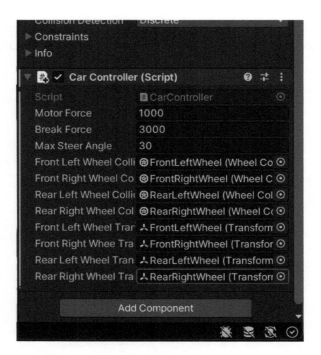

FIGURE 19.39 (*Continued*)

Also, you can follow the other way for the Transforms Sections of the Script by dragging and dropping corresponding components from the hierarchy windows to scripts variables as shown in Figure 19.40.

FIGURE 19.40 Transforms Sections from the hierarchy windows to scripts.

19.4.4 Step 4: First Run and Error

Now, if you run the project, you will see that the car will fall into infinity. That is because the car has nothing to land. The road you select (put) is for visual only; hence, it has no physical property. Then you need to do some more modifications (Figure 19.41).

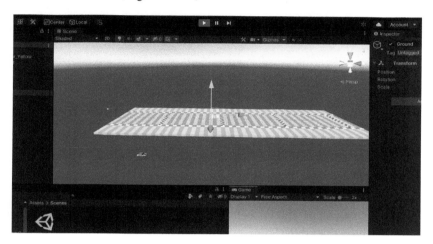

FIGURE 19.41   Car errors.

19.4.5 Step 5: Fix Collider Physics

To solve the mentioned problem, create an empty game object on the project hierarchy and rename it to ground (Figure 19.42).

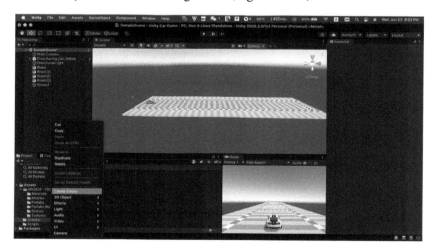

FIGURE 19.42   Create an empty object.

After that, click on the Ground GameObject and click on add component on the inspector. Find Box Collider and add it (Figure 19.43).

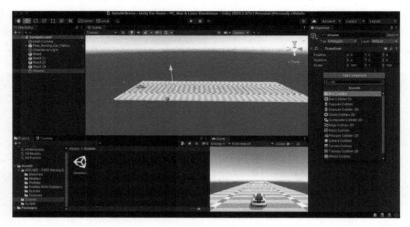

FIGURE 19.43   Box Collider.

Then set values as shown below in inspector window for Transform based on following table (Figure 19.44).

Transform	X	Y	Z
Position	0	−0.33	21.2
Rotation	0	0	0
Scale	2.4	1	10

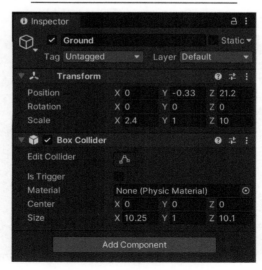

FIGURE 19.44   Inspector window.

After this step, if you run by play option, then the project will work fine as the test stage.

19.4.6 Step 6: Follow the Car on the Screen

To follow the car first; you should fix the Camera and create a new script in the script folder called CameraFollow (Figure 19.45).

FIGURE 19.45 Follow Car in screen.

Then, open the script in visual studio and put the following script there and attach the script to the Main Camera.

```
using System;
using System.Collections;
using System.Collections.Generic;
using UnityEngine;
public class CameraFollow : MonoBehaviour
{
    [SerializeField] private Vector3 offset;
    [SerializeField] private Transform target;
    [SerializeField] private float translateSpeed;
    [SerializeField] private float rotationSpeed;
    private void FixedUpdate()
    {
        HandleTranslation();
        HandleRotation();
```

```
    }
    private void HandleTranslation()
    {
        var targetPosition = target.TransformPoint(offset);
        transform.position = Vector3.Lerp(transform.position, targetPosition,
translateSpeed * Time.deltaTime);
    }
    private void HandleRotation()
    {
        var direction = target.position - transform.position;
        var rotation = Quaternion.LookRotation(direction, Vector3.up);
        transform.rotation = Quaternion.Lerp(transform.rotation, rotation,
rotationSpeed * Time.deltaTime);
    }
}
```

19.4.7 Step 7: Test with Mobile Phone

Connect phone to PC and run the project with Unity Remote. Now, you can see the car movement by changing the motion of your phone (Figure 19.46).

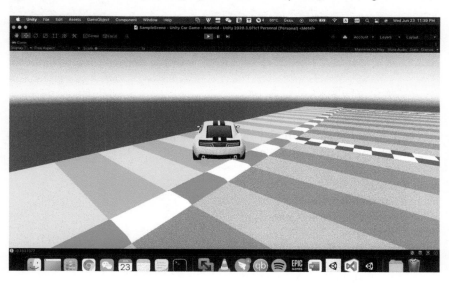

FIGURE 19.46   Final test.

19.4.8 Step 8: A Review of Object Properties

To review all the game object properties in inspector windows, you can refer to the following stage and check the setting to understand the example better.

GameObject	Inspector Properties
A. Main Camera	
B. Free-Racing-Yellow-Car (Car Object)	

C. Road Setting

D. Road Part 1

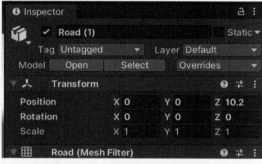

E. Road Part 2

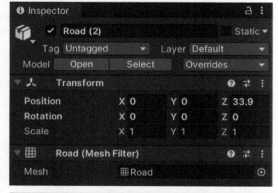

F. Road Part 3

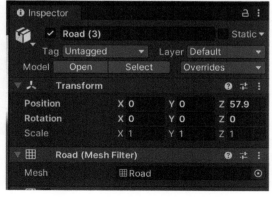

G. Ground

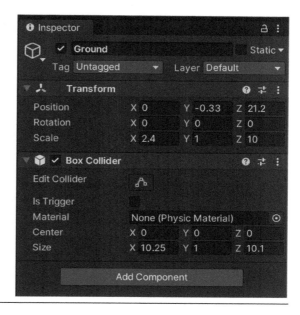

Bibliography

A. Abbasi and A. J. Moshayedi, "Trajectory tracking of two-wheeled mobile robots, using LQR optimal control method, based on computational model of KHEPERA IV," *J. Simul. Anal. Nov. Technol. Mech. Eng.*, vol. 10, no. 3, pp. 41–50, 2018.

A. Abbasi, S. MahmoudZadeh, and A. Yazdani et al., "Feasibility assessment of Kian-I mobile robot for autonomous navigation," *Neural Comput. Applic.*, vol. 34, pp. 1199–1218, 2022. https://doi.org/10.1007/s00521-021-06428-2.

M. Geibollahi and A. J. Moshayedi, "Dynamic modeling, assembly and implementing quadrotor UAV using PID controller," *Journal of Simulation and Analysis of Novel Technologies in Mechanical Engineering*, vol. 11, no. 1, pp. 15–22, 2018.

A. J. Moshayedi and D. C. Gharpure, "Design and development of wind tracker," in 2011 IEEE International Conference on Computer Applications and Industrial Electronics (ICCAIE), 2011, pp. 36–40, doi: 10.1109/ICCAIE.2011.6162100.

A. J. Moshayedi and D. C. Gharpure, "Development of position monitoring system for studying performance of wind tracking algorithms," in ROBOTIK 2012; 7th German Conference on Robotics, 2012, pp. 1–4.

A. J. Moshayedi, D. C. Gharpure, and A.D. Shaligram, "Design and Development Of MOKHTAR Wind Tracker", *International Journal of Soft Computing and Engineering (IJSCE) ISSN*, November 2013, vol. 3, no. 5, pp. 2231–2307.

A. J. Moshayedi and D. C. Gharpure, "Priority based algorithm for plume tracking robot," in 2012 1st International Symposium on Physics and Technology of Sensors (ISPTS-1), 2012, pp. 51–54.

A. J. Moshayedi and D. C. Gharpure, "Path and position monitoring tool for indoor robot application," *Int. J. Appl. Electron. Phys. Robot.*, vol. 1, no. 1, pp. 10–13, Jul. 2013, doi: 10.7575/aiac.ijaepr.v.1n.1p.10.

A. J. Moshayedi and D. Gharpure, "Implementing breath to improve response of gas sensors for leak detection in plume tracker robots," in Proceedings of the Third International Conference on Soft Computing for Problem Solving, 2014, pp. 337–348.

A. J. Moshayedi and D. C. Gharpure, "Evaluation of bio inspired Mokhtar: Odor localization system," in 2017 18th International Carpathian Control Conference (ICCC), 2017, pp. 527–532, doi: 10.1109/CarpathianCC.2017.7970457.

A. J. Moshayedi, A. M. Agda, and M. Arabzadeh, "Designing and implementation a simple algorithm considering the maximum audio frequency of Persian vocabulary in order to robot speech control based on Arduino," vol. 480, 2019.

A. J. Moshayedi, S. S. Fard, L. Liao, and S. A. Eftekhari, "Design and development of pipe inspection robot meant for resizable pipe lines," *Int. J. Robot. Control*, vol. 2, no. 1, p. 25, 2019, doi: 10.5430/ijrc.v2n1p25.

A. J. Moshayedi, A. Abbasi, L. Liao, and S. Li, "Path planning and trajectory tracking of a mobile robot using bio-inspired optimization algorithms and PID control," in 2019 IEEE International Conference on Computational Intelligence and Virtual Environments for Measurement Systems and Applications (CIVEMSA 2019) – Proceedings, pp. 1–8, 2019, doi: 10.1109/CIVEMSA45640.2019.9071596.

A. J. Moshayedi, L. Jinsong, and L. Liao, "AGV (automated guided vehicle) robot: Mission and obstacles in design and performance," *Journal of Simulation and Analysis of Novel Technologies in Mechanical Engineering*, vol. 12, no. 4, pp. 5–18, 2019.

A. J. Moshayedi, Z. Chen, L. Liao, and S. Li, "Kinect based virtual referee for table tennis game: TTV (Table Tennis Var System)," in Proceedings – 2019 6th International Conference on Information Science and Control Engineering (ICISCE 2019), pp. 354–359, 2019.

A. J. Moshayedi, Z. Chen, L. Liao, and S. Li, "Portable image based moon date detection and declaration: System and algorithm code sign," in 2019 IEEE International Conference on Computational Intelligence and Virtual Environments for Measurement Systems and Applications (CIVEMSA), Jun. 2019, pp. 1–6

A. J. Moshayedi, A. S. Roy, and L. Liao, "PID tuning method on AGV (automated guided vehicle) industrial robot," *Journal of Simulation and Analysis of Novel Technologies in Mechanical Engineering*, vol. 12, no. 4, pp. 53–66, 2020.

A. J. Moshayedi, J. Li, and L. Liao, "Simulation study and PID tune of automated guided vehicles (AGV)," in 2021 IEEE International Conference on Computational Intelligence and Virtual Environments for Measurement Systems and Applications (CIVEMSA), 2021, pp. 1–7.

A. J. Moshayedi, M. Gheibollahi, and L. Liao, "The quadrotor dynamic modeling and study of meta-heuristic algorithms performance on optimization of PID controller index to control angles and tracking the route," *IAES Int. J. Robot. Autom.*, vol. 9, no. 4, p. 256, 2020, doi: 10.11591/ijra.v9i4.pp256-270.

A. J. Moshayedi, G. Xu, L. Liao, and A. Kolahdooz, "Gentle survey on MIR industrial service robots: Review & design," *J. Mod. Process. Manuf. Prod.*, vol. 10, no. 1, pp. 31–50, 2021.

A. J. Moshayedi, S. K. Sambo, and A. Kolahdooz, "Design and development of cost-effective exergames for activity incrementation," in 2022 2nd International Conference on Consumer Electronics and Computer Engineering (ICCECE), 2022, pp. 133–137, doi: 10.1109/ICCECE54139.2022.9712844.

A. J. Moshayedi, Z. Chen, L. Liao, and S. Li, "Sunfa Ata Zuyan machine learning models for moon phase detection: Algorithm, prototype and performance comparison," *TELKOMNIKA Telecommun. Comput. Electron. Control*, vol. 20, no. 1, pp. 129–140, 2022.

Index

Note: *Italicized* folios indicate figures and folios in **bold** indicate tables.

For Product Safety Concerns and Information please contact our EU
representative GPSR@taylorandfrancis.com
Taylor & Francis Verlag GmbH, Kaufingerstraße 24, 80331 München, Germany

www.ingramcontent.com/pod-product-compliance
Ingram Content Group UK Ltd.
Pitfield, Milton Keynes, MK11 3LW, UK
UKHW020932180425
457613UK00012B/329